TRAINING COURSE FO

HOW TO WRITE EXCELLENT ELT MATERIALS

Reading And Listening Activities • **Caroline Krantz**
Speaking Activities • **Sarah Cunningham**
Writing Activities • **Rachael Roberts**
Vocabulary Presentations And Practice • **Philip Kerr**
Critical Thinking Activities • **Paul Dummett**
Audio And Video Scripts • **John Hughes**

THE SKILLS SERIES

ELT TEACHER 2 WRITER

How To Write Excellent ELT Materials
The Skills Series

By Caroline Krantz, Sarah Cunningham, Rachael Roberts, Philip Kerr, Paul Dummett, John Hughes

This edition © 2016 ELT Teacher 2 Writer

www.eltteacher2writer.co.uk

Acknowledgements

How To Write Reading and Listening Activities

We would like to thank the following for permission to reproduce their material: Richmond ELT for an extract from *Target FCE Workbook*.

How To Write Writing Activities

We would like to thank Pearson Education Limited for their permission to use extracts from *Real Life Global Advanced Student's Book*, Rachael Roberts and Patricia Reilly, Pearson Education Limited © Pearson Education Limited 2012

How To Write Vocabulary Presentations And Practice

We would like to thank the following for permission to reproduce their material:

What Is Involved In Knowing A Word – From Nation, *Teaching Vocabulary*, 1E. © 2009 Heinle/ELT, a part of Cengage Learning, Inc. Reproduced by permission. www.cengage.com/permissions; From Dellar/Walkley/Hocking. *Innovations Upper-Intermediate*, 2E. © 2004 Heinle/ELT, a part of Cengage Learning, Inc. Reproduced by permission. www.cengage.com/permissions; Extract from: *Global Pre-intermediate* © Lindsay Clandfield; 2010, Published by Macmillan Publishers Limited. Used by Permission. All rights reserved; Extracts from: *New Inside Out Pre-intermediate* © Sue Kay and Vaughan Jones; 2008, Published by Macmillan Publishers Limited. Used by Permission. All rights reserved; Extracts from: *Straightforward Pre-intermediate* © P. Kerr; 2012, Published by Macmillan Publishers Limited. Used by Permission. All rights reserved.

How To Write Critical Thinking Activities

We would like to thank the following for permission to reproduce their material:

From Heinle ELT. *Life Advanced with DVD*, 1E. © 2014 Heinle/ELT, a part of Cengage Learning, Inc. Reproduced by permission. www.cengage.com/permissions; *Life Pre-intermediate with DVD*, 1E. © 2013 Heinle/ELT, a part of Cengage Learning, Inc. Reproduced by permission. www.cengage.com/permissions.

How To Write Audio And Video Scripts

The author would like to thank the following people for giving their time freely and contributing ideas to the book: Mari Tudor Jones (MTJ Media), Diarmuid Carter and James Magrane (Oxford University Press), James Tomalin (Oxford Digital Media), Martyn Gretton (MGvdo) and Tom Dick & Debbie Video Production.

The author and publishers would like to thank the following for permission to reproduce their material: National Geographic Learning, Oxford University Press.

Although every effort has been made to contact copyright holders before publication, this has not always been possible. If notified, ELT Teacher 2 Writer will endeavour to rectify any errors or omissions at the earliest opportunity.

Contents

About The Authors — 6

How To Write Reading And Listening Activities

Introduction	12
An Overview Of Comprehension Activity Types	13
Global Guidelines For Writing Comprehension Exercises	16
Multiple-Choice: Terminology	19
Guidelines For Writing Multiple-Choice Questions	20
Writing Gap-Fill Comprehension Questions	24
Task Commentaries	28
Appendix 1: Vocabulary Exploitation Tasks	33
Appendix 2: Comprehension Questions Bank	34

How To Write Speaking Activities

Aims	36
Introduction: The Difference Between Being The Teacher And The Writer	37
Different Types Of Speaking Activity	39
Choosing The Right Topics And Activities For Your Target Audience	42
Setting The Activity Up To Succeed	49
Maximising Speaking	54
Ensuring The Activity Works Smoothly In The Classroom	68
Writing A Whole Lesson Around Speaking: Checklists For Different Types Of Lesson	77
Task Commentaries	81
Appendix: Activity Bank	90

How To Write Writing Activities

Aims	92
What Are Writing Activities?	93
Different Approaches To Writing	96
Activities To Develop Different Aspects Of The Writing Skill	97
Analysing And Writing A Model Text	106
Staging	110
Writing For Digital	112
A Few Things To Bear In Mind	114
Task Commentaries	115
Appendix	125

How To Write Vocabulary Presentations And Practice

Aims	130
Preliminary Questions	131
Writing Rubrics And Teacher's Notes	141
Presentation Materials	144
Practice Materials	154
Good Vocabulary Material: A Checklist	160
Task Commentaries	161

How To Write Critical Thinking Activities

Aims	165
Getting The Right Mindset	166
What Is Critical Thinking?	168
Why Is Critical Thinking Relevant To Language Learners?	170
Types Of Critical Thinking Activity	171
Writing Your Own Critical Thinking Activities (Receptive Skills)	173
Writing A Critical Thinking Activity At B2 Level (Listening)	175
Writing A Critical Thinking Activity At Lower Levels (Reading)	176
What Is NOT A Critical Thinking Activity?	177
Identifying General Comprehension And Critical Thinking Activities	178
Writing Your Own Critical Thinking Activities (Productive Skills)	179
Writing A Critical Thinking Activity For A Student Talk	180
Task Commentaries	181

How To Write Audio And Video Scripts

Aims And Introductory Task	184
A Short History Of Writing Scripts For ELT Materials	185
How To Write Audio Scripts	192
How To Write Video Scripts	205
Practical Points To Consider About Writing For Video	209
Types Of Video Script	211
Final Checklist	223
Resources And Further Reading	225
Task Commentaries	227

Glossary	231

About The Authors

Caroline Krantz

I live in Oxford where I work as a freelance ELT author. I joined the world of EFL just over 20 years ago, beginning with a two-year stint as a teacher in Barcelona. From there I returned to the UK and worked as an EFL teacher and teacher trainer at a language school in Oxford, before making the move from teacher to writer in 2005. I have since written various titles including Student's Books, Workbooks, Teacher's Books and Teacher's Resource Books for the international adult market and for secondary school students in Spain and Poland. I write for a number of publishers including Oxford University Press, Macmillan Education and Richmond ELT. I also write listening tests for Cambridge ESOL. Most recently I have co-written Student's Books for OUP's new international course for adults, *Navigate*.

Sarah Cunningham

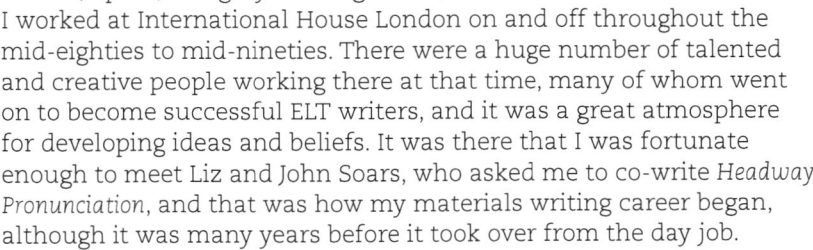

When I started teaching back in the early eighties, the range of teaching materials available was still fairly limited, and I started writing activities for my own classes almost as soon as I started teaching, often finding that I enjoyed preparing my lessons as much as I enjoyed teaching them!

Between stints teaching and training in Greece, Spain, Hungary and Argentina, I worked at International House London on and off throughout the mid-eighties to mid-nineties. There were a huge number of talented and creative people working there at that time, many of whom went on to become successful ELT writers, and it was a great atmosphere for developing ideas and beliefs. It was there that I was fortunate enough to meet Liz and John Soars, who asked me to co-write *Headway Pronunciation*, and that was how my materials writing career began, although it was many years before it took over from the day job.

One of the most talented colleagues that I met at IH London was Peter Moor, and we got married and started writing together at much the same time. Soon, along with having our three children, we began to think about how we could write a course ourselves, and after many ups and downs, *Cutting Edge* was published. For seventeen years we were writing constantly, working on further editions of *Cutting Edge* and the teenage course, *Real Life*. Speaking activities were central to both courses: writing them was always one of the most enjoyable and satisfying parts of the job, and we spent a huge amount of time thinking about how to make them work.

Over the years, we have worked with many experienced and talented editors, publishers and co-authors, who have helped us to understand the needs of different markets, and how to make our writing professional and accessible to all sorts of teachers. At the same time, we have travelled a lot, meeting teachers and observing classes. This, alongside our teacher training experiences, has helped us to appreciate better the wide range of teaching situations that exist around the world, and the many and various ways that different teachers use materials.

There is probably no methodological area in which those differences are more important than speaking, and so I really hope that in this book I can share what I have learnt – from much trial and error – and help you to write successful speaking activities for other teachers to use and enjoy.

Rachael Roberts

Not knowing quite what to do with a degree in English and Drama, I decided to take a year out to teach abroad, and accidentally discovered my vocation. After a couple of years in Portugal I went to Brazil for two years before briefly returning to do an MA in ELT at Warwick. I was already interested in materials design at that point, and one of the modules I took involved writing a sample unit for a coursebook. Putting this idea on the back burner, I got a job as a Director of Studies in Poland, which led into teacher training on CELTA, CELTYL (Young Learners) and DELTA. One of my CELTA trainees happened to be a publisher and he approached me to write a discovery approach grammar book. It pretty much bombed, though I am very proud of a review on Amazon which announces that it is 'better than Murphy'!

Back in the UK, I started working at an FE College, teaching and training, and found myself with a lot of low-level Chinese IELTS students. At that time there was nothing available on the market for them, so, together with two colleagues, I sent in a proposal to Macmillan for a lower level IELTS book. By sheer fluke, they were thinking along the same lines, and didn't yet have an author. *IELTS Foundation* was published in 2004.

Since then I have written a number of Student's Books for Macmillan Education, Pearson and now Oxford University Press, as well as Teacher's Books, Workbooks, photocopiable worksheets and a digital course (MyLab) for PET (Preliminary Test of English).

I pretty much write full time now, though I do teach in short blocks in the summer, or occasionally as a cover teacher. The learning curve has been enormous, and I certainly wish *ELT Teacher 2 Writer* had been around when I was starting out.

Philip Kerr

The first ELT materials that I wrote were during my first job teaching English language in a lycée in Morocco, and I was motivated mostly by frustration with the coursebook I was using. It was called *Practice and Progress* and it was written by Louis Alexander. It has been out of print for a long time but I saw today that a brand new copy of it is available via Amazon for £1,460.68. I can't help wondering how the seller settled on the 68p, but, coincidentally, I recently saw one of my own books on sale for 68 Czech crowns in a remainders box at a conference.

It was a long time before anything I wrote was published. I'd been doing bits and pieces of work for publishers – reader's reports and piloting materials – and eventually I was asked if I would like to write something myself. The first two books I worked on (a grammar book and a coursebook for CAE) were killed by the publishers before they got near to publication. I was naïve and overambitious and I had to learn the hard way.

But I've also been very fortunate. When I worked at International House London in the 1990s my colleagues included some of the best ELT writers of the last 30 years: Ruth Gairns, Sarah Cunningham, Pete Moor, Richard Acklam, Jon Soars, Martin Parrott, Araminta Crace, J.J. Wilson, Chris Redston, Frances Eales, Jane Comyns Carr, Jenny Parsons, Jim Rose, Marisol Gower, Jon Naunton, Sue Leather and Antonia Clare among others. It was a heady place to work and writing was encouraged. I was lucky to be in the right place at the right time.

I was also very fortunate with the first editors I worked with, David Riley and Katy Wright, who encouraged and pushed me to improve my writing, without destroying my confidence. I've now been involved in four coursebook series, and again I've been lucky with my co-writers: Ceri Jones, Lindsay Clandfield, Sue Kay, Vaughan Jones, Luke Prodromou, Marta Rosinska. Writing can be a very solitary occupation and you need good people to share ideas.

As writers, we need to know our limitations. The biography of my life as a writer is mostly about the people that I have worked with. Many have become friends. That, more than anything, is what I have got out of the writing work that I have done.

Paul Dummett

I come across two types of ELT writer*: those who stick mainly to teaching and writing and those who seem to have the energy to teach, do teacher training, blog, present and write. Although I speak from time to time, I definitely fall into the first category. As a teacher and writer, my aim is always to create materials that are stimulating and provoke discussion, whether that be something light and fun or (as tends to be my way) something deeper. Accordingly, I always seek out projects that offer that possibility: *Listening and Speaking Advanced* (Macmillan, 1995) and *Life* (Cengage/National Geographic Learning, 2012/13), *Keynote* (Cengage/National Geographic Learning, 2015/16) are the books I'm proudest of in this respect. (The first one is now out of print but I see you can still get copies on Amazon for as little as £227!)

My teaching career, I guess like many people's careers, has been a quest for greater independence and greater freedom to pursue my interests, in this case methodological. I went from teaching at a private language school in Oxford called Godmer House (1986–90) to designing courses – first task-based learning, then business English, then one-to-one programmes. After a spell as a Director of Studies and Vice-Principal, I set up my own school with two colleagues, servicing contracts with two energy companies in France. That led me to write a book about the Energy Industry – *Energy English* (Cengage, 2010).

Informing my writing and teaching has always been an inquisitive mind and an underlying adherence to the principle of the 'Pedagogy of Question'. I love hearing other people's ideas and I love debate. This goes hand in hand with teaching critical thinking (CT). CT is something that I think I have probably encouraged with students for most of my teaching career, but only more recently (and with the rise of English for Academic Purposes) has it become a more formalized approach. At the heart of it are fundamental and big issues in communication: those of clarity, balance, fairness, truth and effectiveness.

* 'There are two types of people, those who divide people into two types and those who don't.' Edward Murphy Jnr.

John Hughes

Interviewer: What's your name?
Me: John Hughes.
Interviewer: Where are you from?
Me: England. Now I live near Oxford but I've taught students and trained teachers in many other countries.
Interviewer: How did you get into ELT?
Me: I was studying performances of Shakespeare for an MA in central and Eastern Europe and while I was in Poland a university approached me about doing some lecturing on a drama course. They also needed Business English teachers so I started teaching those. I liked teaching Business English straight away because business communication skills are so much about language with performance.
Interviewer: So does your interest in scripts come from your interest in drama?
Me: To some extent. I've studied radio drama and I also worked with TV companies including the satirical *Spitting Image* in the late 80s so I suppose I've spent a number of years listening to scripts and thinking about the key ingredients.
Interviewer: When did you start writing materials for ELT?
Me: As soon as I started teaching in 1992. In particular, I had a lot of Business English and English for Specific Purposes courses, so students would give me texts related to their jobs and I'd turn them into classroom materials.
Interviewer: You published your first ELT book in 2005. How many books have you written since then?
Me: I don't know exactly because I've worked on all sorts of projects either as an author or co-author. For example, I'm a co-author on the series *Business Result* (OUP) and *Life* (National Geographic Learning) and I've also written numerous components such as Teacher's Books and Workbooks for other courses. So I've either written or co-authored well over 30 titles and at least two thirds of those have either an audio or video component. Increasingly, I'm writing online materials which also need scripts, especially for video.
Interviewer: Is that why you've written a chapter for this book? Because materials writers need to write more and more scripts?
Me: Yes, although writing scripts has always been important in ELT; even before recording technology was invented, the earliest examples of textbooks include scripted dialogues on the page. It's a skill that all materials writers need but I also know lots of teachers who like writing their own audio scripts or making videos for their lessons so, hopefully this book will help them to develop that skill.

You can read more of John's writing about ELT, including articles on materials writing, at his blog, elteachertrainer.com.

How To Write Reading And Listening Activities

Introduction

Reading and listening texts can be exploited in a number of ways. They can be used as a vehicle for presenting new language (e.g. grammar and vocabulary), as a springboard for speaking (e.g. discussion of ideas in a text, students retelling a story in a text), or they can be used for skills practice.

As a new writer you are most likely to be asked to write material for supplementary course components such as tests, photocopiable material for a Teacher's Book or Teacher's Resource Book, online material or, further down the line usually, a Workbook.

In these components the main aim of the reading and listening tasks will generally be to give students extra skills practice, as opposed to using texts (reading and listening) as a means of teaching input or as a springboard for discussion.

The focus of this chapter will therefore be on how to write reading and listening comprehension tasks. It is important to note here that while this chapter focuses on the writing of comprehension activities as opposed to the writing/adaptation of texts, it's essential to bear in mind that writing a text/adapting an authentic text and writing comprehension activities need to be done in tandem with one another. Otherwise, it's all too easy to find yourself with a beautifully written and fascinating text, jam-packed with examples of the **target language**, but which yields very few opportunities for comprehension questions. This chapter will therefore also contain examples of how one might fine-tune a text in order to produce better comprehension questions.

An Overview Of Comprehension Activity Types

Some **writing briefs** will stipulate exactly what activity types you need to include. Other briefs will require you to come up with a variety of comprehension activities. The following is a list of some activity types which may be useful for you to have 'in your repertoire' for writing either reading or listening tasks.

1. Pronominal questions

   Pronominal questions are questions beginning with *Who, What, Why, How many, How long*, etc.
   Why is the polar bear endangered?
   How long did the journalist stay in Kerala?
   At lower levels, the question can ask for one-word answers or ask students to copy the answer directly from the passage.
   At higher levels, students can be asked to answer the questions in their own words. This question type is popular with teachers as it is seen to challenge the students. However, you need to make sure that students are likely to have the language to be able to construct an answer which paraphrases what's in the text.

2. Imperatives

   These are similar to the 'answer in your own words' pronominal questions above, in that they require the student to paraphrase, but they use commands instead of questions.
   Describe exposure therapy.
   Explain the three kinds of special effect used in the film.

3. Yes/No questions

   This type of question is suitable for lower levels.
   Does he work better in the afternoon than in the morning?
   Do all students live with host families?

4. True/False sentences or True/False/Not given

   Students can be asked to write T or F (or NG).
   They may also be asked to rewrite the false sentences to make them true.
   Sally is having dinner with Steve tonight.
   Jackson earned very little money working in the hotel.
   True/False sentences are reasonably easy to write, although the false sentences must seem plausible. These exercises can be challenging too if the brief asks you 'squeeze' a large number of True/False questions out of a short text. In these cases, you will have more room for manoeuvre if you can include a few 'NG sentences' which can come from outside the text.

5 Multiple-choice sentences

Multiple-choice sentences are popular exam questions because they are easy to mark and because, unlike True/False questions, students are less likely to get them right just by guessing. For example, if you provide four possible options, students only have a 25% chance of getting the question right. Because of the **backwash effect** (i.e. the effect of testing on teaching) they are also common in coursebooks and supplementary material. Unfortunately, they are the hardest to write! This is because all the wrong choices must seem plausible and not silly.

Why does Maria laugh?
A *She has just heard an amusing story.*
B *She is feeling happy.*
C *She has remembered a funny situation.*
D *She finds Liam's behaviour ridiculous.*

6 Sentence completion

Students complete sentences. They can be asked to complete them with a word from the text, or another specific number of words, e.g. *Complete the gap, using three words from the text.* The words can be the exact words in the reading passage or listening texts. Alternatively, the missing words don't have to appear in the text and students have to use their knowledge of vocabulary to compete the sentence. Gaps can be completed either in individual sentences or in summary paragraphs.

People first started moving to the city because of …
Some people think that visiting local attractions isn't as exciting as …

7 Sentence insertion

Students insert a number of sentences into a gapped text. One or two extra sentences are provided as distractors.

These are the easiest comprehension tasks to write, and, as such, won't be focused on in this chapter. The only points to bear in mind when creating these tasks is to make sure that the sentences which you remove from a text (to be reinserted) are evenly spaced throughout the text and that the text surrounding the gaps (the **co-text**) contains some kind of grammatical or lexical link to the sentences that are to be inserted.

In the following paragraph, for example, not all sentences would be suitable candidates for removal.

The giant panda is a rare type of bear. For many years, however, scientists weren't sure what its closest relatives were. They believed they may be members of the racoon family. Pandas have a very distinctive black and white coat. Giant pandas mainly eat bamboo.

The second sentence contains the **discourse marker**, *however*, which links it to the first sentence. The third sentence contains the pronoun *they* which links grammatically to *scientists*, and the **word family** provides a lexical link to *relatives* in the second sentence. As such any of these three sentences could be removed, to be reinserted. The fourth and fifth sentences, on the other hand, don't contain any links to each other or to the previous sentences and would therefore be unsuitable for removal.

8 Multiple matching

Here students read multiple short texts/a text with several paragraphs or listen to a number of extracts and do tasks such as matching stories with headlines, matching headings or summaries with paragraphs or answering a question, such as *Which speaker/paragraph mentions x, y or z?*

9 Vocabulary exploitation exercises

When writing comprehension tasks, it is likely that you will be asked to produce exercises which exploit the vocabulary from the text (especially for reading texts) or which give students practice in deducing the meaning of unknown words from context. For a list of this type of vocabulary exercise see Appendix 1 on page 33.

Global Guidelines For Writing Comprehension Exercises

The following is a set of guidelines to bear in mind when writing reading and listening comprehension exercises.

1. Make sure that you are not testing students' knowledge of the world. Students need to have read or listened to the text to get the answer.
2. Items should be evenly spread throughout the text. Don't leave chunks of text unexploited.
3. Avoid overlap of items. In other words, don't test the same point in two different questions. If students didn't understand something the first time, they won't understand it the second time.
4. When writing listening items, keep True/False sentences, multiple-choice stems and multiple-choice options clear and concise. They shouldn't require a great deal of processing on the student's part, since the focus should be on listening and not reading comprehension. Also, in practical terms, space on the page is likely to be limited.
5. The questions shouldn't contain the exact words used in the text. If the question repeats part of a sentence from the text, the students will be able to answer it in 'cut and paste' style without needing to understand the text. So the questions need to paraphrase what's in the text. But make sure the language in the questions isn't more difficult than the language in the text.
6. Items should be of roughly the same level of difficulty. If you are writing an exercise that will be used as a test, it is usual to start with a slightly easier question to ease the students into it.
7. The items should be in the same order as the information in the text. Exceptions to this rule are:
   a) if you are writing a matching exercise (e.g. matching summaries/headings with paragraphs, inserting missing sentences)
   b) if students have to answer global questions about the text, e.g. about its purpose or function. This kind of question might appear at the beginning or end of a set of items.
8. If you are writing True/False sentences, or multiple-choice questions, the false sentences and the distractors in the multiple-choice questions need to be as plausible as possible. This is no easy task for the writer!
9. If students are required to complete gaps in sentences, make sure the sentence provides enough context for them to know what to look/listen out for.
10. Ensure a variety of answers across the exercise. E.g. the answers in a True/False exercise should not all be false, or all Cs in a multiple-choice exercise.

How To Write Reading And Listening Activities

Task 1

What's wrong with the comprehension exercise?

In the following reading comprehension exercise the author has not adhered to six of the guidelines listed in the previous section. Read the text and the exercise and identify the six problems. Then check your answers in the task commentary on page 28.

FROM RAGS TO RICHES

Some of the world's billionaires came from humble beginnings. These three entrepreneurs, now retired, are among the richest men in the world. But they weren't born into rich families. They started working at an early age and were never out of work. It was hard work and determination that earned them their enormous wealth.

Leonardo Del Vecchio, producer of Ray-Ban and Oakley sunglasses
Italian industrialist Leonardo del Vecchio became one of the richest men in Italy, but his background was not wealthy. Leonardo's father, who worked in a vegetable market in Milan, died before Leonardo was born. His mother had five children and couldn't afford to bring them up. So Leonardo went to live in an orphanage at the age of seven. He started working at the age of 14, and after that he was never out of work. He worked as an apprentice in a factory, making parts of eyeglasses frames. He was only 26 when he set up his own eyeglasses company. The company grew quickly, and now employs 62,000 people around the world.

Ingvar Kamprad, founder of furniture store, Ikea
Ingvar Kamprad was born in a small village in Sweden. As a child, he lived on a farm, but he was always interested in business. He used to buy large quantities of matches and then sell them for a profit. He reinvested his profits and expanded his business to fish, Christmas decorations, pens and pencils. When he was 17, he got some money from his father for doing well at school. He used the money to set up a mail-order company which later became IKEA. IKEA now has over 200 stores in 31 countries with a total of 75,000 employees. The name IKEA was taken from Ingvar Kamprad's initials (I. K.) and the initials of his farm (Elmtaryd) and village (Agunnaryd).

Amancio Ortega, entrepreneur and owner of fashion store, Zara
His father was a manual worker for a railway company and his mother worked as a cleaner. At the age of 13, Ortega began working for a shirt-maker as a delivery boy. Later, when he became manager of a local shop selling expensive clothes, he realized that only wealthy people could afford nice clothes. He decided to make good quality clothes available to everyone. At the age of 27 he went into business for himself, making and selling bathrobes. He then used the profits to open his first retail store called Zara. It became famous for selling high-quality designer products at reasonable prices. By 1989 there were almost 100 Zara stores in Spain, and the brand continued to grow and expand. There are now 1,603 Zara stores in 73 countries around the world.

Read the article and decide if the statements are true (T) or false (F).
1. The three entrepreneurs are still working.
2. They were occasionally out of work.
3. Del Vecchio had to go and live in an orphanage when he was only seven because his mother and father had both died.
4. He worked as a trainee in a shoe-making factory.
5. When he was a young man he was often without a job.
6. The founder of IKEA was from Finland.
7. Kamprad started his first company when he was 21.
8. Ortega's father worked in an office.
9. Worldwide, IKEA employs fewer than 70,000 staff.

To read a commentary on this task, go to page 28.

Multiple-Choice: Terminology

As I mentioned earlier, multiple-choice comprehension items are notoriously challenging to write. Before we explore this area further, do the following task to familiarize yourself with the terms used to describe multiple-choice items.

Task 2

Do you know your terminology?

Read the following listening comprehension items (1–6) and label the different parts using a word from the list (a–f) below. Then check your answers in the task commentary on page 29.

a) distractor   **b)** key   **c)** option   **d)** rubric   **e)** stem   **f)** text

1 You will hear people talking in six different situations. For each one, choose the best answer, A, B or C.

2 And now for the weather. We're going to see a rather cloudy start to the day today, with outbreaks of rain. These should clear by lunchtime bringing us a very dry, bright and sunny afternoon with temperatures reaching 28 degrees. Tomorrow, again, a cloudy morning, but without the showers, brightening up into another sunny afternoon, though a little cooler than today as there will be an easterly breeze. The current warm spell is expected to continue until well into next week.

3 You will hear a weather forecast. What will the weather tomorrow afternoon be like?
   A) windier than this afternoon
   B) wetter than this afternoon
   C) warmer than this afternoon

4 A, B and C are _____s.

5 B and C are _____s.

6 A is the _____.

To read a commentary on this task, go to page 29.

Guidelines For Writing Multiple-Choice Questions

1. The stem and options should be as short as they can be.
2. The language in the stem and options should be as clear and easy to process as it can be (e.g. no double negatives).
3. The options should be roughly equal in length.
4. Avoid any overlap between the options (i.e. make sure that two options don't say the same thing, or cancel each other out by saying the opposite).
5. Check that the key isn't too obviously right or the distractors too obviously wrong.
6. Make sure that world knowledge isn't coming into play.
7. The options should follow on grammatically and logically from the stem.
8. If using an unfinished sentence, rather than a question, in the stem, check that you have divided it in a logical place (e.g. not in the middle of a fixed expression).
9. Avoid any double keys (i.e. all the other answers must definitely be wrong).
10. Make sure that the key is 'true to text', i.e. that the answer is definitely correct, according to the text.

Task 3

Each of the following reading and listening comprehension items is badly written in at least one way. Can you spot the problem(s) in each? Then check your answers in the task commentary on page 29.

1. According to the text, honey bees are most active
   A) during the day.
   B) in the morning.
   C) late in the afternoon.
   D) at night.

2. Edmund complains that his sister
   A) can be very absent-minded.
   B) spends very little time at home.
   C) doesn't share his sense of humour.
   D) frequently forgets and loses things.

3. What is the speaker's view of violent films?
   A) He suspects they encourage violence in young people.
   B) He doubts they have an effect on people's actions.
   C) He feels that it is impossible to prove that there is a link between violent films and people's behaviour.

4 Giles joined the gym in
   A) order to use the power-lifting facilities.
   B) spite of the high cost of membership.
   C) a street near his office.
   D) an attempt to tone his muscles.

5 What happened after a new manager was appointed at the restaurant?
   A) The quality of service improved.
   B) The service became even worse.
   C) The service was as poor as before.
   D) The décor was modernized.

6 According to the text, the biggest planet in the Solar System is
   A) Mars.
   B) Mercury.
   C) Jupiter.
   D) Earth.

7 Why did Natasha make an appointment at the dentist's?
   A) to enquire about teeth whitening
   B) to find out the cause of her toothache
   C) to have a sight test
   D) to have a check-up

8 When talking about her job, Laura insists that she isn't dissatisfied with
   A) the salary she earns.
   B) the amount of holiday she gets.
   C) the amount of responsibility she is given.
   D) the way she is treated by her manager.

9 Pete wanted to buy a car which
   A) ran on diesel rather than petrol.
   B) was reasonably spacious.
   C) didn't cost too much.
   D) was affordable and spacious.

10 Why didn't Ed stay until the end of the party?
   A) He wasn't enjoying it.
   B) He was tired.
   C) He was feeling unwell.
   D) To get up early the next morning.

To read a commentary on this task, go to page 29.

Task 4

Produce a multiple-choice item.

You are going to write your own multiple-choice item for a listening text, but first, look at the pre-task.

Pre-task
Read the following text and item designed for First (FCE) level. Choose the correct answer A, B or C. Locate the information in the text which contains the key and then identify the information which is used in the distractors.

Text
I've been waiting a very long time for this game to come out and on the whole it lives up to expectations. As with many city-based computer games, it involves getting hold of a vehicle, driving to a destination and accomplishing your mission. The first missions are pretty straightforward. They've been designed that way intentionally to let you get used to the controls. I wish the makers had put more thought into the handling of the vehicles though. The cars are slow and difficult to manoeuvre, which, in my view, takes some of the fun out of it. The graphics, on the other hand, are second to none – it feels like an actual place. Even the weather is convincing. Overall verdict? ... I'd say 8 out of 10.

Item
You hear a young man talking about a computer game. What is his criticism of it?
A) The graphics are unrealistic.
B) Some of the missions are too basic.
C) The vehicles are hard to control.

Now read the text and stem question below, which are also aimed at First (FCE) level.

You hear a conversation between a man and a woman about taekwondo. Why did the woman decide to take up the sport?

Locate the information in the text which contains the key. Identify two more areas which contain information that could be used in the distractors, and then write three options (one key and two distractors). Refer to the guidelines above.

Text
Male So, I hear you've taken up taekwondo!
Female Yeah, I started a few months ago. I reckoned it might be a good way of burning off some of those calories that I'd put on over the holidays.

Male	And a lot better for you than going on a diet, I should think.
Female	Oh yes, totally! And more fun too. But what I hadn't realized is that it's not just a physical sport, it also helps you improve your <u>mental focus</u> and self-discipline.
Male	Really?
Female	Yes, and the other thing is, I now know exactly how to defend myself if I ever need to with one simple kick, so I feel loads more <u>confident</u> when I'm walking around alone at night.

A) gain mental clarity
B) lose extra weight
C) to gain confidence

Compare your answer to the possible answer in the task commentary on page 32.

Writing Gap-Fill Comprehension Questions

Read the guidelines for writing sentence-completion questions and then do the task that follows.

Guidelines for writing gap-fill sentences

1. Your aim is to write a sentence with a gap in which both the correct answer and the distractor(s) can fit logically and grammatically.
2. The sentence to be gap-filled shouldn't be too long or complex to process.
3. However, it needs to be long enough to provide enough context for students to know what they're looking/listening for.
4. Don't let the answer be guessable. Students should be able to work out what kind of word they are looking or listening out for, e.g. a number, a place, a job, but it shouldn't be possible for them to guess the exact word. So, for example, the missing word should not be part of a strong **collocation** (e.g. *earn* _____ .)
5. The words in the sentence should paraphrase the words in the text, not report them directly. In a listening, for example, if the words weren't paraphrased, it would become like a dictation.

How to 'turn up' and 'turn down' the difficulty level of a gap-fill item.

(NB these pointers refer to the writing of the text as well as the items)

1. The incorporation of distractors into a text is one means of adding a level of challenge to a comprehension item. Distractors are designed to 'tempt' the student into choosing the wrong answer if they haven't listened carefully or fully comprehended the text. Providing a distractor in the text makes a sentence harder. Providing two makes it even harder.
2. Sometimes it is very difficult to incorporate a distractor into a text without it sounding forced and unnatural. In this case, there are other ways of raising the challenge level. One is to use challenging language (i.e. **low-frequency** grammar and vocabulary) in the item – within reason, of course. Another is to 'bury' the answer deeply in the text. If the answer is in the middle of the text, it will be harder to 'catch' than if it is at the end of a speaker's utterance.

Task 5.1

The following is an extract from a gap-fill exercise from a First (FCE) listening comprehension.

Read the first part of the listening text and the accompanying gap-fill sentences. Notice how each item paraphrases the language in the text, how each item is buried in the text and how distraction is provided. Locate the key and the distractor(s). Then check your answers in the task commentary on page 32.

You will hear part of a radio interview with an eco-fashion designer called Damien Warner. For questions 1–3, complete the sentences.

Text

Interviewer Tonight my guest is Damien Warner, who is an eco-fashion designer. Tell me, Damien, how did you get into fashion design?

Damien Well, I've been interested in fashion design from the age of 13 when I made my first piece of clothing, a jacket, and then, when I was about 15, I set up my own business designing T-shirts, which I used to sell at school.

Interviewer When did you decide you wanted to make a career out of it?

Damien Well, when I was a teenager, I really had my heart set on studying fashion at university, but in the end I was pressurized by my parents into doing a degree in business studies, which they felt was more 'serious' and more likely to lead to 'a proper job.'

Interviewer And did it?

Damien You could say so – after university I was offered a job as a store manager at a major clothing store but turned that down and took on the role of buyer for the company instead. My parents were thrilled but I realized very quickly that I was never going to enjoy it and that's when I decided to follow my heart and enrol on a fashion design course.

1 The first item of clothing Damien ever designed was a __jacket__.
2 Damien studied __business__ at university.
3 After leaving university, Damien worked as a __buyer__ for a large clothing company.

To read a commentary on this task, go to page 32.

Task 5.2

Now read a later extract from the same interview. The underlined words have been identified as keys that are to be tested through gap-fill sentences.

Write gap-fill sentences, one for each paragraph. The sentences should contain no more than 15 words. The first sentence has been done for you. Then compare your answers to the suggested sentences in the task commentaries on page 32.

Use the guidelines for writing gap-fill sentences to help you.

Text

Interviewer What kind of fabrics do you use?

Damien Mainly natural materials, such as organic cotton. Also, in today's society, where so much stuff is thrown away, I believe very strongly in re-using materials. My most recent collection consists of clothes made entirely of recycled fabrics. For example, there are skirts made from old 1970s' curtains and jackets made from old leather <u>car seats</u>.

Interviewer And is eco-fashion more expensive than ordinary fashion?

Damien Well, eco-fashion, as well as being environmentally-friendly, is also all about making sure that the people who make the clothes are paid a fair price and have good working conditions. There are something like 26 million people around the world employed in the clothes-making business and around <u>19 million</u> of them are underpaid. So if we want to pay these people properly then, yes, they're going to be more expensive to produce and for consumers to buy.

Interviewer What is your biggest challenge at the moment?

Damien I suppose trying to convince people that eco-fashion can actually be trendy. It's had a reputation in the past for being very boring and lacking in colour and style. Fortunately, its image is beginning to change and I have to say I think it's partly thanks to the <u>celebrities</u> who are now buying eco-clothing.

Interviewer Finally, Damien, do you have any advice for any budding fashion designers about how to get into the business?

Damien Competition is pretty tough out there so first of all you need to have lots of determination. I'd also suggest that to improve your chances of getting a place at one of the better fashion schools you should work on perfecting your <u>drawing</u>. There's no point in having good ideas if you can't translate them on to paper so that other people can understand them.

Interviewer Thank you, Damien – it's been great talking to you.

How To Write Reading And Listening Activities

1 Damien's latest collection includes jackets made from _____.
2
3
4

To read a commentary on this task, go to page 32.

Final task

Find a piece of authentic material and adapt it so that you can make a reading or listening comprehension activity. The activity should include either ...
Eight true/false questions OR
Five multiple-choice questions OR
Six gap-fill sentences.

How To Write Reading And Listening Activities

Task commentaries

Task 1 (page 17)

The comprehension task contains the following problems:

Problem 1

2   They were occasionally out of work.

> Question 2 lifts the exact words from the text. Students can cut and paste without understanding what 'out of work' means.

Problem 2

3   Del Vecchio had to go and live in an orphanage when he was only seven because his mother and father had both died.

> Question 3 is far too long-winded.

Problem 3

6   The founder of IKEA was from Finland.

> Question 6 tests world knowledge. Many students wouldn't need to read the text to know the answer.

Problem 4

7   Kamprad started his first company when he was 21.
8   Ortega's father worked in an office.

> Questions 7 and 8 are not in chronological order.

Problem 5

> The text about Amancio Ortega has been underexploited.

Problem 6

> All of the statements are false.

How To Write Reading And Listening Activities

Task 2 (page 19)

1 rubric   **2** text   **3** stem   **4** options   **5** distractors   **6** key

Multiple-choice items consist of:

A **stem**. This can take the form of a question or an incomplete sentence.

Options. These are the sentences or phrases which answer the question or complete the sentence in the stem. There should be at least three options.

A **key**. This is the correct answer.

Distractors. These are the incorrect answers. They are designed to 'tempt' the student and distract them from the key. They should therefore be as plausible as the key.

Task 3 (page 20)

1 According to the text, honey bees are most active
   A) during the day.
   B) in the morning.
   C) late in the afternoon.
   D) at night.

A and **D** are opposites. One of them therefore must be right, which means that students don't need to look at the other two options, as they must be wrong.

Or, the answer may be **B** or **C**, which means that **A** is also correct and therefore we have what's known as 'a double key' i.e. two correct answers.

2 Edmund complains that his sister
   A) can be very absent-minded.
   B) spends very little time at home.
   C) doesn't share his sense of humour.
   D) frequently forgets and loses things.

A and **D** have the same meaning, which would result either in a double key, or students easily rejecting both answers.

Task commentaries

3 What is the speaker's view of violent films?
   A) He suspects they encourage violence in young people.
   B) He doubts they have an effect on people's actions.
   C) He feels that it is impossible to prove that there is a link between violent films and people's behaviour.

> **C** is significantly longer than the other two options. This is an issue not only for the reasons we mentioned earlier (space may be limited on the page, students shouldn't have to process such complicated sentences while listening) but also because it stands out as being longer than the other options. Quite often, though not always, this will suggest to students that it is the correct answer.

4 Giles joined the gym in
   A) order to use the power-lifting facilities.
   B) spite of the high cost of membership.
   C) a street near his office.
   D) an attempt to tone his muscles.

> You should always finish the stem at a logical point, e.g. at the end of a clause. In **A**, **B** and **D** the stem has been cut off in the middle of a fixed expression.

5 What happened after a new manager was appointed at the restaurant?
   A) The quality of service improved.
   B) The service became even worse.
   C) The service was as poor as before.
   D) The décor was modernized.

> The answer has to be **A**, **B** or **C** because the service either got better, got worse or stayed the same – there aren't any more options. Students will therefore discount **D**. (If **D** is also right, then there is a double key.)

6 According to the text, the biggest planet in the Solar System is
   A) Mars.
   B) Mercury.
   C) Jupiter.
   D) Earth.

> Here, world knowledge comes into play and therefore students would not need to read the text to find the answer to the question. This would give an unfair advantage to those who already know the answer to the question. Or indeed it might unfairly disadvantage them if the text says something different.

How To Write Reading And Listening Activities

7   Why did Natasha make an appointment at the dentist's?
    A) to enquire about teeth whitening
    B) to find out the cause of her toothache
    C) to have a sight test
    D) to have a check-up

> In this item **C** is too obviously wrong. Even if the text says the opposite it would be considered unfair to trick students in this way and confound their predictions.

8   When talking about her job, Laura insists that she isn't dissatisfied with
    A) the salary she earns.
    B) the amount of holiday she gets.
    C) the amount of responsibility she is given.
    D) the way she is treated by her manager.

> The stem contains a double negative *isn't dissatisfied*. We should avoid these, especially in a listening, as they are confusing and hard to process.

9   Pete wanted to buy a car which
    A) ran on diesel rather than petrol.
    B) was reasonably spacious.
    C) didn't cost too much.
    D) was affordable and spacious.

> Option **D** includes options **B** and **C**. Even if Pete was looking for a car which was both affordable and spacious, **B** and **C** would also be correct, which would result in a 'triple key'.

10 Why didn't Ed stay until the end of the party?
    A) He wasn't enjoying it.
    B) He was tired.
    C) He was feeling unwell.
    D) To get up early the next morning.

> Option **D** doesn't follow on grammatically or logically from the stem.

Task commentaries

How To Write Reading And Listening Activities

Task 4: possible answer (page 22)

You hear a conversation between a man and a woman about taekwondo. Why did the woman decide to take up the sport?

A) To make her feel more secure.
B) To try to lose weight.
C) To develop her self-control.

The correct answer is **B**.

Task 5.1 (page 25)

The keys are in bold and the distractors are crossed out.

Interviewer Tonight my guest is Damien Warner, who is an eco-fashion designer. Tell me, Damien, how did you get into fashion design?

Damien Well, I've been interested in fashion design from the age of thirteen when I made my first (1) **jacket** and then, when I was about fifteen, I set up my own business designing (1) T-shirts, which I used to sell at school.

Interviewer When did you decide you wanted to make a career out of it?

Damien Well, when I was a teenager, I really had my heart set on studying (2) fashion at university, but in the end I was pressurized by my parents into doing a degree in (2) **business studies**, which they felt was more 'serious' and more likely to lead to 'a proper job.'

Interviewer And did it?

Damien You could say so – after university I was offered a job as a (3) store manager at a major clothing store but turned that down and took on the role of (3) **buyer** for the company instead. My parents were thrilled but I realized very quickly that I was never going to enjoy it and that's when I decided to follow my heart and enrol on a fashion design course.

Task 5.2 Suggested gap-fill sentences (page 26)

2 According to Damien, there are _____ workers in the fashion industry who are not paid enough.
3 Damien thinks that _____ have done a lot to help improve the image of eco-fashion.
4 Damien advised people wanting to get into a good fashion to work on their _____ abilities.

Appendix 1
Vocabulary Exploitation Tasks

The following rubrics may be useful as a checklist of the different exercise types that exploit the vocabulary from a text (especially for reading texts) or which give students practice in deducing the meaning of words from context.

Study the highlighted words in the text. Match them with definitions a–f below.

[definitions a–f]

Find words and phrases in the text which mean:

[definitions – paragraph references or first letter of each word can be given]

Look at the way these words are used in the text.

[words given in a word pool]

Then use the words to complete the following sentences.

[gap-fill sentences]

Find these words in the text and choose the best meaning.

[list of words and options for meaning]

Find synonyms in the text for a–f below.

[list of words a–f]

Find words in the text with the opposite meaning of the words a–f below.

[list of words a–f]

Explain the meaning of [xxxxx] **in your own words.**

Explain the difference between x and y [both taken from text] **in your own words.**

Appendix 2
Comprehension Questions Bank

The following is a list of ready-made question stems which may help you generate your own questions. Think of it as an equivalent of a useful language box for students!

General
When asked about x, Tom says …
What does the writer say about …?
Tom says that when … it's most important to …
According to Tom, …
What advice does Tom have for people who …?
Why does Tom recommend …?
How does Tom feel about …?
What point is made about …?
What does Tom like about …?
What aspect of x did Tom most like/dislike?
What does Tom enjoy most/least about …?
Why did Tom decide to …?
Why did Tom start …?
What does Tom criticize about …?
What is the article about?
What is Tom's advice (about …)?
Why does Tom advise people to/not to …?
What are Tom's plans for the future?
What does Tom plan to do next?
What is Tom's main criticism of …?
Which aspect of x disappointed Tom?
Where does Tom prefer to …?
What is the writer's main point in the first paragraph?
What do we learn about x in the last paragraph?
What do we discover about x in the second paragraph?
The writer's greatest fear (in the mountains) was …?
The writer suggests that …
What does the writer suggest about …?
Why does she recommend …?
Why does he object to the idea?

What helped Tom to decide?
Tom says that when ..., it's most important to ...?
Why was the writer unimpressed by ...?
What do they agree about?
What worries Tom most about ...?
What makes him unhappy?
What does he criticize about it?
What was the main benefit of x for Tom?
What is the article about?

Opinions
What did Tom think about ...?
What's his opinion of ...?
What is Tom's view of ...?
In the writer's opinion, the ideal x is ...
How does Tom view ...?

Feelings
How does Tom feel?
Why does Tom feel proud of ...?
Why is Tom frustrated that ...?
Why is Tom upset that ...?
What is Tom unsure about?
Why is Tom confident about ...?
During his first ... Tom felt ...
How did the writer feel after ...?
How did Tom/Tom's friends/Tom's family react when ...?

Purpose
What is he doing?
Why is he talking about/explaining/advising/discussing/describing ...?
What is the (main) purpose of the conversation?
- to persuade his parents to ...
- to explain how ...
- to suggest that ...

How To Write Speaking Activities

Aims

The main aims of this chapter about writing speaking activities are:

1. to consider the differences between using speaking activities with your own classes and presenting them for use with a wider audience, particularly in print form.
2. to look at different types of speaking activities, and the issues and challenges they may present in a variety of teaching situations.
3. to look at how speaking can be maximised from the point of view of both quantity and quality, and to provide practical examples of how illustration, realia, **rubrics**, staging and teacher's notes can help with this.
4. to provide practical tasks which focus on all these building blocks individually, leading up to writing a full speaking lesson of your own.

NOTE: The example activities I have used in this chapter are deliberately fairly generic and easily recognisable. My aim is to show how any speaking activity can be worked through into a lesson that other teachers can use. It has not been my aim to come up with 'new' or 'original' activities, although of course I hope you do!

All of the example activities can be seen in the Appendix: Activity Bank on page 90.

Introduction: The Difference Between Being The Teacher And The Writer

'Speaking' is a huge area and describes so much of what we do in the language classroom today. It covers activities from oral drills, to quick discussions, to role play, to problem solving, to board games. These activities can have a wide range of different aims, from very controlled practice of grammar, vocabulary, functional language or pronunciation, to freer practice of these areas, to interest creation, discussion of ideas in texts and development of critical thinking skills, and of course pure fluency work.

So perhaps the first thing I need to do is to define the parameters of what I am going to discuss. In terms of materials writing, I think many of the same issues apply to discussions around texts, freer practice speaking activities and 'pure' speaking lessons even though these activities have different aims. On the other hand, very controlled speaking activities, such as drills and pronunciation exercises, throw up completely different issues so I will not be covering these here.

Speaking activities are one of the biggest challenges for materials writers: extended speaking is something that many teachers around the world worry about, and they may feel nervous about trying new ideas. If a teacher is doing a vocabulary gap fill for example, something will always 'happen' in the lesson: even if it is not the most dynamic class, things will not grind to a halt. However, with speaking activities that is often exactly the fear.

In my opinion, this is also the area in which the difference between being the teacher and being the writer is most marked. When you devise a speaking activity for your own learners, you know how old they are, something about their interests, knowledge of the world, cultural sensitivities, group dynamics, sense of humour, and so on. When you write materials for other teachers, whether for teachers in your own school, for supplementary resource books, or for a coursebook, you may not know many of these things. This is of course true when you write any activity, but I think it is a much bigger issue when it comes to speaking.

In your own classroom, you are there to motivate and enthuse your class, to rephrase questions and instructions if they are not working, and to steer things in the right direction if they go off course: in short you can use your experience and personality to make sure the activity works. You may be using an activity type that has worked well for you in the past and this gives you the confidence to persist even if it doesn't take off immediately. Other teachers, who do not have this personal confidence in the material – and with possibly a very different teaching style – may easily conclude that the activity is too complex, ambitious or otherwise unsuitable for their students and be reluctant to give it a try.

Perhaps it is for these reasons that speaking is sometimes rather side-lined in published material: the idea perhaps being that if it is slipped in unobtrusively, then no one will notice if it is passed over quickly. While there may be an argument that it is up to each teacher how much speaking they do, I believe that if a course claims to be **communicative**, then extended speaking has to be given as much prominence as listening, reading or writing. It is much less likely to take place if it is just slipped in as an afterthought. In order to work in the widest range of teaching situations and for the widest range of teachers, speaking activities need to be fully worked through: a speaking lesson with a proper lead-in, stimulus or model, time for preparation and possible follow ups is far less likely to fall flat on its face than something that it is added on half-heartedly. All these stages help to ensure that something does indeed 'happen' in the lesson.

Therefore, perhaps more than with any other types of activity, it is essential to create interest in an imaginative, stimulating way and to provide a genuine reason to communicate, careful staging, clear rubrics and good teacher's notes. As the writer, you have to find ways of motivating learners other than with your own personal enthusiasm, you have to anticipate and pre-empt as many potential sources of misunderstanding or failure as possible, and also consider any necessary variations for different teaching situations. Then it will probably all need to be streamlined so that it does not look dauntingly complicated.

When it comes to speaking activities, I have found that I often spend hours writing and rewriting what ends up as a relatively short series of rubrics on the page. In case all this sounds a bit off-putting, I should add that in my experience, speaking activities are usually the most fun and satisfying activities to write.

Different Types Of Speaking Activity

Before discussing how to write speaking activities, a checklist of different activity types is useful, so here is mine. Obviously terminology can vary and there is overlap between some activity types.

Discussions

Any activity in which learners discuss ideas, including:

- **'Open' discussions** Either standing alone, or leading into or out of a reading, listening text, etc., these can take the form of a list of questions to discuss personal experiences, opinions or current issues; statements to agree or disagree with; quotes to discuss, and so on. They are 'open' because there is no specific goal or end product in mind – the discussion goes on for as long or as little time as the teacher wishes and the class has something to say.
- **List-making and categorising discussions** These differ from open discussions because here there is a goal or 'end product': students discuss in order to compile a list, or are given a list of items and have to categorise them according to certain criteria which they need to discuss and explain.
- **Problem-solving discussions** Here again there is an end goal. Learners have to make a decision or solve a problem based on information and criteria that they have been supplied with.
- **Planning discussions** The end goal here is to discuss and plan the details of an imaginary (or real) event, or schedule of events.

Interviews and surveys

Question and answer activities on a specific topic, often based round a questionnaire, grid, prompt cards or around student-generated materials.

- **Interviews** can be done in pairs or groups, or could involve interviewing a visitor, member of staff, family member, etc.
- **Surveys** are larger scale and more often done as a mingling activity, with another class in the school, members of the public, etc.

Information exchanges/gaps

Activities in which students A and B (and even C and D) are given different information (often on cards or at the back of the book) which they have to share or find out from each other, in order to collect all the information available.

→ Reading

Role plays and simulations

These involve invented characters and scenarios and they can be short or extended, prompted or free, realistic or based on fantasy. They are often set up with role cards, imaginary profiles, etc.

- **Role plays** are done in pairs or groups and learners take on imaginary roles.
- **Simulations** often involve a more complex scenario and are usually done in larger groups. Here learners give their own opinions, but in an imaginary scenario.

Presentations and mini-talks

This could range from formally presenting one group's opinion to the rest of the class to giving a PowerPoint presentation about an area of interest. They include the following when they are done orally either in groups, in front of the class or recorded/filmed:

- **Story-telling** including telling picture stories, personal anecdotes or invented stories.
- **Descriptions** including describing pictures, how something works or how to do something.
- **Summarising** newspaper articles or other information.
- **Reviews** of films, TV programmes, etc.

Games

This category of activities includes a wide range of tasks with the game-like qualities of competing, guessing or winning: from team games to races, board games, and even traditional party games that have been adapted for ELT purposes.

Many speaking lessons are a combination of two or more types (an information exchange might lead to a problem-solving discussion for example, or be part of a game). And of course, these activities may have a number of different aims. A role play, for example, might be used to practise a particular language point, to round off or lead into a reading or listening, or purely for fluency work.

Task 1

1 Read the list of 20 'typical' ELT speaking activities in the Activity Bank on page 90, and match them to the best descriptions above. Which are a combination of more than one activity type?

2 Complete the list with five more speaking activities of your own then match them to the descriptions above. Are any of them combinations of more than one activity type?

(Note that you should keep referring to the list of activities in the Activity Bank on page 90 as it will be used throughout this chapter.)

You can read a commentary on this task on page 81.

Choosing The Right Topics And Activities For Your Target Audience

Choice of topic and activity is at the heart of writing successful speaking lessons, more so, I believe, than with other skills. You can get away with a listening on a topic that learners are not that interested in – they will still answer the questions and do the tasks. But there is a danger that a speaking lesson will fail completely if learners have problems with either the topic or the activity. While the curriculum, and the particular needs of the learners, will dictate general topic choices to a large degree, how these are interpreted in terms of angles and activities is much more in your hands. Of course the materials writer can never absolutely guarantee that a speaking activity will work, but there are a number of considerations that will help to make this more, or less, likely. First and foremost, you need to know as much as you can about your target audience: both learners and teachers.

Writing for a specific audience

If you are writing materials for other teachers in your own school or for your local area, then you are obviously in a strong position to know which topics and activities will go down well and which are a no-no. You may well know the learners' approximate age and something about their knowledge of the world, educational background and interests. You will perhaps know whether students are typically confident about speaking freely in English, or whether they tend to need a lot of guidance and prompting. You may have learnt through experience that classes usually love talking about politics but hate talking about manners, for example. You will know which TV programmes, celebrities, etc. they are likely to be familiar with, whether they are likely to know their way round a smartphone, and so forth. You will probably have a good idea of how open they are to certain 'controversial' topics, and about any cultural or religious taboos. All this information is invaluable in putting together the right speaking activities, so it is worth spending some time working out what you already know about your learners' abilities, tastes and dislikes.

You will probably also know a lot about typical teachers: whether they tend to like group work, games, mingling activities, and so on, whether they have the time and inclination to cut up pieces of paper for role plays, to film their students, or do ambitious group work activities. Or whether on the other hand, they are generally more conservative and tend to prefer whole class discussions and very closely guided and controlled speaking activities. Or perhaps you know that some teachers will be reluctant to try speaking activities at all. Again, this knowledge is invaluable in guiding the choices you make.

If you are writing for a publisher, it can be much more complicated. Sometimes published materials are also aimed at a fairly specific market: sixteen to eighteen-year-old secondary school students in Poland for example; or adults in ESOL groups in the UK. If you have worked in the specific market in question, then again you are in a strong position to draw on personal experience. Sometimes however, you can end up writing for a specific audience that you do not have experience of working with. If this is the case, your publisher should be able to brief you about the key areas of interest, sensitivities and taboos. Ideally you will also visit classes and get the chance talk to teachers about the topics and speaking activities that they like or find problematic. The following points may also be useful, although of course they are only generalisations.

Teenagers and young learners

Writing speaking activities for teenagers and young learners throws up many tricky issues. When it comes to choosing discussion topics, young learners obviously have a more limited experience of the world, and certain issues are more (or less) important to them than they are to adults. While it is good to include a range of teenage-friendly topics and young people's perspectives, it does not follow that everything has to be teenage-oriented, or that serious 'adult' issues like medical science or the future of transport cannot be broached. Teenagers do not *only* think about teenage-related issues. That said, it is important to remember that young learners will not have a lot of the background knowledge and cultural assumptions that adults bring to these topics and that they often need to be approached in a simpler, more informative and less analytical way. (For a more in-depth look at writing ELT primary and secondary materials, see *How To Write Primary Materials* and *How To Write Secondary Materials* in the ELT Teacher 2 Writer series.)

On the other hand, teenagers (much more than adults) are often acutely conscious of anything that they perceive as childish or immature. The worst sin you can commit with fifteen-year-olds is to present a topic that they see as more suitable for twelve-year-olds!

It is also important to bear in mind that teachers have a duty of care towards their young learners and are very aware of how the material might influence them. They are often concerned about being seen to condone anything that is harmful to young people, from violence to drugs and dieting, and may be worried about parents' reaction to the materials their children are using. If you do introduce topics such as these, the approach and tone you take needs to reflect all these concerns. Sometimes, you may be better advised to avoid the topic completely.

As far as choice of activities for young learners is concerned there are important issues too. Class management is one very real problem: young learners can easily get 'over-excited' and forget what they are supposed to be doing in very free, extended, complicated or lively activities. Teachers are often worried about losing control, or about the disruption they may cause to other classes, especially in state schools, and they can therefore be reluctant to do large group work, play noisy games or get their students mingling, for example.

On the other hand, the young learners themselves are often shy or self-conscious about taking risks in front of their peers, which can make them reluctant to 'give' very much in freer discussions or group work. For these reasons teachers often prefer whole class discussions, or favour pair work over group work.

As the materials writer, obviously you cannot solve all these problems, but you can help. For example, where possible you can write discussion activities that work equally as whole class activities, rather needing to be done in groups. Pair work is often perceived as more achievable than group work, but as a general rule, the more structured and focused the activity is, the less the learners are likely to feel that they are sticking their necks out or making fools of themselves. Prompted role plays and interviews, straightforward games, structured information gap activities and list-making activities with clear objectives all often work well as the main 'meat' of speaking lessons for younger learners and teenagers, with freer discussion added on as a more optional extra. Complicated simulations, mingling activities, etc., if included at all, are better offered as alternative suggestions rather than core activities.

Multi- and mono-cultural groups

Some topics work well with mono-lingual/cultural classes but not with multi-lingual/cultural classes, and vice versa. If you are used to working with one or other type but have to write for both, it is important to be aware of the differences.

If you teach groups that contain many different nationalities, whether you are talking about families, social life or the prison system, you can often broaden out the topic in a very generative way by comparing different countries and cultures. With monolingual classes this option doesn't work nearly so well, as everyone's experiences are broadly the same, and learners are not necessarily aware of the difference between their own country and others. If you want learners to compare their culture with another one, then you will need to supply the information, perhaps through a short text, a fact file or an infographic.

In some activities you may even need to supply slightly different discussion questions, or variations on the activity to cover the differences between multi- and mono-cultural classes. Take Activity 13 in the Activity Bank, page 90, in which learners have to devise a list of tips for foreign visitors about social customs in their country. To devise the tips, multicultural groups will have to either work with their compatriots or alone, while mono-cultural classes can work in pairs or groups in the usual way, so this phase of the activity is potentially easier for them. On the other hand, when it comes to presenting their ideas to the group and listening to each other's tips, the multicultural class have a real reason to listen to each other and ask questions, and a long discussion could take off. In the mono-cultural class there will not be much

'natural' comparison or discussion, as their ideas are likely
so here the purpose of the learners listening to other groups
check whether they can add any more ideas to their own li

Writing for a very broad audience

Often, if you write coursebooks or supplementary materials for a publisher, audience is very general, or even as yet unknown, as new markets open up all the time. It may potentially include many different nationalities, religious and racial groups, a wide range of ages, different ability groups, levels of education, monolingual and multilingual groups, and so on. This means in practice that you have to take account of a very wide range of likely curriculum topics, outlooks, life experiences and cultural sensitivities, with the result that a bit like a politician trying to win an election, you end up aiming for 'the middle ground' and 'lowest common denominator', rather than being able to please all of the people all of the time.

This may run counter to your initial instincts. As a teacher, you may feel desperate to get away from 'bland ELT topics' and branch out into something more original, or more intellectually challenging. If you can manage to pull this off and come up with something that engages and is manageable by the range of learners you are writing for, then obviously that is wonderful. However, the quest for originality can sometimes lead to topics that seem odd or obscure to other teachers, and can be difficult in terms of vocabulary and syllabus. Rather than seeking to be original, it is often better to think in terms of finding a 'fresh angle' or a 'new twist' on a more familiar curriculum topic. Often it is the details that bring humour, controversy, emotion or surprise to the topic: a touching human interest story; or an eccentric or interesting personality, or an unusual new way of doing things.

If nothing springs to mind, it often helps to start by brainstorming all the angles you can think of on the broad theme that you are dealing with: cities, travel, money or whatever. Then, as you start to research the different angles, it is sometimes useful just to browse and see where they lead. In the past this has led me to crowdfunding, which gave a new twist to the task of choosing which project to give money to (Activity 15 in the Activity Bank, page 90: Learners decide which of a number of artistic, entrepreneurial and charity ventures to back on a crowdfunding website, and how much to allocate to each one.); or couch-surfing, which brought a new angle to the topic of planning a trip around the world (Activity 20, page 91: In pairs or groups, learners plan a trip round the world, deciding how they will allocate their budget.). Even if you don't find anything as concrete as this, you will almost certainly come across some new issues and considerations that help you to make your material more relevant and up to date.

trying to be too original can cause problems, so, I think, is it easy to estimate the knowledge of the world and analytical skills of the broad spectrum of learners. Of course, one of the aims of speaking activities may well be to develop learners' critical thinking skills, and I am not suggesting that meaty, intelligent topics should be avoided – personally I am all for them – but they do need to be presented carefully. It often works best to open up complex or abstract topics from a concrete human perspective, and in a way that can be discussed on a range of different levels. For example, if you take Activity 11 in the Activity Bank, page 90 (Students talk about a list of questions about a controversial issue such as plastic surgery/gun laws/capital punishment/the ethics of gene editing, etc.), this topic can be discussed from a number of different perspectives: what learners think of various celebrities' plastic surgery; the rights and wrongs of individuals in particular situations having plastic surgery; the rights and wrongs of state-funded plastic surgery operations, possibly leading to a more general discussion about what the state should and should not pay for, how much it is right to interfere with nature, and so on.

As someone who writes materials for a very wide audience of learners, when I read a newspaper or magazine, go on the internet, or simply chat to people in daily life, I am always on the lookout for topics that seem to have the potential to get a wide range of people talking. Sometimes I try to imagine a wide cross-section of people I know being put into a situation where they are obliged to keep a conversation going about the given topic (a scenario not that different from the average language classroom in fact!) and try to decide whether or not they would all manage. Often it is simple everyday subjects such as 'the habits that annoy you', 'shopping habits' or 'coming from a large family' that pass this test most easily.

Level

Lastly, there is of course one issue that makes speaking activities succeed or fail more than other: the level-appropriacy of the topic and activity. Nothing makes learners resort to their own language (or fall silent) faster than being overwhelmed by the pure linguistic difficulty of the task in hand. Key language can be fed in, but if the whole activity is over-ambitious, then no amount of preparation can adequately compensate. And the reverse is of course true: if the topic does not challenge the students sufficiently and they zip through the activity in two minutes. All this may seem incredibly obvious, but away from the classroom at the comfort of my own desk, I know from experience that it is very easy to become over-optimistic about what learners of a particular level can achieve.

If you are writing a series of modules or units, then it is also important that speaking tasks are graded so that they progress in terms of difficulty, especially if learners are starting out without much experience or confidence about speaking in English. This grading is not just a question of linguistic difficulty, although of course that is very important. You also need to consider the accessibility or difficulty of the topic itself (so you might make earlier speaking activities more personalised for example, and later ones more abstract), and finally you need to consider the operational difficulty of the activity: learners who are not very used to pair or group work will initially find a simple interview in pairs easier to cope with than a complicated simulation or class survey.

For this reason, and for all the reasons above, it's invaluable to try to observe classes who will potentially use the material, get feedback on your first draft from the relevant teachers, or, best of all, pilot the materials yourself.

Task 2

1. Before reading the rest of this task, think of one of your favourite classroom speaking activities – a go-to lesson that always works for you, for example, a discussion, a role play, a game, etc.

2. Read about six classes (all real classes that I have visited). Which ones are most/least similar to those you have worked with? What are the potential problems with each when it comes to speaking activities?

CLASS A is a monolingual secondary school class of about twenty bright, lively 16–17-year-olds. They are motivated and enjoy discussing things, but they can be hard to control. L1, topics, some ss dominating

CLASS B is an in-company group of six students aged from about 25 to 50, who range from the receptionist (whose English is rather good) to the managing director (who is less capable). Speaking is supposedly the key skill for them, but in practice they are often reluctant to speak. Level vs company position

CLASS C is a multi-lingual group of fifteen to twenty students attending part-time evening classes at a local authority college in an English-speaking country. Their nationalities, cultures, backgrounds and ages are extremely mixed and attendance is erratic, so even though they are friendly and willing, it is hard to build up a good group dynamic. missing cohesion/ coherence info / language gaps.

CLASS D is a group of 35 university law students doing an English module as a university requirement. On the whole, they are highly motivated and have sophisticated opinions about a wide range of subjects. However, attendance can vary enormously.

CLASS E is a monolingual group of twelve 13–15-year-olds attending a private language school after a day at school. They are being sent by their parents who want them to learn to speak, but they are not always motivated, and are shy about showing themselves up in front of their peers.

CLASS F is a monolingual group of fifteen 17–19-year-old young men attending a technical college, where all are training to be electricians. They are obliged to study English as part of the curriculum, but for many it is not a priority.

3 Think again about the activity you chose in exercise 1 above.
- Would it work well with all these groups? Why / Why not? (You can assume that each class is the correct level for the activity.)
- With which groups would it be unlikely to work, and why? Can you think of any other speaking activities you know that might go down better with these classes? Why?

4 Look at the Activities in the Activity Bank on page 90, including your own ideas. Which topics and activities do you think would work well with each class? Which present potential problems?

You can read a commentary on this task on page 81.

Setting The Activity Up To Succeed
Publishing-friendly ways to create context and stimulate interest

With your own classes, you might create interest and context for a discussion lesson with a chat about a current news story, a thought-provoking *YouTube* clip or an appropriate song. You might kick off a story-telling lesson with your own personal anecdote, or with a short visualising game. A role play might be introduced via a photograph of a local celebrity, or a humorous caricature that you know your students will appreciate: the lazy student or the overbearing parent, for example. And of course, ideas like these should not be ruled out when you are writing for other teachers: if practicable and appropriate they can provide variety and sparkle, particularly if you are writing for a specific context where you know they work well.

But the wider your audience, the more universal and 'dependable' context creation activities need to be. If your material is appearing in print form, you are of course limited to what will work on the written page, but there are many other restrictions too. With any formally published material, permissions for songs or URLs for video clips are usually a minefield. Local and current news stories or celebrities obviously don't always travel or date very well, and neither may your jokey caricatures – with a different age group or culture, they might be irrelevant or even offensive. And although the game or the personal anecdote may work well as additional or alternative suggestions in the teacher's notes, you cannot assume that every teacher who uses your material will have the confidence to carry them off.

It is therefore for good reason that when writing materials for other teachers, authors often start with photographs and illustrations or 'realia': specially written items that have been styled up to look as if they come from a newspaper, the internet, etc. To set up speaking activities you might use short newspaper articles, headlines, fact files, infographics (information represented visually through charts, diagrams, etc.), adverts, brochures, profiles, case studies, quizzes, notices, messages, posters, cartoons or quotes.

At their most basic, pictures and realia create context immediately and can help to make the activity realistic and relevant, whether it is just a photo of a customer complaining in a shop or a simple holiday brochure. And of course they are a straightforward, useful way of pre-teaching any key vocabulary.

On the other hand, you may want to stimulate the learners' imagination: to take them back into the past, forwards into the future, or to set up a fantasy scenario. You may want to create a sense of mystery, give a light-hearted or humorous tone, or provoke curiosity. Well-chosen photos, illustrations and realia can do this instantly, whether you want the learner to contemplate strange laws from around the world, imagine that they are setting up a new civilisation on Mars, or be transported into the world of a 17th-century ghost story.

Photos and realia are also vital in raising the issues that you want to discuss: short articles, quizzes, fact files or infographics can provide background information, plant a few key facts about the topic and present some concrete examples to discuss. A short multiple-choice quiz about how you would behave in various social situations might introduce some of the issues (and vocabulary) to be covered in Activity Bank Activity 13, page 90 (Students decide in pairs on the best tips to give a foreign visitor about manners and behaviour in their country. They then act out a conversation with a foreign tourist in which they make recommendations about the best ways to behave.) or an infographic about gun laws, gun ownership and gun crime might introduce that topic (Activity 11 in the Activity Bank, page 90: Students talk about a list of questions about a controversial issue such as plastic surgery/gun laws/capital punishment/the ethics of gene editing, etc.). Real or imaginary case studies are often a very good way of setting up a discussion too: for example, you could introduce the discussion about plastic surgery with case studies of someone who was attacked and needed plastic surgery, a teenager who has been bullied about a physical feature and wants plastic surgery, a case of someone 'addicted' to plastic surgery, etc. Human stories like this help to bring out the issues in a tangible way, which, as I have mentioned, is often a good way 'into' a topic. And of course photos can bring out issues indirectly too. If you are discussing jobs and employment, for example, a photo of a female plumber or a child sweatshop worker could be used to raise important issues.

These introductory materials also play an important part in making the topic accessible to your target audience: by selecting the people, places and examples in your photos, fact files or case studies carefully, you can help to make the material more relevant to the age group, gender, nationality or ethnic group that you are catering for, or ensure that they reflect the range of groups that you are aiming at. And because you are creating the materials yourself, you can edit out anything that is confusing, irrelevant to the age group, likely to date, too UK- or US-centric, and so on.

If you are working for a publisher, you will have professional photo researchers and designers who can style the material in a way that is realistic, user-friendly and appealing, or can otherwise create the mood and feel that you want. In this case, it is useful to have a concrete example of the kind of picture or feel that you would like, although often the exact picture cannot be used, so if you are basing a lot of work round a particular photo, then it is important to check it out with the publisher in advance.

On the other hand, even if you are working without a publisher, these days there are many royalty-free and Creative Commons photo libraries and other resources available online, including *ELTpics* and *Pixabay*.

Making sure the aims are clear and the activity is set up to achieve them

In your own lessons, you know what your aims are at a given moment: if you only want to focus learners briefly on a topic to create interest, you will ask discussion questions quickly and then move on; if you want learners to talk at length, you will give them time to think or brainstorm ideas in pairs and groups. If you are doing a role play to practise specific language, you will start by prompting and giving examples using the language you are trying to practise; if the aim is fluency, you will instead prompt with ideas to keep the conversation going for as long as possible. When you write materials, you cannot take it for granted that your aims are clear, and the aims of speaking activities in particular can easily get lost, especially if the activity leads into or out of another activity type: a listening or reading, for example. Titles, rubrics (instructions) and examples are therefore particularly important.

Headings

The starting point is a clear heading, preferably mentioning speaking or practice explicitly. If there is a goal or 'end product' in mind, it is a good idea to summarise this succinctly in the heading, so that teachers and students know where everything is leading. Good examples might be:

Speaking: Find out about your partner's family
Practice: Complain about some faulty goods

Rubrics

You can further clarify your aims through rubrics (instructions), for example for a short introductory discussion:

Discuss the questions below **briefly.**

as opposed to an in-depth discussion:

Think about the questions below and make notes. *Then explain your ideas* **in detail** *to your partner.*

Or if your aim is to practise specific language:

Explain to your partner how to use the app, **using the verbs in the box above.**

Examples

Examples are also key in illustrating your aims, as well as showing how the activity works. There often isn't room for many examples on the page, so the ones you choose need to work hard for you. Obviously, examples need to be unambiguous, and it should be clear how the example can be transferred to other items in the exercise or activity. If the activity is there specifically to practise a piece of language, then the target language should be included in the example – you might even put it in bold:

Example (Activity Bank Activity 2, page 90: Students act out a conversation in which a customer is complaining to the manager of a shop about some faulty electrical goods he/she has bought.):

Student A Can I speak to the manager please? **I'd like to make a complaint.**
Student B Yes, of course. **Can I ask what it's about?**

If you want learners to give their opinions and agree/disagree with each other, then this can also be illustrated in the example (Activity Bank Activity 11, page 90: Students talk about a list of questions about a controversial issue such as plastic surgery/gun laws/capital punishment/the ethics of gene editing, etc.):

Example:
Student A **Personally, I don't think** she should have plastic surgery; she's too young.
Student B **I don't agree. I think** she's old enough to decide for herself.

As well as illustrating your aim, the example can be used to get learners started on the task. For example, in Activity 4 in the Activity Bank, page 90, students make a list of annoying habits:

Example:
People who talk loudly on their phones on the bus or the train.

Finally, consistency across different worksheets, units, etc. will help to set up your activity more efficiently. So, if you are writing a series of units with similar, repeated activities (for example, a discussion or role play at the end of each worksheet or unit), it helps users to grasp your aims more quickly if you present examples and phrase headings and rubrics in a similar or consistent way. If you are working for a publisher, especially in a series involving other authors, there may already be a set style for headings, rubrics and examples, but it is always worth keeping in mind their importance in terms of setting out and helping learners to achieve your aims.

Task 3

Look at the Activity Bank on page 90.

1 Find a selection of photos to illustrate Activity 3. (Students explain how to use a favourite app and why they find it useful.) Think about how to make the task relevant and appealing to either the learners you are likely to write materials for, or as wide a range of tastes, age groups, etc. as possible. How can you avoid making the photos date too quickly?

2 Choose one of discussion topics in Activity 11 (Students talk about a list of questions about a controversial issue such as plastic surgery/gun laws/capital punishment/the ethics of gene editing, etc.), or a controversial topic of your own. Decide how you could help learners to appreciate the various issues, using both photos and realia such as fact files, infographics and case studies.
Start researching online. Is the kind of information you require easily available? Can you find any authentic materials that are useable? What can you mock up, based on your research?

3 Find at least one task in the Activity Bank which might:
- act as free practice of a particular language area.
- accompany a reading text, either as a lead-in or as a way of rounding off the lesson.
- be used for fluency work.

4 Think of headings for Activities 3–6 which express clearly and concisely what you want learners to achieve.

   3 Students explain how to use a favourite app and why they find it useful.
   4 In groups, students think of the ten habits that they find most annoying in other people and explain why.
   5 In pairs, students each look at similar pictures on different pages at the back of their student's book and ask questions to find ten differences. The first pair to find all the differences is the winner.
   6 Some/all of the students tell the class about a film they have watched recently and what they thought of it.

5 Decide what example to provide for Activity 5 (In pairs, students each look at similar pictures on different pages at the back of their student's book and ask questions to find ten differences. The first pair to find all the differences is the winner.), in order to help learners understand what is expected of them.

You can read a commentary on this task on page 83.

Setting The Activity Up To Succeed

Maximising Speaking

Having chosen your topic and activity and set it up, you then want to maximise speaking, both in terms of how much learners say and, equally importantly, the ambition and quality of what they say. Depending on the activity type, there are a number of issues you need to consider, and stages you could build in. Not all of the suggestions below are appropriate to every activity, and if you included all of them, your activity would become impossibly lengthy and repetitive. However, as the materials writer, you have the time to work out exactly which help most with which tasks.

Providing a genuine reason to communicate

Ideally your speaking activity should provide learners with a real reason to communicate real information: by comparing their own personal experiences, expressing their own opinions or passing on real knowledge. If this is the case, learners should be more motivated to speak than if they are using language in a more artificial context, and research indicates that they are more likely to acquire language if they are using it in a way that is genuinely meaningful.

Personalisation is often the simplest way to provide a genuine reason to communicate, and many fluency activities and freer practice activities are successfully based round this, particularly at lower levels, for example, Activities 1 (In pairs, students ask each other a list of questions about their families.), 4 (In groups, students think of the ten habits that they find most annoying in other people and explain why.) and 8 (Students tell each other a personal story about a minor childhood accident.) in the Activity Bank on page 90. The key, when writing materials for other teachers, is to make questions relevant but not overly personal (see below) and, as has already been mentioned, to be aware of the potential sensitivities of specific learners (if you were writing for classes of refugees from war zones you might think twice about Activities 13 and 15, for example). There is also a danger of fatigue with certain basic topics after a certain level, so you may need to find a new twist.

Many classroom discussions also provide genuine communication, simply because they are asking learners to give and discuss their own opinions, for example, Activity Bank Activities (page 90) 9, where students talk about shopping habits and consumerism, before and after a reading text about a 'shopaholic' and a 'minimalist', (a person who can fit all his possessions into one rucksack), and 11 where students talk about a list of questions about a controversial issue such as plastic surgery/gun laws/capital punishment/the ethics of gene editing, etc. And sometimes, although the activities that you write might put learners into an imaginary scenario, they are still drawing on their own opinions and judgements to make decisions, and so there is still a strong element of genuine communication. For example, Activity Bank Activities 15 (Learners decide which of a number of artistic, entrepreneurial and charity ventures to back on a crowdfunding website, and how much to allocate to each one.), 16 (In pairs, students each read different information about two candidates for the job of au pair to a family. They ask and answer questions to find out the information that their partner has, then discuss who is best qualified for the job.) and 18 (Learners read some information about a reality TV celebrity charity trek across Africa and have to decide which six candidates should go from a shortlist of ten).

Equally, there are many ways that you can get learners to share real knowledge in the classroom, both incidentally during the course of discussions, and more formally through mini-talks like Activity 3 (Students explain how to use a favourite app and why they find it useful.) or Activity 6 (Some/all of the students tell the class about a film they have watched recently and what they thought of it.) in the Activity Bank. Often though, it is difficult in practice to rely on learners' knowledge of the world and so we 'artificially' create a need to communicate, via information gaps like Activities 16 (In pairs, students each read different information about two candidates for the job of au pair to a family. They ask and answer questions to find out the information that their partner has, then discuss who is best qualified for the job.) and 19 (In groups of three or four learners each read a different article about the topic of online privacy and security, then summarise their article to their group and discuss the issues that it throws up.).

Indeed, not every speaking activity can involve genuine communication. Sometimes in order to practise specific language you have to put learners into an entirely imaginary scenario where they are not acting as themselves or doing anything real. This is often true for activities that practise functional language, like Activity 2 in the Activity Bank, page 90 (Students act out a conversation in which a customer is complaining to the manager of a shop about some faulty electrical goods he/she has bought.). There might also be situations where learners prefer artificial scenarios to discussing real experiences and opinions: perhaps if learners are young and have had relatively few experiences, or have had very traumatic experiences, for example. This kind of speaking activity can still be very generative, and is sometimes the most realistic option, even if it is not the ideal.

Asking the right questions in the right order

Most speaking activities involve discussing questions at some stage, but in your own classroom you can ask as many as you like, and pick up on and reshape your students' answers to lead things in the right direction. If the questions prove beyond the learners' experience, or insensitive for some unexpected reason, then you can rephrase them or move on. But when you write materials for other teachers, you will only have a limited number of questions (a huge list can be intimidating), so if you want to maximise speaking, it is important to phrase questions carefully and build up logically.

Ideally, you want to start from an accessible point and gradually move towards broader or more complex issues, rather than throwing learners into the deep-end of a topic that they have not had time to collect their thoughts about.

Some questions we ask our learners would be difficult to discuss 'off the cuff', even in your own language, and obviously this is much harder in a foreign language. It is better to start out with something simple and specific that sets out the topic but only requires the learner to access information that is easily retrieved. Personal information is typically most easily accessed in the brain, so personalisation is often the most accessible way into a topic. If the subject does not lend itself very well to personalisation, very simple brainstorming is another 'easy' way into a topic: *Think of three facts about (New Zealand)*, and so on.

It is also important to word questions carefully in order to elicit the fullest answers and keep the discussion going. Here are some potential pitfalls based on questions about the topics in the Activity Bank of 'Family' and 'Gun laws'. (I have chosen these topics because it is easy to think of unfortunate questions to ask. Whether or not you would want to use these topics at all depends on other factors.)

The opening question is too broad or vague, and learners have not been prepared for it.

These are exactly the kind of questions that throw learners into the deep-end of a topic they have not had time to focus on. They would be difficult to answer very fully if asked unexpectedly even in one's own language. Opening questions that fall into this category would be:

What do you think of large families?
What do you think about people owning guns?

With the first, a bit of simple personalisation would start things off much better:
Do you come from a large or a small family?
Do you know anyone who comes from a very large family?

The question can be answered with just *yes* or *no*.

This is the opposite problem but likely to be equally ungenerative. It is difficult to avoid these questions totally, but if possible, reword them to elicit a longer answer. For example, *What are the advantages and disadvantages of coming from a large family?* is likely to elicit a longer response than *Would you like to come from a large family?*

The questions ask learners about experience they don't have.

While it is obvious that you should avoid a question like *Have you ever been to New Zealand?* if in all probability no one has, some cases are more difficult. For example, in this set of questions about families, if it is established at the outset that that one of the students in the group is an only child, and/or has no extended family, then many of the other questions are irrelevant.

Do you have brothers and sisters or are you an only child?
Do you spend a lot of time with your brothers and sisters?
Do you have a lot in common or are you very different?

Do you have a large extended family?
Do you see your extended family very often?
Which members of your family do you most take after? In what ways?
Which members are you closest to?
What are the advantages and disadvantages of being an only child or coming from a large family?

That said, it is a potentially generative topic area for the majority of learners, so the questions are still worth asking if they are relevant to the rest of the class. One way round this problem is to get the learners to read and tick the questions that are relevant to them, or to cross out the questions that are irrelevant or which they don't want to discuss.

The question is too personal or sensitive.

As I have said, personalisation is very often the simplest and best way to introduce a discussion topic or indeed practise target language in a way that is natural and relevant. However, some topics and questions are just too personal, sensitive or controversial to bring into the classroom, for example, these questions around the topic of gun ownership:

Do you own a gun?
Do you know anyone who has been the victim of gun crime?
Have you ever been shot? (In case you think this is outlandish, I did once see a teacher ask a class this question!)

Here it would be better to introduce the topic in a more indirect, impersonal way:
What kinds of people generally carry or own guns in your country?
Have there been any stories about gun crime in the news recently?

In other cases, it is more borderline as to whether the question is too personal. For example:
Do you get on well with your siblings/parents/family?
What issues, if any, do you tend to fall out about?

Different individuals feel very differently about this issue: some people positively enjoy discussing matters that are quite personal, others do not, and of course it depends on how well the class know each other and how well they get on. Teachers may be equally divided about whether or not to use such questions. Again, you could get round this by getting learners to tick the questions they want to discuss, or cross out the ones they don't want to answer.

How To Write Speaking Activities

The answer involves knowledge students probably don't have.

Questions like the following may well elicit silence, just because learners don't really know the answers:

Is gun ownership becoming more common in your country?

What are the laws controlling gun ownership in your country?

Adding phrases like *in your country* is not always helpful, as students are not necessarily aware which habits are unique to their country and which are similar to others. In this case it would be much better to provide a fact file about gun laws and ownership in, say, the USA and the UK, and then ask students whether they think the laws in their country are more similar to the USA or the UK.

Everyone is likely to agree about the answer to the question.

For example:

Do you think people with a history of violence should be banned from owning guns?

Better:

What kind of people should be banned from owning a gun? Why?

The question is heavily loaded towards a particular point of view.

For example:

In what ways do you think the gun laws in the USA should be changed?

Better:

Do you think the gun laws in the UK or USA should be changed? In what ways?

Or, in this case, it might work better to base discussion around statements or quotes that learners either agree or disagree with. In that way interesting or extreme points of view that learners may not have thought of, or may not know how to express, can be introduced.

Providing key language

Another frequent reason that learners under-perform in speaking activities is that they do not have the necessary vocabulary or phrases to express their opinions and ideas, or to structure what they want to say. It is therefore often necessary to build in a stage, or several stages, focusing learners on useful language for achieving the task. This is not the same as presenting a lexical set or a functional area like 'expressing opinions' and then using a speaking activity to practise it, so you need to be very clear about your aims at this point: if your main aim is speaking for fluency, then you need to start from what you want the learners to do and work back to the language that is needed to do it.

The best way to find the right key language for a speaking task is to get someone to do the activity that you want the learners to do, or to do it yourself, but without any kind of preconceptions of what language will be used. It is often not what you might have originally imagined. For example, if the task is to discuss a mystery or strange event, you might expect people to speculate using past modals like *could have/might have done/been*. However, you may find that other phrases are more often used instead, for example *I suppose/guess X happened; for all we know, X happened;* or *it seems likely that … .* Having discovered the 'real' language needed to achieve the task however, it will still need editing and paring down to ensure that it is appropriate to the learners' level, and not so idiomatic that it overwhelms them.

Even in a discussion about a specific topic like gun laws, it is interesting that the most useful language is not just a series of topic-based nouns, but a mixed bag of 'general' verbs and other phrases too. So as well as words like *shoot, gun licence* or *self-defence*, there will be a lot of more general vocabulary like *ban, change the law, make it easier/more difficult to …,* etc.

If the task is more extended or ambitious, you may need to feed in different types of language at different points, which will help students perform different **functions**. For example, if the task is to tell a personal anecdote, learners will need:

- the basic vocabulary for describing what happened (*to fall off, a swing, to break your wrist,* etc.). In this case the vocabulary will be different for each learner, and so it is sometimes useful to build in a stage when learners can ask the teacher for personal vocabulary.
- phrases for putting the story together. Different kinds of phrases will be needed at different points too, for example, to introduce the story (*I always remember the time that …, One story I'll never forget is when …*); to recount the events (*to begin with …, so then, anyway, apparently …, so in the end …*)
- phrases to respond with interest when they listen to other people's anecdotes (*No! So what happened? That's terrible,* etc.).

Key phrases like this perform a dual function – as well as helping learners to express their ideas, they illustrate and prompt the kind of interaction you want, which in itself helps to promote greater fluency.

Building in thinking and rehearsal time

While no one needs time to think about whether they have any brothers or sisters, many other speaking tasks do require thought, both about the answer itself and about how to phrase it in English. If learners are to use the best language they are capable of, rather just staying in their linguistic comfort zone, thinking time is invaluable. Generally, the more complex the topic, and the more extended the task, the more thinking time is beneficial. If learners have to speak at length, for example telling an anecdote or giving a presentation, then some kind of run-though or rehearsal will often also improve performance considerably.

Thinking and rehearsal time is also a good way of levelling the playing field between the confident outgoing learners in the group (who often naturally dominate in more spontaneous speaking activities) and more reticent individuals who may be more anxious about making mistakes and who will therefore benefit from some time to formulate their ideas to their satisfaction. Thinking and rehearsal time are obviously also helpful for classes who are generally weaker in speaking skills than in other areas.

While all this might be second nature to you as teacher, you cannot assume that the teachers using your material will automatically incorporate thinking and rehearsal time, so if, as the writer, you think it is necessary to the activity, you should aim to build it in, either in the activity itself or in the teacher's notes. Here are some different ways you can build in thinking and rehearsal time:

- Including a simple rubric which says *Spend a few minutes reading the questions below and thinking about your answers.*
- Staging the activity so that the discussion, role play, etc. is done in pairs first, before being done as a whole class. This is a good way for learners to work out exactly how to phrase their ideas before the more intimidating task of expressing them to the class.
- Extending this previous approach further, so that learners do the activity in pairs, then larger groups or new pairs before finally doing it as a class. If the activity calls for very complex ideas or language, this can be very helpful, or it might be an additional suggestion in the teacher's notes for weaker classes.
- Building in a brainstorming stage, where either in pairs or as a whole class, learners think of a selection of possible answers or ideas to include before working on their own particular answer. This works well as a way of getting learners started on mini-talks or any kind of list-making activity. For example, the class comes up with four or five common annoying habits, or a list of films they might be able to review, before individuals or pairs decide on their own particular list or film.

- Including a stage where learners read though the fact file, advert or whatever stimulus they are looking at and underline key points. For example, in Activity 16 in the Activity Bank, page 91 (In pairs, students each read different information about two candidates for the job of au pair to a family. They ask and answer questions to find out the information that their partner has, then discuss who is best qualified for the job.) they could underline the points in favour of each candidate, and circle the drawbacks of each candidate. They would then think about why it is an advantage or drawback, before discussing their ideas in pairs.
- Including a stage where learners make notes for a few minutes before doing the activity in pairs, groups or as a whole class.
- Including a stage where learners make notes with the guidance of a checklist of bullet points. This is extremely useful for the more extended monologue-type speaking activities such as telling a personal anecdote, giving a talk about an app or summarising a news article. As well as giving learners time to think about how to express their ideas, it can provide a framework for how they will put their talk or story together.
- Including a suggestion that learners rehearse formally by recording or filming themselves on their phones, etc. This works particularly well with role plays or with the kinds of extended monologue-type activities mentioned above, and with the latter you might suggest in the teacher's notes that learners do this on their own at home.

You may well want to combine two, or several, of these stages. For example, you might brainstorm ideas for a film review, then provide a list of bullet points for learners to make notes about, and then build in a stage where learners rehearse their review in pairs, before finally giving their presentation to the class.

Providing a model

In addition to thinking time, it is often useful to provide a model for what you want learners to do. More extensive than the kind of brief examples mentioned earlier, a model conversation for example, illustrates what you want learners to do in a role play better than any description or instructions can. Again, it can also encourage learners to 'raise their game' and be more ambitious, by illustrating how they can elaborate and extend what they have to say.

Listening to a model is in itself a form of thinking time too: if in everyday conversation, someone asked you to tell them about a time you were naughty as a child, off the top of your head you might struggle, but in the course of listening to a couple of other people doing this, there is a good chance that you will come up with a number of stories of your own. Equally, listening to a few people explaining why they find certain habits annoying will probably spark off your own ideas, and this works in the same way in a classroom setting.

Or you may want to illustrate how you expect learners to give reasons and examples to back up their ideas and choices, and again models are an efficient way of doing this. And if learners have no creative ideas of their own, they can often simply follow the format of the model in order to achieve the task at a basic level.

Models are also an excellent way of providing useful language in context. If the task is to discuss a controversial idea, you might provide a few model or example opinions which integrate useful phrases for expressing opinions, agreeing and disagreeing or linking ideas together that can then be highlighted before learners go on to do the activity themselves.

How you go about creating models depends both on your aims and the resources available to you. Models for fluency activities such as personal anecdotes, descriptions or mini-talks should ideally be spoken rather than written, and real, unscripted examples are more convincing, particularly at higher levels, and perhaps more likely to spark off learners' own ideas. You could of course suggest that teachers provide their own model, but for some teachers this may be off-putting, and so it might be better to suggest this as an alternative in the teacher's notes. So ideally, as the author, you will provide some recorded examples. These don't need to be amazingly original or witty, but they do need to be expressed in a reasonably lively and concise way (most people tend to go on for far too long) and, very importantly, they need to be made by people who are able to grade their language while sounding natural.

Whether writing for a publisher or my own class, I have found that other teachers and ELT professionals are usually the best people to provide such models, and once you start, you will soon work out who is naturally good at it. You need to provide a brief explaining what your aims are, how long you want the model to be, and perhaps an example of your own. You usually have to record several more examples than you need in order to get a good selection, and generally if people don't get it right the first or second time, it is best to leave it: those who are not professional actors are not usually very good at sounding natural and spontaneous once they have to repeat things over and over again. However, with a bit of luck you will end up with a selection of ideas, stories etc. that you would never have thought of by yourself, and which bring individuality and **authenticity** to your speaking activity.

On the other hand, at very low levels, or if you are providing models for a freer practice activity in which you want to embed examples of the target language, then you will probably be best with a scripted model. If you are working with a publisher, these can be recorded by actors, who generally deliver scripted material much more naturally than colleagues can. Alternatively, you can provide a written model. These can be especially useful for games, as they show clearly the particular type of interaction you have in mind, like this one for Activity Bank Activity 14, page 90 (Students think of, and elaborate on, four responses to a list of questions such as 'Which common activities have you never done?' 'What surprising things can you do?'. Three of the four responses should be true, but one should be false. In groups, students tell each other their four responses, and the other students have to guess which response is untrue.). This illustrates how the learners should interact and also provides them with useful phrases to help facilitate this.

Student A *Ok, so which of these three things is not true? I've never smoked a cigarette in my life because I absolutely hate smoking. I've never been on a plane because I've got a phobia about flying and I've never broken an arm or a leg – I'm very lucky!*

Student B *Mmm, I'm not sure … you've never smoked, that's probably true because you seem very healthy, I don't know about the others.*

Student C *I think you've been on a plane, because I know you've travelled a lot. I think that's the one that's untrue!*

Sometimes another stimulus works better than a model, and indeed there are cases where a model would do the task for the learners and leave them with nothing to do. If we take the example of the simulation based around the new airport (Activity Bank Activity 12, page 90: Students read some information about an imaginary city and about the requirements of an airport site, then imagine that they are various interested parties (the mayor, local residents, local businessmen, etc.) and discuss the best place to put the new airport in the city.) a model would potentially solve, or partially solve the problem of where to put it in advance. Here a reading or listening presenting some of the pros and cons of various different sites would work much better.

Building in discussion points, controversy and conflicts of interest

In activities where there is a problem solving or decision making element, it's important to build in controversy or conflicts of interest: the decision or choice mustn't be too obvious or the activity will not take off and will be over very quickly.

Take Activity Bank Activity 16, page 91 (In pairs, students each read different information about two candidates for the job of au pair to a family. They ask and answer questions to find out the information that their partner has, then discuss who is best qualified for the job.): let's imagine that the candidate will have to look after two young children, a small girl and an older boy, and that as well as looking after them, the job involves cooking their meals and driving them around. Obviously it makes the choice more difficult if one candidate can cook but can't drive and the other can drive but can't cook, and learners can discuss which skill is most important or easily learnt. You can create more discussion, and perhaps bring out learners' attitudes and prejudices if, for example, one candidate is male, very young or doesn't speak very good English, but on the other hand is more experienced and better qualified than the other candidate.

Or if we go back to the activity in which learners choose which candidates to go on the celebrity charity trek (Activity 18 in the Activity Bank, page 91: Learners read some information about a reality TV celebrity charity trek across Africa and have to decide which six candidates should go from a shortlist of ten.), one candidate may be highly experienced and know the terrain but have an arrogant personality, a secret drink problem or a long-standing feud with another candidate. Another candidate might seem unlikely to cope with the tough conditions, but has a rich father who will make a large donation to the charity if his son is chosen, and so on.

In order to maximise the impact of these conflicts of interest on the discussion, it is important to build in clear stages at which learners read, pick out and explain to each other the implications of these issues. They could read and underline the advantages and disadvantages of each one, then compare answers in pairs, for example. Or each member of the group could present one of the options or candidates, while the others make notes. Completing tables and grids provides a very helpful focus here.

One final word of warning: while you want to make the information you provide complex enough to create plenty of discussion, you need to be careful not to go overboard and make it so detailed that it is impossible for learners to assimilate!

Set an end goal or outcome

Not all speaking activities in the language classroom can be formulated in terms of their end goal: in 'open' discussions for example, it is not leading anywhere in particular. However, where possible, it is useful to set out clearly from the outset what you want the learners to achieve: tell a story (of a childhood accident); give a short talk (about your favourite film); plan (a camping weekend); decide (on the best candidate for the job) or telephone a friend (to arrange a night out).

This way, both teachers and learners know where they are heading and why they are doing all the necessary preparatory stages. When the learners are working in groups or pairs it helps to keep their focus: they know that they need to keep going until they have chosen the best candidate and can explain why, have devised a telephone conversation in which they have successfully made the arrangements, or come up with a story and worked out how to tell it.

In the cases above, the activity has a natural in-built goal, but some discussions have the potential to be rather unfocused, so you may need to think more about how to formulate a clear outcome. List-making and categorising are useful ways of giving a defined purpose to what could otherwise be a rather vague discussion. So for example, instead of just discussing the advantages and disadvantages of coming from a large family, learners have to come up with a list of five advantages and five disadvantages. Instead of just chatting about free-time activities that they like and don't like, learners have to categorise a list of activities into 'things I enjoy', 'things I hate', 'things I feel neutral about' and then explain why.

Include a performance or reporting back stage

Key to this concept is the inclusion of a final feedback, presentation or performance stage, in which learners have to present (or at least *may* have to present) their list, tell their story, or act out their role play, either to a group or the whole class. As well as giving a greater sense of purpose to the activity that they are preparing, this puts a bit of useful pressure on the learners to complete the task to the best of their ability.

If possible, it is also a good idea to provide a task for learners to complete while they are listening to each other's presentations. They could make notes about the decision each individual or pair made, and what their reasons were; they could answer generic comprehension questions about each other's stories or role plays (Where did the story happen? What was the accident? What had the customer bought? What did the manager offer to do? etc.) or they could complete a grid about these questions. If the task was to make a list, they could listen for anything they missed on their own list; or they could listen and decide whose story was the funniest or scariest, then at the end vote as a class.

How To Write Speaking Activities

Finally, if time is likely to be an issue and therefore only a few pairs will be able to perform, you could suggest (perhaps in the teacher's notes) that learners film or record themselves performing the task and send it to their teacher for commentary or marking.

Task 4

Look at the Activity Bank on page 90 again.

1 Read the following questions to accompany an intermediate/upper intermediate level reading text about a shopaholic and a minimalist (Activity 9). Which questions do you feel are inappropriate?
   a) What do you think of consumerism?
   b) Do you enjoy shopping?
   c) What physical possessions do you think we will replace with digital goods in the future? What the advantages and disadvantages of this?
   d) What kind of things do you enjoy shopping for?
   e) 'Happiness is not found in seeking more, but in learning to enjoy less'. Do you agree with this opinion?
   f) How much do you spend on clothes every month roughly?
   g) Do you think being a 'shopaholic' is a psychological problem? Why/Why not?
   h) Do you think our society is too consumerist?
   i) Is there anything that you hate shopping for?
   j) Do you ever buy things you don't need? How do you feel about it later?
   k) Who do you think you are more similar to, the shopaholic or the minimalist?

2 Put the questions in the best order to introduce and develop the topic logically. Which would you put before the text and which after?

3 Look at Activity Bank Activity 6 (Some/all of the students tell the class about a film they have watched recently and what they thought of it.) and decide which different areas of vocabulary you would need to feed in and at what stages.

4 Find at least five tasks in the Activity Bank where learners would benefit from listening to a model before doing the task themselves. What kind of model could you provide?

66 Maximising Speaking

5 Look at Activity 16 (In pairs, students each read different information about two candidates for the job of au pair to a family) again. Can you think of any more ideas for creating controversy and discussion in addition to the ones I have suggested above?

6 Find at least three tasks which would benefit from a reporting or performance stage. What activities could you set for other learners while they listened?

You can read a commentary on this task on page 85.

Ensuring The Activity Works Smoothly In The Classroom

Rubrics and staging

The golden rule for rubrics is to keep them as simple, concise and unambiguous as possible, never using three words if one will do. Similarly, you do not want any more stages than necessary: activities with a multitude of stages can be daunting for users, and from a practical point of view they are space-consuming: very often an issue with printed materials. But while it is relatively easy to keep rubrics and staging simple for, say, grammar gap fills, in extended speaking activities they are bound to be more complicated: what you want learners to do is innately more complex. You may need them to process a lot of different information at different points, and if you add in useful language, models, thinking time, a performance stage, and so on, this adds to the load. While all this is valuable, it is obviously counter-productive if the activity looks so difficult that the teacher decides not to bother! So here are some ways to help keep rubrics and staging as clear and manageable as possible.

Separate information needed to set up the activity from the instructions themselves.

Including background information in the rubrics themselves inevitably makes them long and cumbersome. For example, the following rubric, leading into a mocked up magazine article about the charity trek across Africa for Activity 18 in the Activity Bank, page 91:

'Africa Challenge' is a charity that raises money for education in Africa. This year it is organising a celebrity trek from Cairo to Cape Town. Read the magazine article below and find out what the trek involves and how much money the charity wants to raise.

Wherever possible, find another place for such background information. Here it would be better to put it in the magazine article itself and have the following rubric:

Read the article about the charity 'Africa Challenge' and answer the questions.
- *What is the purpose of the charity?*
- *What event is it organising this year and what does this involve?*
- *How much money are they aiming to raise?*

Separate discussion questions from instructions.

While it is OK to include the odd question in your rubric, a long list of questions can make the activity more complicated than it is. You can avoid this by using bulleted lists, as in the following example rubric (leading into some cartoons of people doing annoying things, such as talking on their phone in a crowded train compartment or tailgating on a motorway – Activity 4 in the Activity Bank, page 90):

1 *Look at the cartoons and discuss the questions in pairs.*
   - *What are the people in the cartoons doing?*
   - *Why might their behaviour annoy others?*
   - *Does this behaviour annoy you? Why / Why not?*

Have one, or maximum two, things to do per stage.

Rather than compressing a lot of mini-stages into one rubric, separate them into a. and b. stages. For example, the following rubric (again for Activity 4 in the Activity Bank, page 90):

Think of any public behaviour that annoys you. Ask your teacher for any words and phrases you need to explain your ideas, then compare answers with your partner to find out if the same things annoy you both.

Could be broken up like this:

a) *Work individually. Make notes about behaviour that annoys you and why. Ask your teacher for any words or phrases you need to explain your ideas.*

b) *Work in pairs and compare answers. Were any of your ideas the same?*

This is actually much more detailed in terms of what learners are doing at any given moment, but appears simpler.

Decide what to do about pair and group work.

You need to decide whether you are going to specify in the rubrics when you want learners to work in pairs, groups, individually or as a whole class, or whether you are going to leave this to the teacher's discretion. Obviously this is an individual decision – it might seem overly-prescriptive to do this all the time, but on the other hand certain activities will only work in pairs and groups. One solution might be to leave it open where it is optional, and only specify pair and group work where it is needed. Another solution is to specify in the teacher's notes even if it is just a suggestion. Everyone will use the materials differently, but it is good to have something to follow as a starting point.

How To Write Speaking Activities

Make use of role cards and instruction cards.

Activities such as role plays, simulations and information exchanges often mean that Student A and Student B have to read different information, which their partners should not read. In your own class, you would probably make role cards or separate handouts for Students A and B, but when you write materials for other teachers you cannot assume that they will read ahead and prepare in advance like this, so normally this kind of material is presented on two different pages, perhaps at the back of the book.

Rubrics are potentially very complicated here, and additional teacher's notes are very helpful, as the teacher herself may not see immediately what is needed. However, it is important to make the student's instructions as clear and self-standing as possible as teachers do not always read teacher's notes.

Sometimes Students A and B are following the same instructions and so these can be included in the main rubric. For example, for Activity 16 in the Activity Bank, page 91, after reading the job advertisement:

Work in pairs. Student A reads about Adam on page 100. Student B reads about Nathalie on page 102.

a) *Complete the correct section of the grid below with brief notes about your candidate.*

	Adam	Nathalie
Age		
Experience	3 years as a nursery school teacher	

b) *In pairs, ask and answer questions to complete the information about the other candidate.*

Example: What experience does she have?

If Student A and Student B need different instructions or ideas to prepare (for example in a simulation or role play) it is easier to put these on their separate role cards and keep the instructions on the page as simple as possible. For example, (for Activity 2 in the Activity Bank, page 90: Students act out a conversation in which a customer is complaining to the manager of a shop about some faulty electrical goods he/she has bought.):

1. a) *Work in pairs. Student A, the customer, reads the instructions on page 101. Student B, the shop manager, reads the instructions on page 102.*

   b) *Spend a few minutes thinking about the questions and ask your teacher about any words and phrases you need.*

2. *In pairs, act out the conversation. You should listen and respond to what the other person says but stick firmly to your point of view.*

And then on page 101 and 102 you would have the following role cards:

Student A: Customer

You have bought some electrical goods in Student B's shop and they do not work.

Decide the answers to these questions:
- What did you buy and when?
- How much did you pay for the goods?
- What is the problem?
- Do you still have the receipt?
- Do you want an exchange or a refund?
- What will you do if you are not satisfied with the manager's response?

Student B: Shop Manager

A customer is bringing back some faulty electrical goods that he/she bought in your shop.

Decide the answers to these questions:
- What information do you need to get from the customer about his/her purchase?
- What is your shop's policy on refunds and exchanges? (For example, does the customer need to have a receipt?)
- Are you prepared to change this policy at all if the customer insists?
- What will you do if the customer gets angry or is not satisfied?

Avoid giving complicated variations on activities.

Generally, variations sit more easily in the teacher's notes, but sometimes they are unavoidable, for example if you need a variation for multi- and mono-cultural classes. If so, try to separate the options as clearly as possible, for example, after devising lists of tips in pairs (for Activity 13 in the Activity Bank, page 90: Students decide in pairs on the best tips to give a foreign visitor about manners and behaviour in their country. They then act out a conversation with a foreign tourist in which they make recommendations about the best ways to behave.):

Listen to the other students' tips and choose one of these options.

a) *(If you all come from the same country) Can you add any more ideas to your own list? Which tips do you think are most important for a foreign visitor? Why?*

b) *(If you come from different countries) Which customs are different from your country? What are the differences?*

How To Write Speaking Activities

Spend time ordering and re-ordering the stages.

Obviously you want the stages to be in the most logical order and this will sometimes take a lot of working out. Do you want to refer learners to the fact file before or after they look at the photos? Do you need the key phrases before or after the model? Do you want learners to make notes individually before or after they discuss their ideas in pairs? At what point do you want learners to read their role card or instruction card? This is going to vary from activity to activity and in my experience this can only be worked out by trial and error – expect to do a lot of cutting and pasting!

Check that the stages don't repeat each other.

Finally, once you have put your activity together, built in all the stages you need, and got it into the right order, it may feel long and unwieldy, so at this point check through to see if any stages repeat each other – this can very easily happen. You may also be able to conflate two stages without any loss to the effectiveness of the activity. Equally, you should check that the interaction-types are not too repetitive. If learners are going in and out of pairs four or five times for example, you might want to vary this with some group work, whole class discussion or individual note-making.

Consider which stages could go into the teacher's notes.

Finally, you may be able to cut back certain stages by putting them into the teacher's notes instead – see below.

Teacher's notes

I have learnt never to work on the assumption that teachers will read teacher's notes and for this reason I would never include any essential stages only in the teacher's notes. However, teacher's notes can really make a difference to how well a speaking activity works, as it is only here that you can address a number of important class management issues. Relatively inexperienced teachers are probably the most likely to read teacher's notes so aim them at about this level of experience, possibly with a few more elaborate suggestions for the more experienced or adventurous. As well as the basic step-by-step instructions, these are the areas that I have found that teachers sometimes need tips about.

Setting up activities

Teachers are often very good at creating interest in the activity, but do not always make it clear enough exactly what the learners have to do once they get into pairs, for example. Suggest that as well as paying careful attention to the examples that you have supplied in the student's exercises, the teacher elicits another example or two to check that learners really know what to do.

Seating and the arrangement of the classroom

It may be obvious to you that group work will not work if the four students in the group are sitting in a line, or talking across three empty desks, but it is surprising how often you see speaking activities being conducted in this way. Obviously there are also certain types of simulation, for example, that might really benefit from re-arranging the classroom a bit. So if seating and layout are important to the activity, they are worth mentioning.

Instructions for more complicated activities

For more complicated activities such as information exchanges, games, role plays and simulations, teacher's notes need to be particularly clear and supportive. Do not work on the assumption that the teacher already knows the activity type that you are talking about. Instead, try and think it through from the point of view of someone who has never done it before. Help with exactly when and how to check key vocabulary / direct learners to the back of the book / hand out cards / put classes into teams, etc. is really useful here.

Checking and supplying key language

In your own classes you would probably automatically check that learners understand key/difficult language in discussion questions or on role cards and fact files, but teachers may not always have read the material through very thoroughly, or may forget to do this, which can have a significant impact on how well the activity works. As you do not want to overload your activity with too many stages, this is a good area to include in the teacher's notes rather than in the main student's instructions.

Equally, as well as the useful language that you have supplied, which will tend to be of general use, you may want to suggest at relevant points during individual or pair work, that teachers supply any specific language that students need in order to express their own ideas.

The role of the teacher in pair and group work

Teachers with a lot of experience of pair and group work activities know that they facilitate them best by taking a backseat and keeping a bird's-eye view of the whole class. They dip in to help individual groups where necessary, but monitor rather than direct, and do not get involved in long conversations with one group at the expense of the others. However, these are very common mistakes amongst inexperienced teachers, or those unused to more student-centred activities, and again it can make the difference between the activity working and failing. If you know your target audience includes a lot of teachers who lack this kind of experience, advice about this is worth including in your teacher's notes where relevant.

Ensuring The Activity Works Smoothly In The Classroom

Correction and feedback

Again, the role of the teacher is very important here. One of the key ways that a speaking activity can be killed dead is by over-correction during the communicative phases, but some teachers find it extremely difficult to hold back on this. On the other hand, learners may not see the value in doing the activity if there is no correction or feedback from the teacher whatsoever, and there are other teachers who focus entirely on the communicative aspect of the activity and do not provide any linguistic feedback whatsoever. While you might argue that this is each and every teacher's own decision, it may also be worthwhile suggesting in the teacher's notes the appropriate points at which to give correction and feedback, and what kind of points to include.

Variations for stronger/weaker classes or smaller/larger classes

As an experienced teacher, when you look at the speaking activity you have written, it may seem obvious to you which stages you would give more attention or miss out, if you were teaching a weaker class, and which you would emphasise more, or skip over, with a very strong class. Equally, there may be ways that the activity can be adapted for a very large or very small class, perhaps simply by omitting or modifying one or two stages. Again, this kind of experience often helps to make the activity work well or less well, and so it is useful to give suggestions about what to miss out, extra stages to add, etc. where you think this would help with these issues.

Additional discussion questions

There may not be enough space in the student's exercises for all of the possible discussion questions, so in the teacher's notes you might want to add some more interest creation questions, personalisation, or follow-up questions that teachers can use if they have time or if learners are sufficiently interested (see Task 5 commentary on page 87).

Options for more adventurous teachers

I have mentioned that for very many reasons it is best to keep your activity relatively simple in the main student's instructions. However, you may have numerous classroom ideas for making the activity more realistic, varied or fun: providing personal models for activities like story-telling, bringing in props for role plays, making posters as a way of feeding back to the group, and so on. The teacher's notes are the ideal place for these.

How To Write Speaking Activities

Task 5

1 Look at Activity 16 in the Activity Bank, page 91 (In pairs, students each read different information about two candidates for the job of au pair to a family. They ask and answer questions to find out the information that their partner has, then discuss who is best qualified for the job.) and put stages a-l into the best order. The first and last ones have been done for you.

a) Learners read the following job advertisement that the Smith family placed on an au pairing website and pick out at least seven important things that the family are looking for.

Wanted, reliable, caring and fun au pair to look after 5-year-old girl and lively 9-year-old boy, starting as soon as possible, and available for minimum six months, preferably one year. Hours 8.00 to 11.00 am and 3.00 to 6.00 pm Monday to Friday. Duties include taking children to and from school, and to sports clubs around local area, cooking children's meals and some family meals, tidying up and light housework. Driver preferred, good English essential.

b) Learners A and B ask each other questions to complete the other column of the grid so that they each have information about both candidates.

c) Learners discuss in pairs which candidate they think is best.

d) Learners look at a photo of the Smiths and their children and read the following caption. (1)

Joanna and Andy Smith are both full-time teachers and are looking for an au pair to look after their children Katie and Ben.

e) Learners work in pairs. A looks at the information about candidate A (Adam) on p.101 and B looks at the information about candidate B (Nathalie) on p.102.

Adam is 25 years old and from Poland.
- has worked as a nursery school assistant for three years and has been driving for three years too.
- speaks intermediate level English and has basic cooking skills.
- available in four weeks' time and can stay for six months, possibly more.
- says about himself, 'I love working with children and having fun together. I love all sports and games and am keen to improve my English.'
- references say, 'Adam is a friendly, fun and reliable person and children love him. He can be a bit disorganised and untidy sometimes.'

Ensuring The Activity Works Smoothly In The Classroom

Nathalie is 19 years old and from France.
- has worked as an au pair for four months in England, and done a lot of babysitting for friends' families.
- has taken driving lessons but failed her driving test.
- is a very good cook and speaks advanced English.
- available now and can stay for a year.
- says about herself, 'I love children and I think I am very kind. I am trying hard to pass my driving test as soon as possible.'
- references say, 'Nathalie is a kind, thoughtful and well-organised person. She is quite quiet and not always very confident.'

f) Learners listen to other pairs' opinions and compare and discuss their answers. (12)

g) Learners focus on an example of the type of question they should ask to find out about the second candidate, then think of other questions to ask.

h) Learners discuss why a family might need an au pair and what qualities they might look for.

i) Learners A and B each complete one column of a grid about the candidate that they have read about.

j) Individual pairs present their decision to the class, explaining their reasons.

k) Learners read through the information about the two candidates and underline the pros and cons of each one.

l) Learners check that they understand all the key vocabulary that they need to discuss the candidates such as *lively, experienced, nursery school assistant*, etc.

2 Write the rubrics for the activity, deciding which stages to conflate and which, if any, to leave for the teacher's notes.

3 Apart from basic step-by-step instructions, what further tips and support would you include in the teacher's notes?

You can read a commentary on this task on page 87.

Writing A Whole Lesson Around Speaking: Checklists For Different Types Of Lesson

Task 6

Choose at least one of the activities in the Activity Bank on page 90 (not Activity 16), including your own ideas, and work out the entire lesson: realia, photos, illustrations, recorded models, etc., rubrics and staging, and teacher's notes. Use the appropriate checklist below to help you.

An open discussion or a discussion around a text

- What photos/illustrations are needed to create the scenario and stimulate interest?
- Do you need to provide any key language? How, and at what stage?
- Is any personal language needed? How will you build this in?
- Are there any points at which you need to provide examples, prompts or even short models of what you want?
- Have you chosen the best questions you can?
- Do the questions move logically from easily accessible topics to more complex ones?
- Is there any need or value in getting learners to select the questions they want to ask/answer?
- Do learners need thinking time? If so, how will you provide this?
- How is the discussion going to be concluded?

A problem-solving, list-making or planning discussion

- What photos, illustrations or realia are needed to create interest, set the scenario or provide key information?
- Do the title and subsequent rubrics set out clearly what you want learners to achieve?
- Is fluency the aim, or do you want learners to practise any specific language? If so, is it clear from rubrics, examples, etc. what language you want learners to practise?
- Do you need to provide any key language? How, and at what stage?
- Would a model be useful? What kind?
- Do you need to provide any fact files at the back of the book, etc.?
- Are there any ways that you can build in more discussion points or controversy?
- What kind of reporting back stage will you incorporate?

An interview or survey

- What photos or illustrations would help to set the topic or create interest?
- Do you want learners to practise any specific language or is fluency the aim? If so, is it clear from examples, rubrics, etc. what language you want learners to practise?
- Do the title and subsequent rubrics set out clearly what you want learners to achieve?
- Do you need to provide any further key language? How, and at what stage?
- Are you providing the questions or will you get the learners to think of the questions themselves? If so, what prompts will you give?
- Have you chosen the best topics for questions that you can?
- Do learners need time to prepare their questions?
- Is any personal language needed? How will you build this in?
- Do you need to provide a way for learners to record answers – a grid or table, for example?
- If the activity is a survey, can you think of alternatives for classes where this is not practicable?
- Will you include a reporting back stage? What form will this take?

A role play or simulation

- What photos/illustrations or realia are needed to create interest/set the scenario or provide key information?
- Is fluency the aim or do you want learners to practise any specific language? If so, is it clear from rubrics, examples, etc. what language you want learners to practise?
- Do the title and subsequent rubrics set out clearly what you want learners to achieve?
- Do you need to provide any fact files, role cards, etc.? If so, do any of these need to be at the back of the book, etc.?
- Would a model be useful? What kind?
- Do you need to provide any further key language? How and at what stage?
- Would thinking/rehearsal time be useful? If so, how and when will you integrate these?
- Will there be a performance or reporting back stage? What will it be?
- Are there any variations that you could include in the teacher's notes?

An information exchange
- What photos/illustrations or realia are needed to create interest/set the scenario or provide key information?
- Is fluency the aim or do you want learners to practise any specific language? If so, is it clear from rubrics, examples, etc. what language you want learners to practise?
- Do the title and subsequent rubrics set out clearly what you want learners to achieve?
- Do you need to provide any further key language? How, and at what stage?
- What information and rubrics will you include in the main student's instructions and what will be provided elsewhere (at the back of the book, etc.)?
- Do learners need thinking time at any stage?
- Do you need to provide a way for learners to record their answers – a grid or table for example?
- What are learners going to do with the information once they have collected it? What is the end goal?
- Are there any ways that you can build in more discussion points or controversy?
- What kind of reporting back stage will you incorporate?

A presentation, mini-talk, story-telling activity, etc.
- What photos/illustrations are needed to create the scenario/create interest?
- Do the title and subsequent rubrics set out clearly what the end-product is?
- Is fluency the aim or do you want learners to practise any specific language? If so, is it clear from rubrics, examples, etc. what language you want learners to use?
- Do you need to provide any key language? How, and at what stage?
- Is any personal language needed? How will you build this in?
- Would a model be useful? What kind?
- How will you build in thinking and planning time?
- What guidance will you give as to how to structure the presentation? (Headings for notes, etc.)
- What are the best ways to get learners to prepare and rehearse their ideas?
- How will learners give their presentation/tell their story to other learners?
- Are there any variations that you could provide in the teacher's notes?

How To Write Speaking Activities

A game
- What photos/illustrations are needed to create the scenario/create interest?
- Do the title and subsequent rubrics set out clearly what the game is?
- Is fluency the aim or do you want learners to practise any specific language? If so, is it clear from rubrics, examples, etc. what language you want learners to use?
- Do you need to provide any key further language? How and at what stage?
- Do learners need thinking time at any stage?
- How exactly will the game be conducted?
- Would a model be useful? What kind?
- Do you need to provide any further instructions, such as a list of rules?
- Do you need to provide any variations for different types of classes?

Good luck with this task and with your future writing projects, whatever they may be, and I hope that this chapter has been useful in helping you to work through your ideas!

Task Commentaries

Task 1 (page 41)

1. Interview (possibly leading to an open discussion)
2. Role play
3. Description-type presentation (possibly leading to an open discussion)
4. List-making discussion (possibly leading to an open discussion)
5. Information exchange with a game element
6. Review-type presentation (possibly leading to an open discussion)
7. Categorising discussion (possibly leading to an open discussion)
8. Narrative-type presentation
9. Open discussion
10. Survey (possibly leading to an open discussion)
11. Open discussion
12. Role play/problem solving discussion
13. List-making leading to a role play
14. Guessing game
15. Simulation/problem solving discussion
16. information exchange leading to a problem solving discussion
17. Team (guessing) game
18. Simulation/problem solving discussion
19. Summarising and information exchange leading to an open discussion
20. Planning discussion

Task 2 (page 47)

I included this task to demonstrate how diverse the range of users might be if you are writing for a 'general English' market, and even for a supposedly specific market many of the same issues are true. I do not think you can eliminate all activities or topics that might potentially cause problems to any of these classes or you would be left with nothing. Teachers can, and do, adapt and miss things out if they are really unsuitable for their students. However, in general I think the variety of classes on this list bears out the need for structured activities and the value of simplicity from the class management point of view, and underlines the importance of varying topics from the serious and adult, to the lighter and more personalised.

CLASS A Quite a wide range of activities and topics could potentially be used with this class and it may depend more on what the teacher is comfortable with than the learners themselves. The size and class management issues might make certain lively games (Activity 14 in the Activity Bank, for example), mingling activities (Activity 10) or large-scale simulations (Activity 12) hard to cope with. The age of the students and the fact that they come from a monocultural background might mean that Activities like 2, 12 and 13 are hard for them to relate to. On the other hand, class discussions (like Activities 9 and 11) and carefully prepared mini-talks (like Activities 6 and 8), role plays in pairs, information exchanges and so on, should work well.

CLASS B It is difficult to make generalisations about this class but speaking may well be a bit tricky. Firstly, there is the issue of class size. It is worth bearing in mind that as well as large classes, your material might also be used with very small classes, so it is important not to include too many activities that depend on larger groups – for example team games, large-scale simulations, and so on. A lot of personalisation and discussion of opinions might be tricky here (for example, Activity Bank activities 4, 8, 9 or 11) because of the difficult personal relationships. So it is always worth remembering that you cannot rely too much on these approaches – it is best to alternate them with other less 'personal' ideas, such as problem-solving discussions (Activities 12 and 16 for example) or informative mini-talks like Activities 3 and 6.

CLASS C Lots of activities might work well with this class, from role plays based on everyday situations that they might find themselves in, to discussion of cultural differences, to games and problem-solving discussions. Some very abstract discussions might be difficult due to the wide variety of educational backgrounds in the class and certain personal or culturally sensitive topics (families, home towns, capital punishment, gun laws, etc.) might be tricky for some members of the class. Learners might also find it difficult to adapt to a more learner-centred teaching style, so it is probably best to introduce these kinds of activities progressively.

CLASS D With this class a large range of topics might work well, but the teacher will clearly be restricted by the size of the class. Activities that potentially involve a lot of role cards or different pieces of paper (for example, Activities 12 or 16) will be difficult just because of the amount of time needed to prepare and set up the activity. Information exchange activities might also be difficult because of having to monitor so many students closely. It is always worth bearing in mind the problems of very large classes and supplying the necessary materials at the back of the book if they are needed, or offering alternatives in the teacher's notes if you can. On the other hand, discussions of 'intellectual' topics like gene-editing or gun laws would probably go very well. Mini-talks, problem-solving discussions, etc. could also work well, if you included suggestions for how to do these with larger classes in the teacher's notes.

How To Write Speaking Activities

CLASS E This is a very tricky age group and class type to do speaking activities with, although classes can vary. If you are writing for this age group, bear in mind all the comments I have already made about writing for teenagers and about Class A above.

CLASS F I included this class, because it showed me when I observed them that you can never quite predict what type of class might end up using your materials. Obviously this might be quite a tricky class to do speaking activities with, and many topics might not work here – for example very people-orientated or abstract topics. Again, I think the most structured and prompted activities, requiring the least personal input from the learners would probably work best: Activities 2, 3, 5, 10 or 17, for example. As writers we cannot possibly predict every situation that the users of our materials will find themselves in, but we can ensure that the speaking activities are varied and do not rely too heavily on certain kinds of learner or interests.

Task 3 (page 53)

1. Any photos relating to technology are notoriously difficult – as the design of both gadgets and software tends to change constantly and therefore the photos date very quickly, while photos of people looking at smartphones or laptops are normally not very exciting. So unless you are in a position to update photos regularly, or you know that your material only has a limited lifespan, you will need to think of a way round this. I would instead focus on the kind of things that people might use apps for, and then look for photos that illustrate these activities (and ideally also show that the person has a phone, without its design being too clear): someone doing exercises in the gym with their phone on the ground next to them or jogging with their phone in their hand for example, someone using their phone to scan the barcodes on food items, walking down the street using their phone to guide them or getting into a taxi with their phone in their hand, etc. Ideally, the photos should be as dynamic and varied as possible, involve people of a similar age, etc. to your target audience, and clearly suggest what the purpose of the app is. Having all of these features is of course a very big ask!

2. **Plastic surgery** Photos of people who need or have had plastic surgery might be a bit insensitive or disturbing, so a photo of someone lying on the operating table or with a plaster over their nose for example may be more appropriate. As I have mentioned, I think case studies of various people wanting plastic surgery would work well here.

    Gun crime Photos directly relating to gun crime might also be upsetting, so it would be better to use more indirect photos which still raise the issues, for example, someone out in the countryside carrying a hunting rifle over their shoulder; a policeman who is armed with a gun; some people protesting about gun crime, etc. I think a fact file or short article contrasting gun laws in different countries would work well, but I would choose English-speaking countries to avoid appearing to point the finger of accusation at learners' own countries.

Capital punishment This is extremely difficult to illustrate sensitively (and indeed a subject that may be too sensitive for some situations). A fact file or infographic about the history of capital punishment around the world would work, including statistics, dates, famous miscarriages of justice, etc., possibly with some historical photos or illustrations. The last woman to be hanged in Britain might be a good example here.

Gene editing Again, this is difficult to illustrate, so I would probably go for some photos of parents with newborn babies, scientists using microscopes in laboratories, cells in Petri dishes, etc. Either a short article summarising the pros and cons, or some case studies would help to bring out the main issues.

3   NB: **All** of the activities (page 90) could be used for fluency work without any specific language aim, but the following might well also be used as freer practice activities:

Activity 1 (to practise vocabulary for talking about families/relationships such as *to get on well with, have a lot in common with, be close to*, etc.)

Activity 2 (to practise phrases for complaining in a shop such as *I'd like a refund, Have you got the receipt*, etc.)

Activity 3 (to practise vocabulary for using technology such as *swipe, tap, enter*, etc.)

Activity 5 (to practise prepositions of place, *there is / there are*, vocabulary such as scenery, furniture, etc.)

Activity 6 (to practise vocabulary for describing films such as *set in, well-acted, special effects*, etc.)

Activity 7 (to practise vocabulary for free time activities)

Activity 8 (to practise past tenses, linkers, etc.)

Activity 10 (to practise vocabulary for describing towns)

Activity 13 (to practise language for making generalisations such as *it's usual / common to; people tend to*, etc.)

Activity 14 (to practise the present perfect, *can* or other structures planted in the examples)

Activity 16 (to practise vocabulary related to jobs: *experienced, references, available*, etc., and/or personal qualities: *confident, well-organised*, etc.)

Activity 17 (to practise language for describing objects: *round, made of metal; lid, handle*, etc.)

Activity 20 (to practise language for making suggestions and/or future forms)

Activity 9 is intended to lead in and out of a reading text, but others might also perform this function for example Activity 1, Activity 4, Activity 11, Activity 13, etc.

All the activities could be intended for pure fluency work especially Activities 1, 6, 9, 11, 12, 13, 15, 16, 18, 19 and 20.

How To Write Speaking Activities

4   Suggested answers:
    Activity 3 Speaking: Explain how to use your favourite app.
    Activity 4 Speaking: Make a list of habits that annoy you.
    Activity 5 Speaking/Practice: In pairs, find the differences between two pictures.
    Activity 6 Speaking/Practice: Tell the class about a film you have seen recently.

5   Suggested answer, depending on the content of the pictures obviously, and possibly laid out as A and B speech balloons:
    Example:
    Student A *Is there a tree on the left in your picture?*
    Student B *There's a tree but it's on the right, not on the left.*
    Student A *Ok, that's one difference.*
    Student B *Is there ... ?*

Task 4 (page 66)

1   I would omit question a (too broad), question b (if learners answer 'no' the topic does not get off to a very positive start), question f (too personal), and question h. (Question e covers much the same ground but in a more concrete and less abstract way.)

2   I would present the other questions in roughly this order:
    (before the text)
    d) What kind of things do you enjoy shopping for?
    i) Is there anything that you hate shopping for?
    j) Do you ever buy things you don't need? How do you feel about it later?
    (after the text)
    k) Who do you think you are more similar to, the shopaholic or the minimalist?
    g) Do you think being a 'shopaholic' is a psychological problem? Why/Why not?
    e) 'Happiness is not found in seeking more, but in learning to enjoy less'. Do you agree with this opinion?
    c) What physical possessions do you think we will replace with digital goods in the future? What are the advantages and disadvantages of this?

3   A lot of vocabulary is needed here – both general and personalised.
    - Feeding in some vocabulary for different types of films (*costume drama, action film, rom com,* etc.) is a good way of introducing the topic and getting the learners thinking about films they have seen.

- Some generic phrases for describing films such as *set in, starring, the soundtrack, the special effects,* are also needed. Some models could be presented and these could be used to highlight such phrases.
- Once learners are planning their own presentations, it would also be useful to build in a stage during which they can ask the teacher for personalised vocabulary to describe their particular film.

4 I think the following activities would particularly benefit from a model:

Activity 2 A recorded or written model of a customer complaining to the manager about some other kind of goods, which contextualises the necessary language and can easily be adapted by learners.

Activity 3 A recorded (or written) example of someone describing and recommending a favourite app of approximately the same length as you expect from learners, and exemplifying the kind of language you want them to use and/or points you want them to make – the teacher's personal model would work well here and I would suggest this in the teacher's notes.

Activity 4 A few recorded or written examples of people describing behaviour that annoys them. Ideally these should not be too obvious, as this might help to spark off more original ideas from learners.

Activity 8 Recorded (or written) examples of two or three people telling the stories of minor childhood accidents. These should be of approximately the same length as you expect from learners, and exemplify the kind of language you want them to use and perhaps be structured according to the pattern that you want them to follow. The teacher's personal model would also work well here and I would suggest this in the teacher's notes.

Activity 6 Recorded (or written) examples of two or three people describing good films they have seen recently. These should be of approximately the same length as you expect from learners, and exemplify the kind of language you want them to use and/or the areas that you want them to elaborate on (or summarise – for example you probably only want them to summarise the plot). The teacher's personal model would also work well here and I would suggest this in the teacher's notes.

Activity 13 A few short examples of people from around the world giving tips about various areas where cultural differences tend to exist: meeting and greeting; eating, etc.

Activity 14 (example already provided on page 63)

Activity 17 A few short recorded or written examples of what you want. This would also work well if the teacher gave the model, and this could be suggested in the teacher's notes.

How To Write Speaking Activities

5. You could build in more discussion points by giving quotes from each candidate's references about their personalities (one could be very extrovert and fun but a bit disorganised, the other could be very well-organised but a bit quiet, for example); the job advertisement could also include specifications about availability, length of stay, etc. which the two candidates match in different ways.

6. There could be some kind of whole class feedback stage for nearly all the tasks in the Activity Bank (possibly excluding the games) but the performance stage would be particularly important in activities 2, 3, 6, 8 and 13. Brief comprehension questions or grids to complete would work well in all these cases.

Task 5 (page 75)

1. My answers:

   1 d   2 h   3 a   4 l   5 e   6 i   7 g   8 b   9 k   10 c
   11 j   12 f

2. Since twelve stages are a lot, I have conflated some and where two stages are linked I have combined them into a and b stages of the same exercise. Some stages go in the teacher's notes, stages l and g for example. This is my answer:

   1. a) Look at the photo of the Smith family and read the caption. What are they looking for?
      b) Discuss with other students why you think a family might want this kind of help. What qualities and skills do you think the Smith family are looking for?
   2. Read the online advertisement that the Smiths placed. Find at least seven skills and qualities that they need in their au pair.
   3. The Smiths have shortlisted two candidates for the job. Work in pairs. Student A reads about Adam on page 101. Student B reads about Nathalie on page 102.
      a) Complete the grid below with brief notes about your candidate.

	Adam	Nathalie
Age		
Experience	3 years as a nursery school teacher	

      b) In pairs, ask and answer questions to complete the information about the other candidate.

      Example: What experience does she have?

4   a) Read your notes. Underline the plus points and circle the negative points of each candidate.

   b) Discuss the pros and cons of each candidate with your partner, and decide together who is the best candidate and why.

5   Explain your opinion to the rest of the class and discuss together who is the best candidate.

3 These are the teacher's notes I would supply, with additional ideas in bold. You may of course have many more ideas of your own!

1   a) Focus on the Smith family photo and the caption, and elicit what they are looking for. **Discuss these questions briefly: What is an au pair? What kind of work do they do? Can you imagine what problems there might be if you were doing this job? What sort of problems might there be for the family?**

   b) Get the learners to guess what the au pair's duties will be and what personal qualities the family are probably looking for.

2   Focus on the online advertisement and **check the meaning of any unknown vocabulary, e.g. *caring, available, lively*.** Get learners to find six qualities and skills that the Smiths are looking for.

3   a) Explain that the Smiths have found two candidates that they are interested in and that the learners are going to choose the better one.

   Before directing learners to the pages at the back of the book check the following vocabulary: *nursery school assistant, references*.

   Divide learners into pairs, telling each student that they are either A or B. Direct them to the correct page, focusing them on the photos and fact files for Adam and Nathalie.

   Show learners how you want them to complete the grid using the example given for Adam. **Elicit an example for Nathalie too** and ensure that they know what they are doing. As they make notes, monitor closely.

   b) Explain that learners are going to ask questions to find out about the other candidate, and focus on the example question. **Elicit (some of) the other questions that they need to ask to check that they understand what they have to do.** Put learners into pairs to ask and answer the questions. **Monitor closely, eliciting questions and answers if necessary.**

4 a) Ask learners to give you an example of a plus and negative point for Adam, and show how they have to underline/circle these points in their notes. Give them a minute or two to do the task individually.

   b) In their pairs, ask learners to compare the plus and negative points for each candidate, explaining why. Tell them to discuss and decide who they think is the best candidate. **Monitor, asking extra questions to prompt further discussion if necessary. For example, *Ben is very lively. Who do you think will be better at looking after him? Who do you think the children might prefer and why?*** Tell learners that they will have to explain their decision to the class.

5 Get four or five pairs to give their opinion to the class, explaining their reasons. **You could collect their ideas onto the board into two columns.** If you have a larger class, ask the other pairs to tell you briefly who they decided on without going into everyone's reasoning as this will become repetitive. Ask pairs with different opinions to try and persuade each other that they are right, and if necessary ask further questions to get learners to justify their opinions.

Further discussion questions: *Would you like to do this job? Why/Why not? If you want to travel and work abroad, what are the advantages of being an au pair? Would you like to travel and work abroad doing another job? Why/Why not?*

Alternative suggestion: Learners work in new pairs and act out a conversation between Mr and Mrs Smith. You could make this more fun by giving each parent slightly different concerns; Mrs Smith is very worried about safety and doesn't like the idea of an inexperienced driver driving her children around, Mr Smith wants someone who is a good cook, etc.

Appendix
Activity Bank

1. In pairs, students ask each other a list of questions about their families.
2. Students act out a conversation in which a customer is complaining to the manager of a shop about some faulty electrical goods he/she has bought.
3. Students explain how to use a favourite app and why they find it useful.
4. In groups, students think of the ten habits that they find most annoying in other people and explain why.
5. In pairs, students each look at similar pictures on different pages at the back of their Student's Book and ask questions to find ten differences. The first pair to find all the differences is the winner.
6. Some/all of the students tell the class about a film they have watched recently and what they thought of it.
7. Learners look at a list of free time activities and talk about which they like doing in their free time, which they don't like and which they have never tried.
8. Students tell each other a personal story about a minor childhood accident.
9. Students talk about shopping habits and consumerism, before and after a reading text about a 'shopaholic' and a 'minimalist' (a person who can fit all his possessions into one rucksack).
10. Learners devise a list of questions about features and facilities in their town then circulate around the class asking each other their questions.
11. Students talk about a list of questions about a controversial issue such as plastic surgery/gun laws/capital punishment/the ethics of gene editing, etc.
12. Students read some information about an imaginary city and about the requirements of an airport site, then imagine that they are various interested parties (the mayor, local residents, local businessmen, etc.) and discuss the best place to put the new airport in the city.
13. Students decide in pairs on the best tips to give a foreign visitor about manners and behaviour in their country. They then act out a conversation with a foreign tourist in which they make recommendations about the best ways to behave.
14. Students think of, and elaborate on, four responses to a list of questions such as 'Which common activities have you never done?' 'What surprising things can you do?' Three of the four responses should be true, but one should be false. In groups, students tell each other their four responses, and the other students have to guess which response is untrue.
15. Learners decide which of a number of artistic, entrepreneurial and charity ventures to back on a crowdfunding website, and how much to allocate to each one.

16 In pairs, students each read different information about two candidates for the job of au pair to a family. They ask and answer questions to find out the information that their partner has, then discuss who is better qualified for the job.
17 In teams, learners give short descriptions of everyday items without saying what they are, and the opposite team has to guess what they are describing.
18 Learners read some information about a reality TV celebrity charity trek across Africa and have to decide which six candidates should go from a shortlist of ten.
19 In groups of three or four learners each read a different article about the topic of online privacy and security, then summarise their article to their group and discuss the issues that it throws up.
20 In pairs or groups, learners plan a trip round the world, deciding how they will allocate their budget.
21 _____
22 _____
23 _____
24 _____

How To Write Writing Activities

Aims

The basic aims of this chapter about creating writing activities are to:

1. Understand what we mean by 'writing activities' in the context of this chapter, and the approaches to writing that can be used.
2. Look in detail at the different aspects of the writing skill and explore what kind of writing activities you could create to focus on each of them, whether for your own classroom, for a publisher, or for online sharing.
3. Learn how to write a good model text, and look in detail at how you can use one as a basis for a writing activity.
4. Understand how writing for digital differs from writing for print, and how you can adapt your skills to suit the medium.
5. Be aware of some of the practical constraints, and key things to consider when producing writing materials.

People sometimes think that writing is not as relevant as it used to be, because our students now spend so much time online that the traditional writing tasks and text types seem outmoded. However, although it is true that most people don't handwrite as much as they used to, the growth of online activity means that we are generally writing much, much more than we did. So, writing is, in fact, a vital **21st century skill** which needs to take a central role in any set of learning materials.

Careful staging is really key to writing a successful writing activity, and it should guide the students step by step through the process. In order to do this successfully, you will need to have a really good understanding of what exactly is involved in the skill of writing, and what the aims of each stage of your activity are. This chapter aims to equip you to do this with confidence, as well as giving you plenty of ideas and examples of how you can produce a variety of writing activities.

Note The chapter focuses primarily on materials for adult and secondary school learners. It also looks mostly at printed, as opposed to digital, materials although there is a section on writing for digital. For more detail on primary and digital, you should supplement your reading of this chapter with the titles *How to Write For Primary* and *How to Write For Digital Media*.

What Are Writing Activities?

Task 1

Before you read further it will be helpful to complete this brief task.

Let's start by considering exactly what we mean by a writing activity.

1 Make a list of all the different types of writing activities that you might find in Student's Books, Workbooks, worksheets or online. If you are able to, you might like to take a look at some published materials to help you compile the list.

Then compare your list against the list on page 115.

2 Which of the activities below do you consider to be writing activities? Think about the reasons for your decision in each case.
   a) Copying words or sentences from the board
   b) Making notes while listening
   c) Writing sentences about things you used to do when you were a child
   d) Filling in the gaps in a **cloze text**
   e) Writing a text message
   f) Practising forming letters

Read the task commentary on page 115.

Controlled to free writing

While some of the activities in Task 1 might have been too controlled to count as writing activities for the purposes of this chapter, it is nonetheless important to say that writing activities often are quite controlled.

What exactly do we mean by 'controlled', or 'free'? The terms derive from the **audiolingual approach**, where there was a general principle that students needed to be guided carefully so as to avoid making errors. In speaking, this would mean drilling and practising dialogues before the students were gradually given more and more freedom to express their own ideas and choose the language they wanted to use. Writing was similarly sequential, from more to less controlled, and students started off by being given all or most of the language and possibly all or most of the content as well.

How To Write Writing Activities

With the advent of the **communicative approach**, the idea that mistakes were to be avoided at all costs disappeared, and there was a new emphasis on students being able to express their own ideas – to use language to communicate. Obviously, this is still very much the case today, but there is still a lot of value in controlled writing because these are the activities where the nuts and bolts of writing are taught. Few published writing activities are completely free, because they usually need to focus on teaching a particular aspect of writing, or practising specific language.

Task 2

Put the following writing activities in order, from the most controlled to the least controlled. Remember that the term refers to controlling the language or content, not the students!

1 Using a **writing frame** to write a report or letter.

2 Writing a **parallel text** – one that is almost the same as a model, but substituting different items of vocabulary.

3 Writing a description of a painting.

4 Writing a 'for or against' type of essay. Students write an introduction, then arguments for, then arguments against, and finally give their own opinion.

5 Reading an article about a famous place, then writing a similar article about another famous place that the student has visited.

6 Rewriting a paragraph to put it in the past tense.

7 Writing a story using a picture sequence as a guide to content.

8 Rewriting a paragraph to add conjunctions and other linking words.

Now read the task commentary on page 116.

Purpose of writing activities

Writing activities can be created for various different purposes. As we saw in the list of writing activities in Task 1, a key purpose is to teach students how to produce different **genres** of writing, such as an informal letter or an essay. However, writing can be used for other purposes, such as consolidating language, encouraging creativity, or, as a means of direct communication between students.

Task 3

Can you think of a writing activity which could have all of the

- To consolidate a set of phrasal verbs
- For students to get to know each other better
- For students to develop their creativity

Now read the task commentary on page 117.

The kind of task you have just considered is often found in Student's Books, towards the end of a lesson. It is not focused on producing a particular type of writing, but is rather a way of consolidating language or wrapping up the lesson. For example, after a lesson on *will* for predictions, students might be asked to write predictions about themselves or each other. Clearly the purpose of a writing activity informs the kind of activity you will design.

Different Approaches To Writing

Product/genre approach

The traditional approach to teaching writing, which we looked at in the previous section, is often known as the '**product approach**'. It is very much in line with the idea of Presentation – Practice – Production. Typically, there will be a model text which the students will analyse to see how it is organised or what language is used. The students will then carry out a quite controlled activity either focusing on the organisation (such as putting paragraphs in order) or on the language (perhaps completing gaps in the model). Finally they will write their own version of the model. The '**genre approach**' is superficially similar to the product approach, in that it involves analysing features of a model, but it is rather more sophisticated. Whereas the product approach is mainly about copying the model, and focuses mainly on using language correctly, the genre approach is also focused on the purpose and the audience of the piece of writing.

Process approach

In the early 1990s another approach emerged, called the '**process approach**'. This took as its starting point the cyclical way that people write in real life. In a process writing lesson, students will begin by brainstorming ideas, then write out a brief plan before drafting, and redrafting, until they reach a final version.

Task 4

What are the advantages and disadvantages of the two approaches?

Read the task commentary on page 117.

Many published writing materials, especially Student's Books, nowadays take a process-product or process-genre approach to writing, where, hopefully, the best of both approaches is combined. There is a model, which is analysed in some way, more controlled writing activities and a final product, but students are also encouraged to brainstorm ideas together and to write and review drafts. Very often the process elements form a kind of sandwich to the product elements. The activity starts with brainstorming or a discussion, then focuses on a model, and then encourages students to write a plan and create and share a draft.

Obviously, if you are writing a self-study worksheet, it is much less likely that the process elements will be included. And if you are writing for your own class, you may just include the process elements in your plan, rather than in the piece of material itself.

If you are writing a Workbook activity, you may just give a writing task as a kind of test, rather than setting out to teach students how to write the text type, or the activity you create may focus on just one of the aspects of writing a text which is similar to that in the Student's Book.

Activities To Develop Different Aspects Of The Writing Skill

Writing is a complex process, and creating writing activities can be just as complicated. It is important to consider exactly which aspects of the writing skill you are aiming to help the learners to develop.

In a shorter Student's Book activity, or in a Workbook activity, you might just be focusing on one aspect, while in a longer (maybe page-length) activity in a Student's Book, or in a self-contained worksheet, you are likely to be focusing on several different aspects.

Here are some of the aspects that you might choose to focus on:
- Content/audience/purpose
- Layout
- Organisation (of the text as a whole and of the paragraphs)
- Register
- **Syntax** and grammar
- Vocabulary (including phrases)
- Mechanics (spelling, punctuation, handwriting)

If you look back at the list in Task 1 on page 93, you will see that each of the activities listed is related to one or more of these aspects. Copying words or sentences from the board would have a particular focus on mechanics and writing sentences about things you used to do when you were a child would have a particular emphasis on grammar. Many writing activities could focus on more than one aspect, presenting a choice to the materials writer. Let's take the example of writing a text message. Probably the most obvious areas to focus on would be audience and register (because text messages are often very informal). However, you could also focus on some set phrases (vocabulary) or on a particular grammatical area (perhaps imperatives).

Task 5

Find an example of a longer writing activity, either in a Student's Book or in a worksheet. Which of those aspects listed above does the activity focus on?

Tasks to focus on content/audience/purpose

Obviously the content of a writing task is always important, and it is also a good idea to get students to think about the purpose of any piece of writing (to inform, persuade, etc.) and to consider who they are writing for. However, these aspects are absolutely central to many exam-type writing tasks, as students will lose marks if they don't follow the rubric very carefully. If you are writing exam-type tasks, you will need to be able to write a rubric which makes it very clear exactly what the students have to do.

How To Write Writing Activities

For example, look at this PET (Cambridge Preliminary Test of English) type task:

> A friend in your English class, Sophia, has invited you to her birthday party.
>
> Write an email to Sophia. In your email you should:
> - Thank her for the invitation
> - Say how pleased you are to be invited
> - Ask her what she wants for her birthday.

This rubric makes it very clear who the audience is (a friend in your English class), what the purpose of the task is (to respond to an invitation) and what the content is (the three bullet points).

When writing rubrics for a particular exam, look carefully at plenty of examples so that you can recreate the correct wording, length and style.

If you are writing exam practice materials, you may simply have to write the rubrics for a set of exam-type tasks (and possibly matching model answers). Alternatively, you may also have to write tasks which support the students in understanding the rubric.

For instance, you could ask them to underline the key words in a question, such as the key words underlined in this typical IELTS question:

> It seems that most news stories that we read or see on television are about bad news. Why might this be the case? What factors do you think make an event newsworthy?

The key words would mainly be those which identify the content (news stories, bad news, etc.). However, key words could also tell you something about the audience (write a letter/email to a friend), or the purpose (replying to their invitation), or the organisation of the piece of writing (what factors and why). Therefore, you could design a task which gets students to identify key words in all or any of these areas.

In a non-exam writing task, the rubric may well not need so much analysis, but you will still need to ensure that you have included some kind of activity where students focus on content. It is rarely a good idea to plunge students straight into writing without giving them a chance to marshal some ideas.

Usually a longer piece of writing will come as a culmination to a series of activities in which students may have already listened to, or read a text about the topic, which will have given them some ideas. They may also have had a chance to personalise or discuss their opinions. Even if they have done both of these things, it might still be a good idea to include another short task where they gather their ideas together.

Activities To Develop Different Aspects Of The Writing Skill

Here are some possible tasks for stimulating and gathering ideas about content:
- Speedwriting. Ask students to write about the topic for a few minutes. They should write whatever comes into their head, without editing themselves – the important thing is to generate ideas.
- Looping. This is a variation of speedwriting where the student, or their partner, picks out the most interesting ideas from a speedwriting session and then writes about those ideas for another few minutes. This can be repeated several times.
- **Mind-mapping**. Either individually, in small groups, or as a whole class, students group their ideas into related clusters around the central topic.
- Questioning. Students write questions they would like to see answered in the piece of writing. One way of doing this is to use all the question words. For example: What are the issues? Who is affected? Where and when does this happen?
- Listing. Ask students to make lists with a specific number of points. For example, think of five reasons why bad news is more often reported than good news.

Tasks to focus on layout

Focusing on layout is only really applicable to genres where the layout is very fixed, and an important element of the genre. For example, a formal letter, with the address, or even addresses, date, salutation, and so on. With the advent of the internet, it is more usual to teach students to write emails, but layout might also be important for writing a CV, or particular kinds of reports.

Students will need to see a clear model of the layout, and will then need some kind of task which requires them to notice the features of the layout. For example, you might get them to match labels to different features (e.g. your address, the salutation). An obvious task here is to get students to put the right sections in the right order, or the right place. However, while this might work fine in class, on a printed page, you want to avoid having a model in which the sections are all muddled up because this won't provide a clear reference for students and may even mislead them.

Once students are aware of what the layout should be, you can then go on to ask them to write a parallel text using the correct layout.

Tasks to focus on text organisation

All text types require some organisation, or **coherence**, but some text types require a particular emphasis on this. For example, academic essays, narratives, and letters or emails with a clear **function** (complaint, application and so on).

How To Write Writing Activities

A typical essay, such as the example below, could be organised in the following way:

> Some people consider that encouraging children to compete in sports is healthy, whereas others think that children should be encouraged to co-operate, rather than compete against each other. Discuss both views and give your own opinion.

1. Introduction
2. Arguments in favour
3. Arguments against
4. Your own opinion
5. Conclusion

There are various ways of getting students to focus on the organisation of an essay like this. One common way, especially if students are new to this kind of writing, is to provide a model for students to analyse.

It is usually good practice to set some kind of task which requires students to read the model first: for example, to find out what the opinion of the writer is, or to identify two arguments for and two arguments against.

Then you could ask students to label the different sections of the model (introductions, arguments for, etc.), or match the paragraphs of a model with the main topics. Sometimes, you could put ONE paragraph in the wrong place and ask students to identify which one, and say where it should go. In general, though, as mentioned under layout, try to keep the model on the page clear and easy to refer to.

Another way to approach this aspect is through **lexical chunks**. For example, you could have some typical phrases used in an introduction, a conclusion and so on, and ask students which section of the essay they would put them in. They could then read the model essay to check.

Task 6

Read the following model answer for the essay question above and identify some typical phrases that could be used in any essay of this type.

Some years ago it was generally accepted that promoting competition between children was a good thing. Children in a class were often ranked in order of academic achievement, and sports day was all about winning races. In recent years, however, there has been a shift towards encouraging more co-operation, and it is now quite common for schools to avoid having individual winners and losers in sporting activities.

> Some people believe that the experience of constantly losing at sports can be damaging for children's self-esteem. Whereas a child may do badly in a test without the others in the class having to know, if they do badly at sports, it can be very publicly humiliating. Competitive sports can, they argue, also lead to bullying and aggression. For example, if a child misses a goal, his or her team-mates may get angry with them.
>
> On the other hand, those who argue in favour of competitive sports point out that wanting to win provides a strong motivation for children to take part in physical activity, something which is very important as children are becoming less fit and more overweight. They also say that competing against others can actually help children to learn to keep their temper.
>
> Clearly there are good arguments on both sides. Personally, I think that it is important that sports are inclusive, and that everyone should be encouraged to enjoy physical activity. If children constantly fail at sports, they are unlikely to become active and healthy adults. On the other hand, it seems unnecessary to completely ban competitive sports, as many children do enjoy these.
>
> In conclusion, the answer seems to be that educators should consider the impacts of both co-operative and competitive sports and ensure that both kinds of activities are provided.
>
> Read the task commentary on page 118.

Other text types also have typical ways of organising the content, which students can focus on in similar ways. For example, a narrative will usually be organised chronologically or a letter of complaint will usually begin by giving the background details (e.g. when and where the item was purchased), then explain the problem, and then say what the writer would like to happen (e.g. a refund).

Tasks to focus on paragraph organisation

Paragraph organisation is something which is very often dealt with in IELTS or **EAP** material, and much less often in General English, even when the focus is on writing an essay. It is well worth including this focus, however, as it can really help students to write more coherently.

A paragraph always has a **topic sentence**, which encapsulates the main idea of the paragraph. This is usually the first sentence, but not always. To start raising students' awareness of topic sentences, a good task can be to ask them to identify these sentences in a model text.

How To Write Writing Activities

> **Task 7**
>
> Read the model answer for Task 6 again, and identify the topic sentences in each paragraph.
>
> Read the task commentary on page 118.

To take this a little further, students could be asked to identify the topic sentence, supporting sentence(s) and examples. For example:

> **Some people believe that the experience of constantly losing at sports can be damaging for children's self-esteem.** *Whereas a child may do badly in a test without the others in the class having to know, if they do badly at sports, it can be very publicly humiliating.* Competitive sports can, they argue, also lead to bullying and aggression. *Example, if a child misses a goal, his or her team-mates may get angry with them.*

Key:

Topic sentence

Supporting argument 1

Supporting argument 2

Example

Students could simply underline and label these as above, or they could be asked to match highlighted sentences with these three types of sentence, or do a multiple choice type activity, e.g. *Is sentence 'a' a topic sentence, a supporting sentence or an example?*

Another possibility is to give students all the topic sentences, in the right order, and ask them to add supporting sentences and examples. (This is a little like using a writing frame, as discussed in *What Are Writing Activities* on page 94.) Or the topic sentences could be missing and they only have the supporting sentences (but that would be quite a bit more challenging).

Alternatively, students could be provided with a range of topic sentences for each paragraph and ask them to choose the best one, and say why. For example:

> _____. Personally, I think that it is important that sports are inclusive, and that everyone should be encouraged to enjoy physical activity. If children constantly fail at sports, they are unlikely to become active, and healthy, adults. On the other hand, it seems unnecessary to completely ban competitive sports, as many children do enjoy these.
>
> a) There can be no justification for banning competitive sports
> b) Clearly there are good arguments on both sides

c) Another argument in favour of competitive sports is that our future sportsmen and women need to learn to compete internationally

Having worked receptively on paragraph organisation, students could then be asked to start a piece of writing by writing just the topic sentences – in effect creating their own writing frame. They could then go on to complete this with supporting sentences and examples, or they could even swap papers and complete each other's frames.

Tasks to focus on register

Again, you could use a model text and ask students to find examples of the features of formal or informal language. At lower levels, you might say what these are and ask them to find examples; at higher levels they could try and find a specific number of different examples. For example:

Read the following model text. What features of formal language can you identify?

Dear Mr Smith,

Thank you for your email of 3rd July. I was concerned to hear about your experiences at our hotel, and would like to extend my sincere apologies.

The manager in question has been reprimanded, and we are confident that such an incident will not happen again.

In compensation, we would like to offer you a voucher for either a free night's stay, or a free meal in our restaurant. Please let us know which you would prefer.

Thank you for your understanding. I look forward to your reply.

Yours sincerely,

JA Green

Alternatively, you could give them some informal phrases and ask them to find formal equivalents in the model text (or vice versa). E.g. *I was really shocked when you told me what happened to you* – *I was concerned to hear about your experiences.*

Students could also be asked to complete gaps in formal sentences, where the missing words or phrases have to be quite formal. You could give them options, or leave the gap completely blank (if the context is clear). For example,

I _____ your reply.
a) can't wait to get
b) look forward to
c) am looking forward to

At higher levels, you could ask students to rewrite sentences, or even whole texts, to make them more or less formal, but bear in mind that this will often require them to change a lot more than the odd word or two. It is quite a sophisticated task.

Note too, that at lower levels, we often contrast formal and informal, but, in fact, most writing that general English students will have to do will be in a semi-formal style.

Tasks to focus on syntax and grammar

Obviously the kind of syntax and grammar you might focus on will be dictated by the level and the type of text. A narrative will necessarily involve a use of narrative tenses, a description of a process will probably demand a focus on the passive, and at higher levels, the focus might be on something like sentence inversion in a formal text.

However, a really useful focus at all levels is conjunctions and linkers. At lower levels, this might just be about using simple conjunctions, like *and* and *but*; at higher levels you could look at the subtle differences between *although*, *though* and *even though*.

Linkers are probably the key way in which texts are made **cohesive**, and anyone producing writing activities needs to be familiar with them. For this reason, I have included an appendix (see page 125) with a (far from exhaustive) list of linkers often focused on at different levels.

The line between a grammar activity and a writing activity could be a bit blurred, but if you are focusing on linkers as a stage towards a final writing activity, where you hope students will put what they have learnt into practice, then it's at least partly a writing task. Some of these preparatory activities could include sentences where students have to choose the correct linker, either choosing from limited options, or, for more challenge, choosing from a selection in a box. You could also have an activity where the 'wrong' linkers have been used (they either don't make sense, or don't work grammatically) and students have to replace them with something more suitable, or rewrite the sentences so that they do make sense or work grammatically.

You could then give students a model text with the linkers missing, so that they have to complete it with, for example, the most appropriate linkers. But be aware that, again, you do want to have a clear (and correct) model for students to follow. If they make a lot of mistakes filling in the gaps, the model could end up being impossible to follow.

Tasks to focus on vocabulary

A Useful Language box is a common feature in Student's Books. These boxes typically contain level-appropriate **exponents** of the target language. And there's no reason not to include them in worksheets as well. If you have a

Useful Language box, you could either get students to complete it with phrases taken from the model, or find phrases from the box in the model text.

If the students are writing about a particular topic, you can also include a focus on topic-related vocabulary. One economical way of doing this is to create a task where students find vocabulary in a previous reading or listening, then give some controlled practice, before encouraging students to use the language in their own writing.

A useful tip in identifying topic-related vocabulary is to find several texts on the topic and put them into a programme that highlights the most frequent words (e.g. *Wordle* or *Tagcrowd*).

For example, this is the result of putting in two texts about climate change.

You can see that some of the words are quite obvious (*drought, emissions*), but others are words you might not have considered teaching (*crisis, regions, forest fires*). The choice of words will depend on level, and on the task you set.

Tasks to focus on mechanics (spelling and punctuation)

Problems with spelling can be caused by a number of different reasons – they are often related to the students' first language background, to hearing the sounds incorrectly, to having difficulties with the Roman **script**, or to being influenced by the spelling of related words in their own language. For this reason, spelling rarely has much of a focus in published materials for a global market, apart from an exhortation to 'check your spelling' when looking at a first draft. When included, usually at beginner and elementary levels, it will focus on commonly misspelt words, such as *friend*, or on spelling related to certain grammar areas, such as double letters in present continuous forms. That said, if you are writing materials for your own classroom, you might well want to have a greater focus on spelling, and will be in a much better position than I am to know where your students' spelling weaknesses might lie.

Punctuation also tends to be something which is focused on at lower levels (though not always). One common exercise is to give a paragraph with no punctuation, and ask students to add it in. You could also ask students to correct the punctuation in a paragraph. Both of these activities are fairly straightforward while you are focusing on capital letters and full stops, but can get complicated very quickly if you are looking at commas. Comma usage is often transferred incorrectly from other languages, but there are also disagreements among English speakers. Take, for example, the Oxford comma

How To Write Writing Activities

(also called 'Harvard comma', 'serial comma' and 'series comma'), which comes before the word *and* at the end of a list. Some publishers like it, while others prefer no comma. However, most people agree that it's a good idea to include the comma if it prevents a lack of clarity or ambiguity. An example often quoted to illustrate why this is a good idea is, 'I dedicate this book to my parents, Ayn Rand and God'!

Analysing And Writing A Model Text

Model texts are often used for writing exam tasks, academic tasks and letters and emails because the features are central to the successful completion of the task. However, other forms of writing, such as narratives or reviews, also have specific features which students can benefit from being made aware of. Whether you are using an authentic text as a model, or writing your own, you need to be able to identify what the key features are of the genre you want the students to be able to reproduce.

Task 8

Look at two example texts, both taken from an upper secondary Student's Book at B2/C1 level. Answer the questions that follow for each text.

Writing & Vocabulary
Describing data

Chart A: The chart gives information about participation in different sports or physical activities on at least one occasion in the last four weeks, looking at different age groups.

1 Discuss the questions in pairs.
- How often do you take part in sport or other physical activity?
- Who takes the most exercise in your family? Children? Teens? Parents? Grandparents?
- Do you take more or less exercise than your parents did at your age? Why?

2 Look at chart A and compare the data with your answers to exercise 1. Does anything surprise you?

3 a STRUCTURE Read the report. Match the paragraphs (1–5) with the topics (a–e).

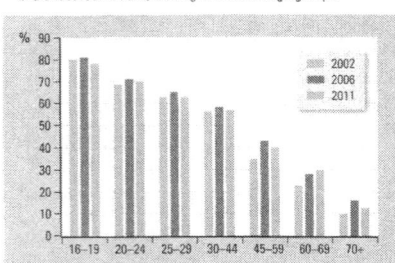

1.12

Summarise the information by selecting and reporting the main features and make comparisons where relevant.

① The chart shows how many people in different age groups took part in a sporting or physical activity at least once in a four-week period, and how this changed between 2002 and 2011.

② Generally speaking, the younger age groups participated in sporting or physical activities much more than the older age groups. Around eighty percent of those aged between 16 and 19 took part in some activity, compared with less than twenty percent of those aged 70 plus.

③ Overall, for most age groups there was not a very noticeable increase in activity levels over the nine years. Participation by most of the age groups climbed between 2002 and 2006 but this had dropped back down by 2011.

④ A striking point is that for the 60 to 69 age group activity levels rose steadily over the period and there was quite a significant increase for the other two older age groups between 2002 and 2006, though this fell a little in 2011.

⑤ In contrast, the youngest age group were the only group participating less in 2011 than they did in 2000, despite a brief rise in 2006.

Tripped up on a trip to London

As I came out of the railway station it was raining heavily and the wind was blowing hard. The sky was glowing a dark bronze, lit up by the streetlamps, and all around me people were rushing to get home, huddled under umbrellas or half hidden by their hoods and hats.

It was my first visit to London and I had stupidly arrived there at rush hour. Keen to start seeing something of the city, I hailed a cab and asked to be taken to Leicester Square. 'What square?' grunted the taxi driver. '*Lee-kester*,' I replied, pronouncing it carefully. 'Oh,' he laughed, 'You mean *Lester* Square. The pronunciation is a bit strange, I suppose.'

We drove off slowly through the rush-hour traffic. By now the sun was setting, like a big scarlet ball behind the black silhouettes of the London skyline. I looked out of the window, hoping to catch a glimpse of some of the famous sights. Big Ben, perhaps, or Buckingham Palace.

'First time in London, is it?' asked the taxi driver, chattily. I nodded, catching his eye in the mirror. 'Nice day tomorrow, they say' he added helpfully.

'That'll be good,' I said. 'I was thinking of going to Greenwich.'

This time the taxi driver laughed so hard that I began to worry we would have an accident.

'Green witch!' he snorted, 'That's a good one! Do you mean *Grenitch*?'

Oh dear, would I ever master the English language? I decided that, for the rest of my stay in London, I would simply point at my destination on a map.

1. What genre is the text?
2. How would you describe the overall organisation of the text?
3. What happens in each paragraph?
4. What do you notice about the grammar? What tenses are used?
5. Is the register formal or informal? How do you know?
6. What linkers are used?
7. What other set phrases or **formulae** can you identify?
8. Is there any other language that you could usefully focus on?
9. How long is the text, and at what level of complexity?

Read the task commentary on page 119.

How To Write Writing Activities

Task 9

Now write your own model text describing the following diagram. Look at your answers in the previous task, where you analysed a model text for describing data, and try to include all the features you identified.

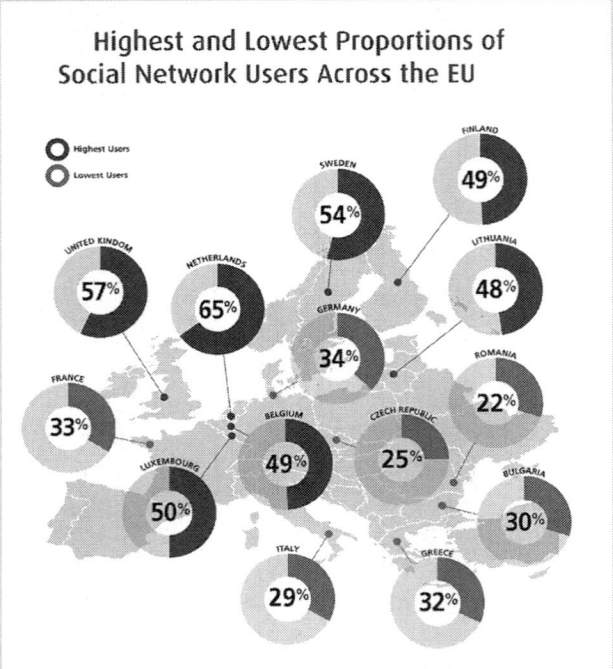

Copyright Office for National Statistics. Contains public sector information licensed under the Open Government Licence v1.0.

Read the task commentary on page 121.

So, to summarise, in order to write a good model text, you first need to look at examples and analyse what the key features are. Examples of different text types might be found on exam board websites or in books or on practice papers (for exam type tasks) or online (blog posts, articles, etc.). Once you have analysed the key features, you can then try to write a text which reproduces these features as closely as possible.

Don't forget to also consider the *content* of what you write. If you are writing a model 'balanced argument' essay, for example, you will need to give some reasoned arguments as well as organising the text appropriately, using suitable vocabulary, and so on.

One final issue to bear in mind is that of level. A good model text needs to be written in a way that a (very) good student at the right level might be able to produce themselves.

Analysing And Writing A Model Text

Task 10

Read the following film reviews. Which one would (not) be appropriate as a model for a good intermediate level learner (B1/B2), and why?

Based on a novel by John Green (the best-selling author of the young adult book/film The Fault In Our Stars), Paper Towns is also aimed at the teenage market.

The film stars the model Cara Delevingne, who plays Margo, a free-spirited high school student. Nat Wolff plays her childhood friend, Quentin. He has been in love with her for years, but nowadays she barely notices him. Until she appears at his house one night to take him on an all-night adventure around the town. They become closer, but the next morning she has disappeared, and the rest of the film covers the trip that Quentin and his friends make as they go looking for Margo, in order to bring her back for the 'prom' (final school-leaving dance).

The character of Margo is rather irritating, which means that it's actually a much better film once she has disappeared. There are some nice moments, and a good soundtrack, but, overall, it's a bit predictable.

The manic pixie dream girl lead of Paper Towns, played by Cara Delevingne, is clearly a girl as written by a male author. Based on a young adult novel by John Green, who wrote the huge hit weepie, The Fault In Our Stars, this will probably be a big success as well, but I'm not sure it deserves to be.

Paper Towns begins as a romance, turns into a mystery and finally becomes a road trip. Nat Wolff's portrayal of Quentin, who has been in unrequited love with Margo since kindergarten, is natural and endearing and once Margo disappears (the mystery), the film starts to pick up pace. The scenes between Quentin and his friends as they wind their way up the east coast to find her are quite engaging, but nothing feels particularly original.

A great high school movie stays with you into adulthood. This is entertaining enough, but no one will remember it in ten years' time.

Read the task commentary on page 121.

Grading texts is a complex skill. There are various online tools, such as the Oxford 3000 Text Checker, that you can use to check the level of vocabulary in a text, but don't forget to consider the other aspects mentioned in the task commentary as well.

Staging

Careful staging is really key to writing a successful writing activity. If you are writing for publication, author briefs almost inevitably use the terms *step by step* and **scaffolded**.

As well as considering the stages from the point of view of which aspects of writing you'd like to focus on, you also need to think about it from the other angle, and consider whether students have or know everything they need in order to be able to produce the final product.

But bear in mind that you can't include everything, or the run up to producing a piece of writing could take the students several weeks!

Staging needs to be logical. This can mean going from more controlled to less controlled, or simply that each stage builds on the last one.

Task 11

Decide what might be the most logical order in which to put the following stages of a writing lesson. (There may well be more than one correct answer.)

1 Write a paragraph plan for the essay.

2 Check your draft against a checklist.

3 Read a model essay entitled *The education a child receives at home is more important than their education in school. To what extent do you agree or disagree?* and make a list of arguments the author makes for and against the statement.

4 Listen to a short audio discussion about home-schooling.

5 Identify the topic sentences in each paragraph of the model essay.

6 Write the first draft of the essay.

7 Underline any passive phrases in the model essay.

8 Find the **thesis statement** in the first paragraph of the model essay.

9 Rewrite a set of sentences, using passives where appropriate.

10 Write a final draft.

11 Discuss with a partner what you think the advantages and disadvantages of home-schooling might be.

Read the task commentary on page 122.

If you are writing for your own class, you can easily add 'process' elements, such as brainstorming together, planning and self- or peer-evaluating against a checklist to your lesson plan. If you are writing for publication, however, you might or might not include these in the rubrics, depending on the brief.

Task 12

Look at the second text from Task 8 on page 106 and carry out the following tasks. Remember that this is B2/C1 level for upper secondary. You have a **double-page spread** with room for about 1,000 words including the text itself, which is 250 words.

1 Decide which of the different aspects of writing covered in *Activities To Develop Different Aspects Of The Writing Skill* (page 97) might be appropriate to focus on.

2 Write the following exercises around this model text.
   a) A lead-in activity which will set the scene and get students to read and start to engage with the text.
   b) An activity to focus on how the text is organised. Look back at *Tasks To Focus On Text Organisation* for some ideas on this.
   c) An activity to focus on either grammar or vocabulary found in the text. Look back at *Tasks To Focus On Syntax And Grammar* for some ideas on this.
   d) A further practice activity focusing on the language chosen in the previous stage.
   e) An activity to help students start to gather ideas for the content of what they are going to write. Look back at *Tasks To Focus On Content/Audience/Purpose* for some ideas on this.

When you have finished, look at the original exploitation of the model, and read the task commentary on page 123.

Writing Activities

For Digital

In this chapter we have mainly focused on writing for traditional print materials for our own classes. However, increasingly, you are likely to be asked to write material for digital media which needs to be approached slightly differently.

Probably the most obvious difference between writing for digital and writing for your own class (or for a class which will have a 'live' teacher) is how you deal with feedback on exercises. If students are studying alone at home, they won't have a teacher to help them understand something, or to explain why an answer is right or wrong.

Providing a model answer can work well, especially if you can also write some commentary, explaining why it is a good answer (or not). However, you might be asked to create digital materials where you need to devise tasks which can be marked completely objectively, with right or wrong answers, which is much trickier.

Essentially, you need to identify which aspect(s) of the writing skill you want to focus on (see the list in *Activities To Develop Different Aspects Of The Writing Skill*, page 97) and consider how you could make the answers **closed** rather than **open**.

For example, let's look at a typical question from Part 2 of the Writing Test in the Cambridge English Preliminary English Test (PET). I chose an exam task because the criteria are very clear, but the approach could obviously apply just as well to any writing task at this level.

> Your friend, Julia, invited you to her house for dinner last night.
>
> Write a card to her. In your card, you should
> - thank Julia for the dinner
> - say what you enjoyed most about the evening
> - invite her to dinner at your house.
>
> Write 35–45 words.

Here are some tasks with closed answers, which would test the skills needed to write a good answer to this question:
- Focus on the rubric. Students need to follow the instructions carefully, so you could have some true/false questions about the rubric.
- You could have two sample answers and ask the students which one covers all the points in the rubric.
- The students will need to use certain functions and formulae, so you could have a task which focused on that. For instance, matching the function of thanking or inviting with some exponents.
- Looking at the whole task, you could have a sample answer with gaps which have to be completed from a wordpool, or students could put the sentences of a sample answer in the correct order.

All of these tasks could have a clear, objective key.

> **Task 13**
>
> Look at the rubric for a typical PET Writing Test Part 3 task. Think of four or five exercises that you could create for a digital product, which would focus on the relevant aspects of writing needed to complete the task, but that would have an objective, closed set of answers.
>
> This is part of a letter you receive from an English friend.
>
> > I'm so excited about my holiday this year. We are going to Spain for two weeks. What are your plans for the summer? Do you prefer to go abroad or stay in your own country?
>
> Now write a letter, answering your friend's questions. Write about 100 words.
>
> Read the task commentary on page 124.

Another big difference between print and digital, is that digital material does not necessarily have to be used in a linear way. Rather than beginning with the first activity and gradually building up to more and more complex activities, students are often able to skip about, which might mean that you need to work out different paths through the material. For example, if you were writing a PET writing test preparation course, rather than working through each part of the exam in turn, it might be possible to work on all the text organisation focused activities first. You can achieve this by **tagging** activities, so that it's easy to search and find related activities. The developer or publisher would explain how to do this in the platform that you're using.

Digital products can also adapt to the learner, suggesting what activities they need to do next, based on what they can and can't already do well. The potential is enormous, though the restriction on activity types (largely variations on multiple choice, drag and drop, true/false) is still quite limiting.

While it can be challenging if you're new to it, writing for digital can give you a lot more freedom than writing for print. You will probably still have the same constraints on what will fit on a page – and these constraints may be even more limited if the product is going to be used on mobile phones, where not much will fit on a screen, or if you're instructed to avoid anything so long as to need students to scroll. On the other hand, overall word limits tend to be more flexible as you don't have to worry about how much paper you're using.

The big downside for digital writing, at least as far as I'm concerned, is that the key often needs to assume that there won't be a teacher. This means that you have to put a response for every possible answer, and explain why a wrong answer is wrong as well as giving the correct answer. It can take a very long time, and it can be rather mechanical work. Of course, this applies to print self-study material too, but, probably because of the amount of paper it would take up, this level of detail in a key rarely seems to happen in print.

For more on writing for digital, see *How To Write For Digital Media*.

A Few Things To Bear In Mind

Both students and teachers tend to avoid writing activities. They often get given for homework, rather than being done in class, or missed off the end of a lesson plan because the teacher runs out of time. Yet writing is increasingly important in our daily lives, thanks to how much time we all now spend communicating online.

Good writing activities need to be central to the students' learning, not just tacked onto the end of a lesson or a unit in a Student's Book, and they need to be written in such a way that students (and teachers) can easily see how completing the tasks will help them to improve and develop their writing.

If you are writing exam material, you may have no choice but to present learners with fairly dry topics (the environment for the nth time, anyone?), but you can look for ways to make the topics as relevant to the students' lives as possible, and use a variety of different task types to engage and motivate.

I cannot stress enough the importance of trying tasks out yourself. You won't always need to provide a model answer, but you should always write one. It's the only way to really see just how easy (or difficult) that essay is to write. If you can't come up with any ideas yourself, it probably isn't a very good task. And make sure that the model is appropriate for the level you're writing for. If it's too sophisticated, it may mean that your task is too difficult for the level, and it will probably demotivate the learners.

Remember that staging is absolutely key. Don't try and do too much at once, and make sure that there is a clear, logical progression, so that students feel supported along the way.

Finally, you may find the Appendix (page 125) useful. As well as the list of linkers commonly taught at different levels, I have also gathered together some common task types, and aspects of writing tackled at different levels. I hope these give you some ideas of where you could start when writing your own materials, either for your class or for publication.

Final task

Look at the Appendix and choose a task type that would be suitable for a group of learners you teach, or a level you are familiar with. Decide on which aspects of the writing skill would be a good 'fit' with this task. This might include a focus on linkers, but does not need to. Then write a double page spread (about 1,000 words), including a lead-in, a model, some controlled practice and culminating in the students producing their own piece of writing.

Task Commentaries

Task 1 (page 93)

1. Here is a list of some common writing activities, based on looking through several coursebooks, secondary and adult, at different levels:

Writing skill	Writing genre
Avoiding repetition	Writing a biography
Beginning and endings of letters and emails	Writing a CV and covering letter
	Writing a description
Checking your work	Writing a film review
Giving examples	Writing a leaflet
Making generalisations	Writing a short note
Organising ideas	Writing a story
Using adverbs	Writing a summary
Using an informal style	Writing an informal email
Using capital letters and full stops	Writing an opinion essay
Using linkers	Writing paragraphs

No doubt you can think of, or find, many more. You may have noticed that there are different kinds of writing activities. Some seem to focus on producing a particular genre, others are focused on organisation, or on particular aspects of language. We will look at the different types of writing activities in more detail later in the chapter.

2. a) **Copying words or sentences from the board** In the very early stages of learning to write, learners may well need to copy words and sentences, especially if the script of their first language is different from that of English. However, this activity would, for the purposes of this chapter, come under the heading of a **literacy** activity rather than a writing activity.

   b) **Making notes while listening** While learners would be using their writing skills, the aim of this activity would probably not be to develop those writing skills, but to develop listening skills. That said, it would be possible to devise an activity where students were explicitly taught how to write effective notes (in an EAP course, for example), in which case this *would* be a writing activity.

   c) **Writing sentences about things you used to do as a child** Whether this is a writing activity or not very much depends on the aim of the activity. If the focus is on practising the structure *used to*, then I would argue that this is not a writing activity. On the other hand, if the focus is on writing an account of childhood, and the language is mentioned in order to help you do that effectively, then it would count as a writing activity.

How To Write Writing Activities

   d) **Filling in the gaps in a cloze test** This is such a controlled activity that it cannot really be seen as a writing activity. The students may be physically writing, but none of their focus is likely to be on any of the skills of writing.
   e) **Writing a text message** Although this is likely to be quite short, it is definitely a writing activity. The focus is on getting a message across using writing – and there may also be a focus on using abbreviations.
   f) **Practising forming letters** This would definitely come under the heading of literacy rather than writing for the purposes of this chapter.

Task 2 (page 94)

6   **Rewriting a paragraph to put it in the past tense** This is probably the most controlled, as the students don't make any choices at all, they simply have to be able to produce the correct past forms. It is arguable whether this is in fact a writing activity – it's more of a grammar activity – but it could be part of a sequence of activities for lower level students preparing to write a past narrative.

2   **Writing a parallel text – one that is almost the same as a model, but substituting different items of vocabulary** Using a model, then writing a parallel text could be quite free, but because all the students can change are certain items of vocabulary, this is actually the second most controlled activity. It's the written version of a **substitution drill**.

8   **Rewriting a paragraph to add conjunctions and other linking words** This is actually quite a lot less controlled (and a lot harder) than the previous activity because the students will have quite a lot of choice about how to rewrite the paragraph. They can choose which conjunctions and linkers to use, and which sentences to combine. They will also have to make other small changes to make the paragraph flow or to make it grammatical. If you were writing an activity like this and you felt it was too free for the level of the learners, you could restrict or control these choices by giving the learners options rather than free rein.

1   **Using a writing frame to write a report or letter** This is quite controlled because the structure of the task is set, plus the beginning of each paragraph is given. However, within these constraints, students can then actually say anything they like. This is a very good writing activity for situations where you want to support students in writing something which has a very fixed organisation and/or fixed phrases.

7   **Writing a story, using a picture sequence as a guide to content** I hesitated about whether to put this one here or before 1, because they are both quite controlled in different ways. This activity controls the content of the writing, but not the language. Picture stories are rarely found in published material these days, but I included it as a useful reminder that you can control content as well as organisation or language.

4 **Writing a 'for or against' type essay. Students write an introduction, then arguments for, then arguments against and finally give their own opinion** This is an example of controlling the organisation, but not the content, or the language. In practice, however, you are likely to combine this with work on other aspects of the task. For example, it might follow an activity where students identified useful phrases they could use.

5 **Reading an article about a famous place, then writing a similar article about another famous place that the student has visited** This is a much freer example of parallel writing (see 2). In fact, it's probably a little too free to stand on its own in published material. Students are likely to need a little more guidance than this.

3 **Writing a description of a painting** This is completely free, and, again, probably wouldn't be suitable for published material without some other more controlled stages coming first. For more about staging, see *Staging*, page 110.

Task 3 (page 95)

Clearly there is no one 'correct' answer here. You might, for example, write an activity where the students have to use as many of the phrasal verbs as possible to write a story about themselves, which may or may not be true. They then have to share the story with others in the class, who have to decide if the story is true or not.

Task 4 (page 96)

Product approaches are still very popular, probably because they recognise that students (and teachers) like to have a step-by-step guide to producing a piece of writing. They also work very nicely on a page, and take up an amount of space which represents the amount of time an activity takes. The model is useful as a reference for students (and teachers) both during the activity and afterwards. If you are taking more of a genre approach, you can help students to notice really useful features of the genre that they would probably otherwise miss, and reinforce the idea that all writing has an audience.

The disadvantage of product writing is that it can be very teacher-centred – though you can, of course, write a task in such a way that the students are given more autonomy than they would have had traditionally. For example, by asking them to find examples of useful language in the text, rather than just giving the examples to them.

Process approaches encourage more learner independence, and many teachers feel that writing in the classroom (or at home) should reflect a more natural process of brainstorming, planning and drafting. However, as a materials writer, pure process writing activities are pretty impossible to write. There's simply nothing much to put on the page.

How To Write Writing Activities

Task 6 (page 100)

This task is naturally fairly subjective, but the phrases I would choose to focus on are underlined below.

<u>Some years ago it was generally accepted that</u> promoting competition between children was a good thing. Children in a class were often ranked in order of academic achievement, and sports day was all about winning races. <u>In recent years, however,</u> there has been a shift towards encouraging more co-operation, and it is now quite common for schools to avoid having individual winners and losers in sporting activities.

<u>Some people believe that</u> the experience of constantly losing at sports can be damaging for children's self-esteem. Whereas a child may do badly in a test without the others in the class having to know, if they do badly at sports, it can be very publicly humiliating. Competitive sports can, <u>they argue,</u> also lead to bullying and aggression. For example, if a child misses a goal, his or her team-mates may get angry with them.

<u>On the other hand, those who argue in favour of</u> competitive sports point out that wanting to win provides a strong motivation for children to take part in physical activity, something which is very important as children are becoming less fit and more overweight. <u>They also say that</u> competing against others can actually help children to learn to keep their temper.

<u>Clearly there are good arguments on both sides. Personally, I think that</u> it is important that sports are inclusive, and that everyone should be encouraged to enjoy physical activity. If children constantly fail at sports, they are unlikely to become active and healthy adults. That said, it seems unnecessary to completely ban competitive sports, as many children do enjoy these.

<u>In conclusion, the answer seems to be that</u> educators should consider the impacts of both co-operative and competitive sports and ensure that both kinds of activities are provided.

Task 7 (page 102)

Para 1: In recent years, however, there has been a shift towards encouraging more co-operation, and it is now quite common for schools to avoid having individual winners and losers in sporting activities.

> Note that this is not the first sentence, but it is the sentence which carries the main idea of the paragraph – the move from a focus on competition towards more co-operation.

Para 2: Some people believe that the experience of constantly losing at sports can be damaging for children's self-esteem.

> This summarises the main idea as the second sentence is linked to, and supports this idea. The third sentence extends the idea further.

Task Commentaries

How To Write Writing Activities

Para 3: On the other hand, those who argue in favour of competitive sports point out that wanting to win provides a strong motivation for children to take part in physical activity, something which is very important as children are becoming less fit and more overweight.

> This sentence contains the main argument in favour of competitive sports.

Para 4: Clearly there are good arguments on both sides.

> This is the topic sentence here because it sets up the idea that the writer is going to agree partially with both arguments.

Para 5: In conclusion, the answer seems to be that educators should consider the impacts of both co-operative and competitive sports and ensure that both kinds of activities are provided.

> In this paragraph there is only one sentence, so it has to be considered the topic sentence – this is not unusual for a conclusion.

Task 8 (page 106)

Text 1

1 **What genre is the text?**
   Description of data

2 **How would you describe the overall organisation of the text?**
   It goes from a more general description of what the chart shows to the specifics.

3 **What happens in each paragraph?**
   Para 1 – the introduction says what the chart shows. It is noticeable that the author has not used the same words as those in the rubric describing the chart.
   Para 2 – an overview of what the chart shows, the bigger picture
   Para 3 – another more general point
   Para 4 – a more specific point
   Para 5 – another more specific point
   It is also noticeable that there is no summarising comment or opinion – in this kind of task the students are not asked to interpret the data, just to describe it.

4 **What do you notice about the grammar? What tenses are used?**
   The chart describes a past situation and the text is mostly written in the past simple tense, with one example of past perfect.

5 **Is the register more formal or informal? How do you know?**
   The register is quite formal, with more formal word choices such as *a significant increase* and *participated*.

Task Commentaries

6 **What linkers are used?**

   generally speaking, overall, compared with, in contrast

7 **What other set phrases or formulae can you identify?**

   Language to talk about charts and graphs such as *a noticeable increase, climb, drop, rise steadily,* etc.

8 **Is there any other language that you could usefully focus on?**

   There is a cleft sentence, *A striking point is that* … You could also look at how the author avoids repetition by using synonyms, *took part* and *participated in* for example, or the way that they have reworded the rubric of the chart.

9 **How long is the text?**

   It is around 150 words (the exam requirement).

Text 2

1 **What genre is the text?**

   A narrative

2 **How would you describe the overall organisation of the text?**

   It starts by setting the scene, then goes through a sequence of events until it gets to the key event or turning point (when the taxi driver laughs at him/her). It then concludes with the narrator stepping outside the action to comment.

3 **What happens in each paragraph?**

   Para 1 – setting the scene

   Para 2 – first event

   Para 3 – more scene setting and what happened in the taxi at first

   Para 4 – start of the conversation with the taxi driver, leading to the taxi driver laughing

   Last para – comment on what happened

4 **What do you notice about the grammar? What tenses are used?**

   It's a narrative, so past continuous, and some past simple, is used to give the background, while past simple and occasionally past perfect are used to relate the events.

5 **Is the register more formal or informal? How do you know?**

   It's fairly informal and conversational, with vocabulary like *stupidly, snorted, grunted.*

6 **What linkers are used?**

   as, by now, this time – sequencers

7 **What other set phrases, or formulae can you identify?**

   As I …, It was my first visit

How To Write Writing Activities

8 **Is there any other language that you could usefully focus on?**
   Adverbs of manner, place and time; verbs to describe how someone says something (*snorted*, *grunted*); colours

9 **How long is the text?**
   250 words (a typical length in exams for this kind of text)

Task 9 (page 108)

This diagram shows which countries in the European Union have the highest and lowest proportions of social network users.

In half of the countries more than 50% of the population use social networks, and in the other half, less than 50% do so. However, while the difference between the highest proportion of users (in the Netherlands) and the lowest (in Romania) is quite marked, generally the differences are not so great.

It is immediately noticeable that many of the countries with a higher proportion of social network users are situated in the north of Europe. For example, Finland, where 49% of the population use social networks, Sweden where 54% do so, Lithuania with 48% and the United Kingdom with 57%. Luxembourg, Belgium and the Netherlands also have a high proportion of people using social networks, with the Netherlands having the highest figure overall, at 65%.

Although France and Germany are geographically very close to these last three countries, the proportion of social network users in these countries is considerably lower, at only 33% and 34% respectively.

The lowest proportion of users is in Romania, with only 22%, and the Czech Republic is only a little higher, at 25%. In the south of Europe, Bulgaria, Greece and Italy are only a little lower than France and Germany, with between 29% and 32% of the population being social network users.

Task 10 (page 109)

The first text would be more appropriate for the following reasons:

It is organised in a more logical way – it starts by saying what the film is, then describes what happens, then gives the writer's opinion. Newspaper reviews are more likely to be like the second text, but we are not teaching students to become professional film reviewers.

The second text is full of cultural references – readers need to know quite a lot about typical features of movies – the road trip, the idea of a *manic pixie dream girl* – a stereotypical female character that is charming and quirky and unusual, and so on.

There are also a lot of USA-specific references.

How To Write Writing Activities

The vocabulary in the second text is generally pitched rather high, and uses a lot of infrequent words and expressions (*weepie, portrayal, endearing*).

The syntax is also more complex than it needs to be, making many sentences difficult to understand.

Task 11 (page 110)

A logical order would probably be:

4   Listen to a short audio discussion about home-schooling.
11 Discuss with a partner what you think the advantages and disadvantages of home-schooling might be.

(These two stages could go the other way around, but either way they both provide input and a chance for students to gather their own ideas and opinions.)

3   Read a model essay entitled *The education a child receives at home is more important than their education in school. To what extent do you agree or disagree?* and make a list of arguments the author makes for and against the statement.
8   Find the thesis statement in the first paragraph of the model essay.

(I would put this first in the analysis of the model because it contains the central idea of the essay, and the other paragraphs should be related to it.)

5   Identify the topic sentences in each paragraph of the model essay.
7   Underline any passive phrases in the model essay.

(You could focus on language before structure, but tasks 8 and 5 will help with understanding the content of the text, so it seems logical to do these first.)

9   Rewrite a set of sentences, using passives where appropriate.

(This is a controlled practice activity, before students use passives more freely in their essays.)

1   Write a paragraph plan for the essay.
6   Write the first draft of the essay.
2   Check your draft against a checklist.
10 Write a final draft.

Task 12 (page 111)

Clearly, there is not just one way in which this text could be successfully exploited. The examples below are simply how it was exploited in *Real Life Advanced*, and reflect the level and audience, as well as what had already been covered in the unit (for example, there had already been a focus on colours and ways of speaking).

Writing & Vocabulary

A narrative

1 Discuss the questions in small groups.
- What do you think is the most challenging aspect of visiting another country?
  - Different food
  - Not speaking the language (well)
  - Different customs or behaviour
  - Different weather
  - Not understanding the money
- Do you enjoy these differences? Why? Why not?
- What do you think a foreigner might find challenging about visiting your country?

2 Read the following narrative essay and answer the questions.
1 What was the writer's first impression of London?
2 What was it that the taxi driver found amusing?
3 Why did the writer decide that 'for the rest of my stay in London, I would simply point at my destination on a map.'?

3 a STRUCTURE Look at the story again and decide which lines are:
1 an introduction or background (Who? Where? When?)
2 the main sequence of events
3 the key event or turning point (may be unexpected, funny, strange, etc.)
4 the conclusion

b Choose the correct tense to answer the questions about the story.
1 Which tense is most often used to give descriptions? Past simple or past continuous?
2 Which tense is most used to give the main events of the story? Past simple or past perfect?
3 Which tense is used to talk about something which happened before the main events of the story? Past continuous or past perfect?
4 Which two structures are used to talk about the future? Would, was going to, will?

4 LANGUAGE Read *Language4writing* and find examples of adverbs of manner, place and time in the story.

Language 4 writing

We use adverbs to add extra description to the verbs in a story. They can, for example, describe how someone does something or where or when something happens.

Adverbs of manner
delicately, fast, heavily, quickly

Adverbs of place
abroad, everywhere, here, nearby, outside, somewhere, underground, upstairs

Adverbs of time
early, in the morning, never, now, often, soon, then, today, tomorrow

There are three usual positions for adverbs.
1 At the end of a clause – this is the most common position for adverbs of manner, place and time
*I'm sure I left it **here**.*
2 In a middle position, next to the main verb – adverbs of manner can go in this position
*He **quickly** ran over to the desk and hid the papers in a drawer.*
3 At the beginning of a clause – adverbs of place and time can go in this position, especially to add emphasis
***Outside** it was cold.*
If all three types of adverb are used in the same clause, the order is usually manner, place, time.
*I **stupidly** left it **here yesterday**.*

5 Find the mistake in the sentences and correct it.
1 She told me that she was leaving gruffly.
She told me gruffly that she was leaving.
2 The car drove away fastly.
3 He asked me if rudely I was going to be much longer.
4 In the taxi I realised I had left my wallet.
5 How did the exam go? Do you think you did good?
6 I need to finish by the end of the week this homework.
7 She ran before he arrived quickly up the stairs.
8 She well plays the piano.
9 She waited for over an hour patiently.
10 She spoke to me friendly.

6 a Think of a story about something which happened to you or someone you know while travelling and make notes to answer the questions.
1 Introduction/background
- Where and when does the story take place? Who is involved? What colours or other adjectives could you use to describe the background?
2 Main events
- What are the main events of the story? What tenses will you use to describe them?
- What could the characters say? How could they say it?
3 Key event or turning point
- What happened that was particularly interesting/ surprising/funny?
4 Conclusion
- How did the story end?

b Now write your story.

How To Write Writing Activities

The lesson begins with a lead-in to the topic, then gets students to analyse the model, looking at the structure and an aspect of language and giving some practice in these areas, before asking students to put it all together and write a parallel task. This is obviously not the only way of structuring a writing lesson, but it can provide a useful template to play about with.

Task 13 (page 113)

Obviously there are lots of possibilities here. Some ideas:

- Give a sample answer, but with some sentences which are NOT related to the topic of the letter – the students must identify which ones.
- Put the paragraphs of a sample letter in the correct order.
- Choose the most appropriate linkers to join sentences, either standalone, or within a sample answer.
- Choose the sample answer which is written in the most appropriate register (or a similar activity with standalone sentences).

Appendix

List of linkers, task types and aspects of writing found in coursebooks at different levels

A1/A2

Linkers

and and *but*

and, *but* or *then* and *after that*

and, *so*, *but*, *because*

because, *when*, *until*

although, *because of*

who, *that*, *which*

too, *also*, *as well*

because and *so*

Task types

Biography

Blog entry

Describing a holiday

Description of a friend

Form filling

Instructions

Invitation

Online profile

Postcard

Simple letter to a friend

Story

Thank you letter

Aspect of writing skill

Capital letters and full stops

Layout of an email vs a letter

Learn to use paragraphs

How To Write Writing Activities

Spelling y-i (e.g. *beauty-beautiful*), plurals, double letters

Use commas correctly

Useful phrases for email (beginnings and endings)

B1

Linkers

and and *also*

first, then, after that, after a while, finally

to begin with, firstly, lastly, secondly, next, finally

Task types

A memory

Advice for a problem page

Description of a friend

Description of a product

Diary/blog entry

Email of complaint

Formal letter

Give opinion (web comment)

Informal email

Write about event in your life

Aspect of writing skill

Abbreviations in text messages

Correcting mistakes

Formal/informal language

it's vs its

Organising (order) an email

Pronouns

Spelling (homophones)

Starting/ending an email

B1+
Linkers
anyway, naturally, nevertheless, fortunately

Adverbs of attitude: *luckily, unfortunately, personally*

Arguing for and against: *in my opinion, another point is, in my view, I disagree that …*

in this way, first of all, for example, for this reason

however, moreover

Task types
A CV

A report

Arguing for and against

Biography

Describing a person

Describing a place

Description of a favourite room

Discursive essay

Formal letter

Informal letter

Magazine article

Semi-formal writing

Telling a story (historic event)

Aspect of writing skill
Beginnings and endings of emails

Complex sentences

Correcting mistakes

Expanding sentences

Formal/informal emails

Planning

Using dashes

B2

Linkers

Contrast linkers: *however, nevertheless, although, in spite of, whereas, on the other hand*

Linkers of addition: *not only, as well as, in addition, furthermore*

Time and sequence: *as soon as, while, by the time, then, when, as, during, until, after, just as*

In spite of/despite, even so, even though, even if

Task types

Advantages and disadvantages essay

Article

Discursive essay

Formal letter of complaint

Letter of application

Letter to a friend

Persuasive letter/email

Report

Review (book and/or film)

Short story

Summary

Aspect of writing skill

Adjectives and adverbs

Apostrophes

Arguing persuasively

Formal language

Making your stories more memorable

Organising your ideas in a text

Relative clauses

Topic sentences

Writing a paragraph plan

C1

Linkers

Addition linkers: *another, also, furthermore, a further* …

Referring: *for this reason, regarding*

Text organisation: *the second, the third*

Discourse markers: contrasting, adding, drawing conclusions

Task types

Autobiographical statements

Cause and effect essays

Different types of correspondence: letter of apology, letter of application

Formal emails

Magazine article

Report

Restaurant review

Short newspaper story

Short story

Tabloid article

Transactional letters

Aspect of writing skill

Adding colour and variety to a story

Apologising / giving bad news / making and responding to requests / complaining / responding to an invitation

Essay introductions

Fronting

Inversion

Redrafting

Reference

Register in for and against essays

Writing in an appropriate style

How To Write Vocabulary Presentations And Practice

Task 1
Before you start this chapter it will be helpful to complete this brief task.

1 If you look for vocabulary materials online (and the internet is awash with them!), what kind of task types do you expect to find? Try to think of at least three different task types.

2 Do a quick internet search (no more than five minutes), using 'English Vocabulary Exercises' as your search words. How many different task types can you find?

3 Evaluate these task types as material for the classroom.

4 Take a coursebook that you know quite well. Look, at random, at four double-page spreads. What is the proportion of space devoted to vocabulary compared to the space devoted to grammar? Then, looking only at the vocabulary material, what is the proportion of space devoted to practice compared to the space devoted to presentation?

Read the task commentary on page 161.

Aims
The basic aims of this chapter about writing vocabulary materials are to:

1 provide an overview of the theoretical and practical issues involved in writing vocabulary materials.
2 provide you with a framework which can guide you in the planning of vocabulary materials.
3 provide practical suggestions on writing vocabulary materials (and **rubrics**) and to provide a wide range of models.
4 suggest ways of using teacher's notes to support and extend the vocabulary materials that the students see.
5 encourage you to think critically about vocabulary materials.

Note

This chapter focuses primarily on materials for adult and secondary school learners. It also looks mostly at printed, as opposed to digital, materials. For these other areas, you should supplement your reading of this chapter with the ELT Teacher 2 Writer titles, *How To Write For Primary* and *How To Write For Digital Media*.

Preliminary Questions

Your approach to writing vocabulary materials will inevitably be influenced by your beliefs about language learning and teaching, and more specifically your beliefs about the role of vocabulary in this process.

I am old enough to remember a time when published teaching materials were almost exclusively concerned with grammar (mostly tenses) and vocabulary was introduced (usually in the form of word lists) as a way of practising the grammar. Things changed in 1984 with the publication of *The Cambridge English Course* (CUP) by Michael Swan and Catherine Walter – the first major international coursebook series with a strong **lexical** strand to the syllabus. The importance of vocabulary in language learning materials was given further boosts in 1990 with the publication of Dave Willis's *The Lexical Syllabus* (Cobuild) and in 1993 with the publication of Michael Lewis's *The Lexical Approach* (LTP). Now, in the second decade of the 21st century, it almost goes without saying that vocabulary tasks will form a substantial part of any package of language learning/teaching materials.

We've come a long way in 30 years. There is now general agreement about syllabus priorities, but the devil is in the detail and here we are a long way from any consensus. It may well be the case that no consensus will ever be reached, as we increasingly recognize that there is no single 'right way'. The right way to do things will be informed by insights from research, but equally from the requirements of particular teaching contexts. The best teaching material is invariably very aware of the particular contexts in which it will be used. As you think about the contentious issues that are discussed below, keep the context for which you are writing materials firmly in mind.

How To Write Vocabulary Presentations And Practice

Which vocabulary items?

If the vocabulary set that you need to write an exercise for has already been determined for you, you may feel that this question does not concern you. However, the chances are that you may want to modify, even if only slightly, some of the items in the set in the light of the considerations below.

It has often been suggested that we should select vocabulary items by considering their **frequency**. It seems reasonable to give priority to high frequency items, as these have a greater surrender value. The frequency of an item is easy to check by looking at a good online dictionary for learners, such as one of the following:

The *Longman Dictionary of Contemporary English* will tell you if a word is in the top 1,000, 2,000 or 3,000 words, and also specifies if these frequencies are for a written or spoken **corpus**.

The *Macmillan Dictionary* has a system of one, two or three red stars to indicate frequency.

The *Oxford Advanced Learner's Dictionary* shows a key symbol if the word is in their list of top words, the Oxford 3000™.

A useful and simple tool for getting an idea of frequency is a search engine like Google or Bing which will tell you the number of results returned by a particular item. If you want to check which of two items is more frequent (at least, online), you can use *GoogleBATTLE* which allows you to compare the frequency of two keywords. This is only a rough-and-ready guide (because it only gives you information about the frequency of items that come up in Google search results), but it's a huge and totally up-to-date corpus, nevertheless.

How To Write Vocabulary Presentations And Practice

Task 2

Before reading further, you might like to compare your intuitive knowledge of some vocabulary items with actual frequency data. Native speakers, in particular, often overestimate their ability to 'judge' a word.

1 The vocabulary set below was presented in the opening unit of a B1 (Pre-intermediate) coursebook. Divide the words into three groups:
   a) seven words that are in the top 3,000 words
   b) three words that some databases list in the top 3,000, and others don't
   c) six words that are not included in the top 3,000

   Why do you think the writer chose to include the six lower frequency words?

   aunt   best friend   classmate   colleague   cousin   daughter
   grandfather   mother-in-law   pet   neighbour   niece   roommate
   son   son-in-law   uncle

2 The set of phrasal verbs below was presented near the beginning of a B1 (Intermediate) coursebook. What are the two least common phrasal verbs? Why do you think the writer chose to include these two low-frequency phrasal verbs?

   He was able to **sort** the problem **out**. / They **came across** the bear near a river. / Tizio **got over** his injury. / Their friends and families **saw** them **off**. / A van **picked** her **up** after only five minutes. / The van **dropped** her **off** near the finishing line.

3 The set of reflexive verbs below was presented near the end of a B2 (Upper Intermediate) coursebook. Which of these words could you expect students at this level to understand the meaning of (even if they cannot use the words accurately)?

   adapt yourself   content yourself   deceive yourself   destroy yourself
   distinguish yourself   endanger yourself   express yourself   pride yourself
   remind yourself   sacrifice yourself

When you have finished, you can compare your answers with the commentary on page 161.

The frequency of a word is determined by looking at its occurrence in a computerized corpus. Obviously, the choice of corpus will affect the frequency of a word. Do the students that you are writing the material for need a particular variety of English, such as British English, American English or **English as a Lingua Franca (ELF)**? As a materials writer, you'll need to check out the properties of the vocabulary items that you are considering for inclusion in an exercise. A couple of good learner's dictionaries near your desk or on your desktop will prove very helpful.

Preliminary Questions

How To Write Vocabulary Presentations And Practice

You may also be interested in checking the appropriacy of vocabulary items for the level of the students. *English Profile* has a corpus of learner English that can be searched in order to find out at which level students typically use a given vocabulary item. At the time of writing, subscription to this service is free, but this may change at some point in the future.

You may, of course, have good reasons for wanting to focus on vocabulary items that are neither high-frequency nor typically used by learners of the appropriate level. These reasons may include such things as the usefulness of the item for tasks which will follow on from the vocabulary work (e.g. a reading or listening task) or the fact that the item may be included as part of a list which the students will be tested on.

Although we typically think of vocabulary items as being single words, there are very good reasons to broaden the range of items that we want to expose learners to. Many applied linguists have discussed the importance of lexical chunks in the way that language is both used and learnt. **Chunks** may be collocations, grammatical patterns that are typically associated with a word (e.g. dependent prepositions or adjectives followed by a gerund or an infinitive), set phrases and idioms, sentence frames (e.g. *There are very good reasons to* + infinitive), etc.

Longer stretches of language, such as 'useful phrases', may be easier for students to learn and use than individual items. The **learnability** of a vocabulary item does not necessarily correspond to its frequency or usefulness, but it may be a justification for teaching it, especially at low levels. Good examples of such learnability are phrases like *Happy birthday* that are widely used in non-English-speaking cultures or words that are '**true friends**' (e.g. *fitness, job, piercing* and *steak* in French, German and many other languages).

How should we group vocabulary items?

Vocabulary items are most commonly grouped and taught in **semantic** sets (i.e. which are related in terms of meaning), such as days of the week, parts of the body, or adjectives of personality. The second most common approach to grouping vocabulary items is by using lexico-grammatical categories, such as pairs of gradable and ungradable adjectives, words beginning with a particular prefix, or phrasal verbs that contain the particle *out*.

This approach seems logical and published material rarely does anything different. However, research suggests that, especially at lower levels, this may not be a terribly good idea, as learners mix up very similar items. *Tuesday* and *Thursday*, for example, are easily confused and there is no compelling reason to teach them at the same time.

An alternative approach is to (1) look at the material (e.g. texts and tasks) that students will be using in the next lesson or two, (2) predict the items that will be problematic, (3) select a set of these in the light of the considerations of the above section, and (4) write material that will introduce these items.

Vocabulary breadth or vocabulary depth?

The vocabulary syllabuses of most coursebooks and vocabulary study books is driven by a desire to provide as wide a coverage as possible (**vocabulary breadth**): the more words the better. This seems to be popular with many teachers and the best-selling coursebook *New English File Upper Intermediate* (Oxford University Press, 2008), for example, has 'Vocabulary Banks' with dozens of new vocabulary items on a single page.

An alternative strategy may be to devise materials that encourage learners to extend their knowledge of high-frequency words, as opposed to broadening their repertoire of low frequency words. Learning a word (especially a high frequency word), after all, is a gradual, incremental process. The table on page 136 provides a good summary of what is involved in word knowledge. It is clearly impossible to learn all the things that one needs to know about a word in one go!

How To Write Vocabulary Presentations And Practice

Form	spoken	R	What does the word sound like?
		P	How is the word pronounced?
	written	R	What does the word look like?
		P	How is the word written and spelled?
	word parts	R	What parts are recognizable in the word?
		P	What word parts are needed to express the meaning?
Meaning	form and meaning	R	What meaning does this word form signal?
		P	What word form can be used to express this meaning?
	concept and referents	R	What is included in the concept?
		P	What items can the concept refer to?
	associations	R	What other words does this make us think of?
		P	What other words could we use instead of this one?
Use	grammatical functions	R	In what patterns does the word occur?
		P	In what patterns must we use this word?
	collocations	R	What words or types of words occur with this one?
		P	What words or types of words must we use with this one?
	constraints on use (register, frequency, ...)	R	Where, when, and how often would we expect to meet this word?
		P	Where, when, and how often can we use this word?
In column 3, R = receptive knowledge P = productive knowledge			
What Is Involved In Knowing A Word – From Nation, *Teaching Vocabulary*, 1E. © 2009 Heinle/ELT, a part of Cengage Learning, Inc. Reproduced by permission. www.cengage.com/permissions			

Consider, for example, the fourth most common noun in English, *way*. Look at the following exercise, which is designed to extend low-level (A2/B1) German-speaking learners' ability to use this word. Here, learners' knowledge of a high-frequency word (i.e. vocabulary depth) is extended through a simple translation task.

How To Write Vocabulary Presentations And Practice

Rearrange the words to make translations of the German phrases.

1 Wie macht man das am besten?
   best   do   the   this   to   way   what's
   What's the best way to do this?

2 Wir sind weit weg von zuhause.
   a   from   home   long   way   we're

3 Wie geht's nach Hause?
   home   is   way   which

4 Wir müssen eine Lösung finden.
   a   find   must   way   we

5 So mag ich es.
   I   it   like   that's   the   way

6 Ich hab's auf eine andere Weise gemacht.
   another   did   I   it   way

7 Nur so macht man es.
   do   it   only   that's   the   to   way

8 Er hat sich verirrt.
   he   his   lost   way

Task 3

The sixth most common noun in English is *thing*. Use a dictionary, your own language knowledge or online resources to write a list of seven or eight sentences/phrases which could form the basis of an exercise to develop students' (level A2/B1) ability to use this word. Think particularly about common collocations of this word.

Read the commentary for this task on page 163.

Materials for the classroom or for self-study?

There is, or there should be, a difference between materials that have been written for classroom use and materials that have been written for self-study. It seems to me that classroom time is best used by making optimal use of the key classroom resources, i.e. the other students and the teacher. **Communicative** oral exercises, for example, are possible in a classroom, but not at home, unless the learner is working in an interactive online environment. Exercises that encourage memorization, a necessary but unfashionable part of vocabulary acquisition, on the other hand, may be better done as part of self-study.

Good communicative vocabulary exercises for the classroom are often hard to find. Vocabulary gap-fills, which seem more appropriate for self-study, are easier to locate, both online and in printed books. If you need material of the latter kind, it's worth having a look at material that already exists: as a teacher, you may be able to use it as it is, or you may want to make minor modifications. As a writer, you will want to avoid writing anything that is too similar to what has already been published. The *English Vocabulary in Use* series from Cambridge University Press is an excellent source of self-study material. These books are also very valuable as reference sources: to check, for example, which items have been included in the lexical sets.

What is the aim of the materials you plan to write?

The example task below is fairly representative of much published vocabulary material. This kind of task is so familiar that we may not stop to consider what the point of it is. It obviously deals with a particular set of vocabulary, but what exactly is it trying to achieve?

Fill in the gaps with a word from the list below.

best man   bride   bridegroom   bridesmaid   engaged   guests   honeymoon   reception

1 The couple were _____ for ten months before they got married.
2 On the day of the wedding, the _____ arrived at the church with her father.
3 Her ten-year-old niece was the _____ and she stood behind her aunt during the ceremony.
4 The _____ waited for his future wife to arrive.
5 The _____ were relations and friends of the two families.
6 After the ceremony, everyone went to the _____.
7 The _____, a good friend of the husband, gave a speech.
8 At the end of the day, the couple left for their _____ in the Seychelles.

As a task type, a gap fill like this is problematic. Is it to introduce a set of new words? If so, it does not do a very good job. If students do not know the words, they cannot do the task – unless, of course, they consult a dictionary, a classmate or the teacher. If they do not know the words, but are given the answers, the meaning is still not evident. Or is, perhaps, the task intended to practise a set of words that the students have already come across? If so, it still does not do a very good job, because the amount of practice that students will get for each word is very, very minimal.

As a task type, a gap fill like this seems best suited to testing. It could be used as a **diagnostic** test, to find out what students know before helping them further with unknown items. Alternatively, it could be used as a **summative** test. It is, however, rather dull. Materials writers, including myself, sometimes resort to gap fills because they can't think of anything more interesting or original.

Gap fills can, however, be made more interesting. Jim Scrivener (in the Teacher's Book for Straightforward Pre-intermediate 2nd Edition, Macmillan, 2012, p150–151) suggests the following ideas:

1 Turn the gap fill into an intensive listening exercise. The teacher reads out the sentences while the students' books are closed, and indicates (with some sort of noise, or by clicking the fingers) that there is a gap. The students write down the missing word. They then open their books and compare answers in pairs before the teacher goes through the exercise with the whole class.

2 The teacher does the work herself on the board. She gives the answers and explains her reasons for choosing particular words. However, she makes a few deliberate mistakes along the way, and the students' task is to spot these.

3 The students do the work individually or in pairs. Then, get one student to take the teacher's role in feedback to the exercise. Provide this student with the correct answers. She/He elicits answers from the class and corrects as appropriate. Encourage the other students to ask for explanations.

Such ideas, good as they are, are probably best suggested in teacher's notes, rather than in the material which is given to the students.

The more aware we are of the aims of the materials we write, the more likely it is that those aims can be achieved. For more practical suggestions, see section 3 of this chapter Writing rubrics and teacher's notes.

What is not covered in this chapter?

The ideas that we will be looking at in this chapter are with teenage (or older) students in mind. For younger learners, a different approach will be needed. There are three other areas that will not be covered in this chapter:
- extensive reading activities for vocabulary development
- dictionary and other learner training activities
- exam preparation activities

Writing Rubrics And Teacher's Notes

The task types that we will look at in the rest of this chapter will be divided into two broad groups: presentation tasks and practice tasks. Presentation tasks assume that students are encountering the items for the first time; practice tasks (often following on immediately from a presentation task) assume a previous encounter. In reality, however, there is no hard and fast distinction between the two. In much published material, exercises intended to present new language would be more appropriate as practice tasks. They can be made into practice tasks with relatively minor tweaking to either the rubric or the accompanying teacher's notes.

More generally, it's worth bearing in mind that the job of a materials writer is to write materials, rather than prepare lesson plans. Teachers will do whatever they want with the materials that we write: it is impossible to write 'teacher-proof' materials. Believe me, I've tried! Materials alone do not make for good teaching. Good teaching only comes from the teacher herself, and the way she uses the materials. We can give guidelines and suggestions, and materials that are rich in possibilities, but there is little that we can do to counteract the tendency of many teachers to test rather than teach. When it comes to vocabulary materials, we can try our best to suggest approaches that teach rather than test, but things will never be entirely clear-cut.

For the reasons discussed above, we will look at rubrics and teacher's notes before looking at a range of task types.

Rubrics

Few writers enjoy writing rubrics. Before going to the printer, an editor will check that rubrics conform to a house or series style and that they are consistent. However, the writer should ask the editor for style guidelines during the writing process, which will save time and effort in the long run.

The first issue to be resolved is the language in which the rubrics will be written. With materials for monolingual groups at a very low level, there seems to be no compelling reason not to use the students' own language. In general, however, it is likely that you will prefer to use English. It will help to follow a few simple guidelines:

- Make sure that the language of the rubric is less complicated than the language that is being presented or practised.
- Stick to a small set of words for your rubrics.
- Use the same rubric for all activities of the same type.
- If an activity can only be explained with a very long rubric, it's probably the wrong activity. (I have even written what I thought were quite simple tasks, and when I looked at them again later, I couldn't understand or remember exactly what I was intending!)

How To Write Vocabulary Presentations And Practice

- Stage the parts of the rubric very carefully. Think hard about which parts of the rubric should come before the main body of the exercise, and which should come after. Remember, too, that's it's sometimes a good idea to break an activity down into two or more activities.

The examples below should provide you with enough rubric ammunition for most purposes.

Rubrics that come before the main body of the exercise:

Match the words in the box to the definitions.
Complete the sentences with a word from the box.
Label the picture with the words in the box.
Match the pictures with the words in the box.
Look at XXX. Match the words in **bold** to the definitions below.
Match the words from column A with words from column B.
Replace the words in *italics* with a word from the box.
Choose the correct words to complete the sentences.
Complete the sentences with the correct word.
Complete the words by putting vowels (*a, e, i, o, u*) in the spaces.
Put the words in the box into three groups.
Put the text in the correct order.
Complete the sentences in column A with a phrase from column B.

Rubrics that come after the main body of the exercise:

Use a dictionary to check your answers.
Listen to the recording to check your answers.
Work in pairs. Compare your answers to exercise 0.
Work in pairs. Ask and answer the questions in exercise 0.
Work in pairs. Do you agree or disagree with the sentences in exercise 0?
Change the sentences in exercise 0 so that they are true for you.

It is common to use a different font for the rubrics (often a sans serif font like Arial or Calibri) and the main body of an exercise (often a serif font like Times New Roman or Garamond). This is simply to make it easier for users to differentiate the material on the page. You may also want to use bold, italics and highlighting, bullet points, boxing, colour and shading to make the material more easily readable, but beware of 'over-styling'. When it comes to design, less is often more. For professionally published material, these formatting decisions are usually the responsibility of an editor.

Teacher's notes

Teacher's notes offer a lot of scope to a writer. Complicated information gap activities, where the materials typically do not contain any rubric (such as those written by Jill Hadfield, *Intermediate Vocabulary Games*, Longman, 1999), will need explanatory notes for the teacher. Other materials, which could stand alone, may also benefit from suggestions for how to manage them in class.

Besides these procedural notes, you will normally be required to provide an answer key (or suggested answers) for any materials that you write. Teachers will also be pleased to get language notes that are related to the vocabulary that is being presented or practised. These may contain information about the target items that is not immediately relevant to the exercise, but that will be useful for the teacher to bear in mind. These language notes may also contain the following:

- Help with pronunciation
- Dictionary definitions and/or translations
- Problems that one may anticipate students having (e.g. easily confused words, **false friends**, etc.)

In addition, teacher's notes may include:

- Alternative procedures (suggestions for different ways of exploiting the material)
- Suggestions for stronger and weaker students/classes
- Lead-ins and follow-ups
- Suggestions for additional activities

Task 4

In a B1 level coursebook that I wrote (*Straightforward Pre-intermediate* 2nd Edition, Macmillan, 2012), I began one unit with a very simple exercise which asked students to put the following set of words into four groups: art gallery, bar, bus, cinema, crime, flat, house, library, Metro, nightclub, park, pollution, restaurant, studio, theatre, traffic, tram. The four groups were (1) public transport, (2) types of accommodation, (3) nightlife, culture, (4) other. The students were then asked if they could add any more words to these groups. Finally, they were asked to rank these items in order of importance in terms of their desirability if they were to move to a new town. The aim was to revise a set of words (and introduce a few new ones), and to provide some practice of using these words. The students would encounter these words later in the lesson in a reading task.

Apart from an answer key and language notes, what might you consider including in the teacher's notes? Spend ten minutes brainstorming ideas before turning to the commentary for this task on page 163.

Presentation Materials

Much published material that is ostensibly intended for vocabulary presentation is problematic because the task requires students to do something with words they do not know. Before students do anything at all with a word, they need to know, at the very least, what it means. It is perhaps surprising how frequently published materials do not actually help with meaning. For this reason, the first section that follows suggests the most basic approaches to meaning.

Basics

The most basic approach in vocabulary presentation materials is to provide a list of words and their pictorial equivalents. This could be, for example, in the form of a picture with labels or a series of matching words and pictures (e.g. word cards). If you are writing materials of this kind, you will need to provide an **artwork brief**: clear instructions about the kind of illustration that you want to be commissioned or found in an archive. Artwork of whatever kind is expensive, and you need to be aware of your budget. If you are writing for a publishing company, make sure you are fully informed about the whole area of permissions and cost restrictions.

Pictorial representation, besides being expensive, is also necessarily limited to words that can be represented pictorially. Even some sets of concrete nouns do not always lend themselves to this approach. You will probably have come across illustrations for 'Parts of the Body' where it is far from clear whether the arrow is pointing to the heel or the ankle or the foot, or to the throat, the neck or the shoulder blade. Less interesting visually, but often clearer, is to use translations or definitions (or opposites) in place of illustrations. The students' task is simply to study the lists and learn the words. This approach is widely used in materials for younger learners, but has gone out of fashion in materials for more adult learners. It remains, however, popular with many learners themselves and research suggests unequivocally that memorisation of word lists can be a very effective learning strategy. With a growing awareness in recent years of the importance of memory in language learning, one may expect word lists to stage something of a come-back. At the same time, technological developments now allow us to produce digital word cards that work as apps for smart phones and other devices. We can expect to see publishing companies commissioning more and more of this kind of material in the future (material which will be mostly used as a marketing add-on for major coursebook series).

Learner involvement

Word lists, however interactive or glossy they may be, are not massively involving, to put it mildly. If a student's task is simply to study and learn, their engagement in the learning process is not likely to be terribly high. In an attempt to involve learners more actively in learning tasks, vocabulary materials have shifted from simply saying what words mean to some sort of engagement in the process of finding out. Much more common these days is a task which (1) gives students a picture which they must label themselves, (2) a series of pictures and words that they must match, or (3) variations on the same approach with definitions (or opposites) or translations.

As mentioned earlier, a problem arises when students do not know the words and so cannot do the task without help from the teacher, an answer key, another student or a dictionary ... or by simply guessing. If, of course, they can already do the task because they know the words, one may wonder what the point of the task is! There are, however, a good number of variations of these most basic task types.

providing students with words and meaning	variations	students must match words to meanings
zero or minimal student involvement		student involvement

The three variations below are examples of ways in which the extent of student involvement can be modified.

Variation 1

In this variation, some of the items that students must match are already matched. The example below asks students to identify three wrongly matched pairs, but the number of wrongly matched items could be greater or smaller, or could be stipulated or not stipulated.

How To Write Vocabulary Presentations And Practice

Look at the criminals and definitions. Three criminals are in the wrong place. Correct them.

a blackmailer	damages property
a burglar	steals from houses
a dealer	sells drugs
a forger	makes illegal copies of something (e.g. banknotes)
a kidnapper	makes someone a prisoner and asks their family or friends for money
a mugger	has information about someone else and asks for money to keep the secret
a murderer	kills another person
a pickpocket	steals from someone's bag or pockets
a shoplifter	steals from shops
a smuggler	takes something illegally into another country
a vandal	attacks and robs someone in the street
an arsonist	burns buildings

The same approach can be used with word-picture or word-translation pairs. In addition, of course, the familiar sentence gap fills (with the target words given in a box) can serve the same function. These can be made rather more challenging by including a small number of extra words in the box that do not have a corresponding gapped sentence.

It is sometimes claimed that there is a danger in activities of this kind that students will remember the wrong information. I don't share this fear, but it is clearly important that the teacher makes a big point of highlighting the errors.

Variation 2

Multiple choice is another option to introduce a degree of support. Pictures, definitions or gapped sentences can be connected to two, three or more multiple choice items. This approach can also be inverted so that students must select from multiple definitions for each of the target words.

Variation 3

In this variation, an element of word play is introduced. One of the simplest approaches is to ask students to match pictures or definitions to **anagrammed** words. Another, very similar, approach is to delete/gap certain letters (e.g. the vowels) from the words. A further element of challenge can be introduced by jumbling up the order of the anagrammed or gapped words.

Crosswords, wordsquares, word searches and wordsnakes can all be used to make such tasks appear more game-like.

Previous knowledge

It often makes sense to find out what students already know. The most straightforward way of doing this is illustrated in the example below:

> Mark the objects below (Y) if it's a word you know, (?) if you're not sure, (N) if you don't know.
>
> blender   bowl   chopping board   cup   fork   grater   jug
> kettle   knife   ladle   mixer   pan   peeler   plate   pot
> scales   scoop   sieve   skewers   spatula spoon   timer   whisk
>
> Compare with a partner and check any unknown words.

More structured, and with a clearer, more measurable end-result is to ask students to give examples. These could be **hyponyms** of a **superordinate** (e.g. think of three different kinds of public transport) or specific examples of the target vocabulary (e.g. can you name one of the following from your country – a chat show, a quiz show, a reality TV show, a soap opera, etc.). This could also be done in a less open-ended way, where the hyponyms and superordinates are given and the student must match them. Often, it is a good idea to begin with a closed task (i.e. where there is only one correct answer) and then invite students to contribute their own knowledge. This is illustrated in the mind-map task below.

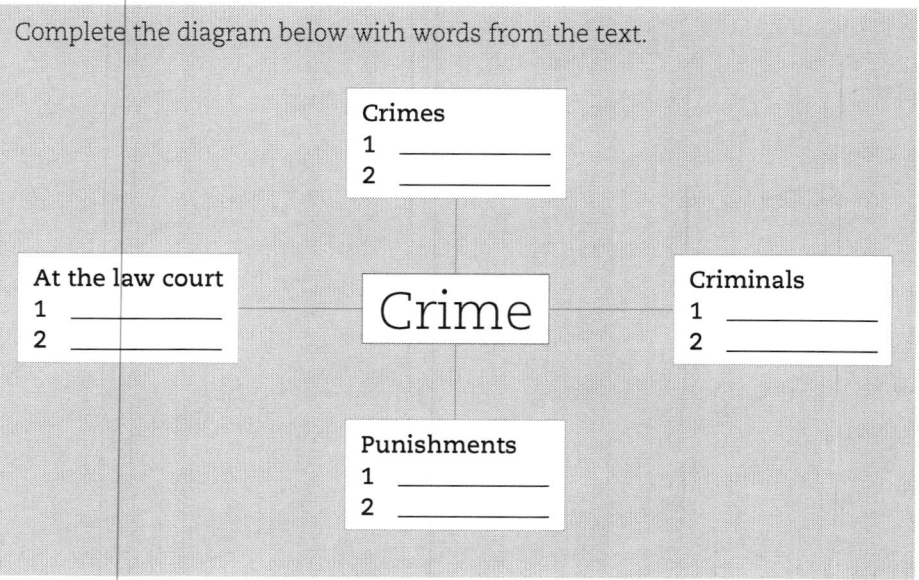

How To Write Vocabulary Presentations And Practice

An example of an approach which combines example-giving with the provision of definitions is given below:

> 1 Work with a partner. Decide what you would say in these situations.
> example
> **Invite** a friend to dinner at your house.
> 'Would you like to come to dinner at my house?'
> 1 **Accuse** someone of not telling the truth.
> 2 **Recommend** a friend to go and see the new Spielberg movie.
> 3 **Deny** eating the last piece of chocolate.
> 4 **Remind** someone to post a letter.
> 5 **Encourage** a colleague to look for a new job.
>
> 2 Work with a partner. Say the verbs.
> | | |
> |---|---|
> | **invite** | ask someone to see you or do something socially |
> | **accuse** | say that someone has done something wrong |
> | **recommend** | advise someone to do something |
> | **deny** | say that something is not true |
> | **remind** | help someone to remember something |
> | **encourage** | try to persuade someone to do something that you think is good |

Finally, here are three ideas that use pictures.
1 Students are asked to look at a picture for, say, 30 seconds. They must then cover the picture and describe what they have seen to a partner. In order to do this well, they will need to use the target vocabulary. If this vocabulary is unknown, a learning gap has been created, and the teacher will then teach the necessary items.
2 Students are given a picture to look at and a short written description of the picture. This description contains a number of factual errors which the students must identify.
3 Students are given two or more pictures which they are asked to discuss/compare using the target words that have been provided in a box.

Text-based approaches

With more adult and higher-level learners, it may be preferable to present new vocabulary in context, i.e. embedded within a text. The contextual information may provide help towards understanding the meaning, and the co-text may give useful information about how the word operates **syntactically**. There are at least two basic variations to this approach.

Variation 1

Having read a text (and having completed some related tasks, such as **skimming** or **scanning**), students are given a series of gapped sentences. These must be completed with words from the text. In order to make this less difficult, various clues may be given. (1) The first letter of the missing word may be provided, (2) the number of letters in the missing word may be indicated, (3) the paragraph where the missing word can be found may be indicated, or (4) the words that will be needed for the exercise may be colour-highlighted in the text.

Variation 2

Again, after having read a text and completed some reading tasks, the attention of students is drawn to particular words in the text. They are asked to guess, using contextual information, what these words mean. Since it is often a lot more difficult to articulate the meaning of a word than it is simply to understand it, this task can be made more structured and do-able by (1) giving students definitions or synonyms to match to the target words in the text, or (2) giving multiple-choice definitions or synonyms.

A neat example of this approach is illustrated below. Here the vocabulary work is tied in to the initial reading task.

> 2   Read the article. Are these statements true or false?
> a) World leaders participated in protest marches and demonstrations.
> b) The protesters carried banners and shouted political messages.
> c) A group of protesters on bicycles went to 10 Downing Street.
> d) They delivered a letter asking world leaders to do something immediately about the economy.
> e) Trafalgar Square was extremely crowded and very busy in the afternoon.
> f) A small group of protesters separated from the peaceful demonstrators and went shopping.
>
> **Climate change march**
>
> In London today, 20,000 people took part in protest marches and demonstrations as world leaders were meeting for climate change talks. The event was organised by the Campaign Against Global Warming.

How To Write Vocabulary Presentations And Practice

> The day started early outside the US embassy with poetry readings and speeches. Protesters then marched slowly to Trafalgar Square, carrying banners and shouting slogans.
>
> A group of protesters on bicycles made their way to 10 Downing Street and delivered a letter to the Prime Minister demanding urgent action on climate change.
>
> By three o'clock in the afternoon, Trafalgar Square was swarming with people and buzzing with activity. There was a carnival atmosphere with music provided by a samba band, a New Orleans jazz band and Scottish pipers.
>
> Most of the protesters marched peacefully, but a small group of people broke away from the peaceful demonstrators. They smashed shop windows and tried to set fire to a supermarket. Five people were arrested.
>
> **3** Look at the highlighted phrases in the article. Find phrases with similar meanings in the sentences (a–f) in Exercise 2.
>
> took part in – *participated in*

Extract from: *New Inside Out Pre-intermediate* © Sue Kay and Vaughan Jones; 2008, Published by Macmillan Publishers Limited. Used by Permission. All rights reserved

The advantages of such text-based approaches are clear: they are linguistically rich and require student involvement. The practical problem for many teachers, is that this forces them to do reading skills work before looking at the vocabulary. If, during the reading work, a student asks what a particular word means, are you going to tell them? They may really feel that they need to understand it (and they won't know whether they really need it until they have understood it!). It seems to me inappropriate to refuse to answer their question just because it will mess up the vocabulary activity that follows (working out meaning from context is utterly pointless if students already know the word). There is, however, the alternative of using similar task types with short, sentence-level texts, and these can be used early in a lesson.

For a writer, this kind of material will almost certainly require a lot of to-ing and fro-ing between the reading exercises and the vocabulary exercises. You will need to write both at the same time: vocabulary considerations will influence the text you are writing or adapting, and the nature of the text and accompanying reading tasks will have an impact on the choice of vocabulary.

Sentence-level approaches

The example below was crafted to serve a number of functions. There is sufficient contextual information in the sentences for most B1 students to make an intelligent guess at the matching task, and the surrounding vocabulary has been carefully graded, so that it does not raise any additional problems. The sentences/questions are all closely related to the theme of the lesson and lead on very naturally to a speaking activity which requires students to use this new vocabulary. An activity like this could be used either before a text (to establish the topic and to pre-teach necessary vocabulary) or after a text (as a follow up).

> Match a word or phrase in *italics* with the underlined words or phrases below.
>
> *important times or events*   *members of your family*   *not generous*
> *present*   *take off the paper*   *very strongly dislike*
>
> 1 Do you have any <u>relatives</u> (e.g. uncles or aunts) who always give you the same present? If so, who and what?
> 2 What is the best <u>gift</u> you have ever received?
> 3 How quickly or slowly do you <u>unwrap</u> presents?
> 4 Do you only give presents to people on special <u>occasions</u>, like birthdays or religious holidays? If not, when and why?
> 5 Do you enjoy shopping for presents or do you <u>loathe</u> it?
> 6 Do you know anyone who does not like giving presents or who is very <u>mean</u> when they give presents? If so, who and how?

A rather different, but increasingly common approach, which provides a lot of contextual information, requires students to match the first half of a sentence to the second half of the sentence. The target items are embedded in the broken sentences. Students can use both semantic and syntactic clues to help them put the sentences together.

In variations of this approach, the chunks of language that need to be put together could be (1) questions and their answers, (2) mini-dialogues, (3) sentences with follow-on sentences. Exercises of this kind can be very tricky to write. A lot of juggling is sometimes needed to make sure that the task requires the students to focus on the target items, that there is only one possible way of matching up the chunks of language, and that it is not too difficult or easy.

A common follow-up for this kind of task type is for students to listen to a recording to check their answers.

How To Write Vocabulary Presentations And Practice

Collocations and forms

Knowing a word, being able to use a word, entails more than knowing what it means. There will be many lexical sets which contain words that may be familiar to the students, but their ability to use them may be more limited. Most of the task types already described in this section (matching, multiple-choice, etc.) can be used to focus on collocations and forms. The three pieces of material below illustrate different ways of working with collocations. The third example shows a way of combining this approach with a text-based approach.

Work in pairs. How many correct phrases can you make with the words in the box?

	glass	coffee
	cup	cola
	mug	juice
a	bottle of	milk
	carton	tea
	can	beer
		water
		wine

Extract from *Global Pre-intermediate* © Lindsay Clandfield; 2010, Published by Macmillan Publishers Limited. Used by Permission. All rights reserved

---

Which phrase in each row does not collocate with the verb at the start of the row?

Example

	get over	a fear of something	an illness	a shock	~~money~~
1	give up	a hobby	a job	smoking	your health
2	look after	a dog	football	the baby	yourself
3	look up	a cup of tea	a definition	a word	the spelling
4	put off	a decision	a meeting	the TV	the wedding
5	turn into	a change	a gas	a movie	a nightmare

Add another collocation to each of the sets below using words and phrases from the article above.

a) to have some time / two weeks / ___*a day off*___ (line 15)
b) to find / lose / _____ a job (line 18)
c) to make a decision / money / _____ (line 26)
d) a well-paid / full-time / _____ job (line 27)

152 Presentation Materials

e)	to have a nap / rest / _____ (line 37)
f)	to ask for advice / a pay-rise / _____ (line 39)

Extract from: *New Inside Out Pre-intermediate* © Sue Kay and Vaughan Jones; 2008, Published by Macmillan Publishers Limited. Used by Permission. All rights reserved

A simple way of focusing students' attention on the syntactic patterns of lexical items is, first, to embed what you wish to illustrate in a text, and then to write a series of sentences which require students to insert, for example, the correct preposition, or to choose between a gerund and an infinitive. Jumbling up the order of words in a sentence may be a good way of focusing students' attention on word order: they can be asked to look in a text to check their answers.

Finally, I should mention a classic task type that focuses on **word families**. Students are asked to complete a table (perhaps already partially completed) which lists the different forms (e.g. adjective, negative adjective, noun, verb, etc.) of the target items.

Concluding comments

There is no single *right* way to present vocabulary. Your choice of approach will depend on many things, including the level of the students and the words that you wish to present, and the institutional and cultural context in which the material will be used. Perhaps most important of all, if you are going to write quite a lot of vocabulary material, is to include plenty of variety. Learners learn in different ways, and they, as well as their teachers, will appreciate and benefit from an avoidance of repetitive formats.

Task 5

Take two coursebooks. These could be either books that you know well or books you have never used. Flick through the two coursebooks, looking only at the sections entitled 'Vocabulary'. How much variety is there in the choice of approaches to vocabulary?

Then, from each of these books, select one vocabulary presentation section at random. Identify the approach that the author(s) has selected. Can you rewrite this exercise using a different approach?

Practice Materials

I suggested earlier that it is not always clear whether some published materials (such as gap fills) are intended for *presentation* of a set of vocabulary or for *practice* (or testing). Such materials leave a lot up to the teacher, and it is rare for teacher's notes to give much support (for example, how to teach the meaning or how to help with pronunciation problems). I also suggested that gap fills may be more suitable for testing, as they provide precious little practice of the target vocabulary. Writing a word in a gap is not unhelpful in trying to learn the item, but it's not especially helpful, either. Learners will need more intensive practice in *using* it.

There is now a great wealth of published material that provides communicative practice of grammar, but the same is not true for vocabulary. Most coursebooks seem to present vocabulary through a gap fill and leave it at that. The situation is beginning to change as the lexical syllabus is given more prominence, but grammar still calls the tune. Teachers often complain of a lack of grammar practice in the coursebooks they are using; it is rare for them to complain of a lack of vocabulary practice.

I will begin the suggestions for vocabulary practice task types with communicative activities – those that require the student to do something reasonably meaningful with the target language. The second section will consider less communicative activities (many of which are no different from the presentation approaches).

Communicative activities

Grouping

Asking students to organize words in to groups can be a communicative activity. There is nothing communicative in the example below, but tasks can be modified to provide an opportunity for communicative practice.

> Put the words in the correct category. Say the words and phrases.
> band   beat   cast   costume   director   instrument   lyrics
> mic   plot   premiere   rhythm   script   set   tune
> Category 1: movies
> Category 2: concerts

Two changes need to be made to activities like this to make them communicative. First of all, there needs to be something to communicate about, and this means that the exercise should not have a wrong or a right answer. It must be reasonably open-ended to provide scope for discussion. In this case, students could be told (in the rubric) to come up with their own categories. Alternatively, they could be told to repeat the task using a different set of categories. Finally, they could be given a set of categories which are open-ended and personal enough to generate discussion (e.g. words you like vs. words you don't like).

Ranking

As with grouping tasks, a **ranking** task becomes communicative when students are told to work in pairs or groups and when they have something to talk about. In the examples below, the first (although it's a perfectly acceptable task) could not be considered communicative as there is clearly only one correct answer. The second example, however, generates a lot more communicative practice of the target vocabulary.

Number the phrases below 1–12 from the least recent to the most recent.	
four months ago	in the 14th century
last Wednesday	30 minutes ago
at four o'clock this afternoon	in the 1990s
on 25th December last year	three years ago
in 2011	last March
on Tuesday evening	yesterday morning

Here are some things that people do in the morning. Which order do you normally do them in? Discuss in pairs or small groups.	
You **brush** your hair.	You have **breakfast**.
You **brush** your teeth.	You put on your **make-up**.
You get dressed.	You read or listen to the **news**.
You have a cup of **tea** or **coffee**.	You have a **shower** or a **bath**.

The criteria for the ranking or ordering will depend on the words in the set that you want to practise. The examples below are for a selection of commonly taught lexical sets.

crimes	order of seriousness
adjectives of personality	order of importance in an 'ideal partner'
jobs	order of how much you think they should be paid
sports	order of personal interest
kinds of TV programme	order of preference
animals	order of suitability as pets
items of clothing	chronological order of when you last bought these items
parts of the face	order in which you notice the features the first time you meet someone
food	order of price

How To Write Vocabulary Presentations And Practice

Questions and answers

With many sets of words or phrases, it is possible to combine a standard gap-fill with communicative (pairwork) question and answer practice by writing gapped questions instead of sentences. In the example below the vocabulary was first introduced with a text reconstruction task – *Sentence-level approaches* on page 151.

> **3** Complete the questions with a word in bold from exercise 1.
> 1. What sort of people do you _____ on well with?
> 2. How often do you and your best friend _____ each other?
> 3. Do you _____ a lot in common with your best friend? What?
> 4. How do you _____ in touch with friends in other towns or countries?
>
> **4** Work in pairs. Ask and answer the questions in exercise 3.

Extract from: *Straightforward Pre-intermediate* © P. Kerr; 2012, Published by Macmillan Publishers Limited. Used by Permission. All rights reserved

Agreeing and disagreeing

Essentially the same as 'Questions and answers' above, this task type requires students first to complete a gap fill before discussing the sentences. Writing this kind of task can be quite tricky because you need to make sure, first, that the gap fill is watertight, and, secondly, that the sentences will lead to some sort of discussion.

> Complete the sentences below with the words and phrases in the box.
>
> against   anti   believe   don't feel   in favour   really care   support
>
> a) I'm not anti-cars – I just think more people should use public transport.
> b) I don't _____ about people. They can look after themselves.
> c) I'm _____ of small family run companies.
> d) I _____ in responsible tourism.
> e) I'm _____ cars in the city centre.
> f) I _____ local farmers.
> g) I _____ strongly about politics.
>
> Which statements do you agree with? What other things do you feel strongly about? Discuss with your partner.

Extract from: *New Inside Out Pre-intermediate* © Sue Kay and Vaughan Jones; 2008, Published by Macmillan Publishers Limited. Used by Permission. All rights reserved

With some sets of sentences, you will need to replace the rubric line, *Which statements do you agree with?*, with *Which sentences are true for you?* or *Which* sentences are true for your country? (if the material is intended for a multilingual/multicultural class).

A good variation of this task type is to gap a series of sentences, and the students' task is to compare answers.

> Complete each of the sentences below so they are true for you. Then compare your answers with a partner. What are the most important differences between you?
> 1 My favourite subjects at school were _____ and _____.
> 2 I didn't usually get very good grades for _____.
> 3 If we failed an exam, we had to _____.
> 4 During the breaks at school, I used to _____.
> 5 I wore _____ to school and carried _____.
> 6 One of the strictest teachers in my school was _____.
> 7 The school had a rule which said that _____.
> 8 The most usual punishment at my school was _____.

Describe or discuss

After presentation of a lexical set, students are asked to use the language to describe something (ideally this will not be a purely physical description which is likely to be more fact-based than opinion-based) or discuss something. This may require artwork of some kind, but any knowledge that is shared by all the students in the class can be used (e.g. the local environment, shared cultural phenomena such as celebrities). The example below does this well, but also illustrates the danger of such personalized tasks: it is not difficult to think of classes where this discussion could become uncomfortable! Writers are usually advised to steer well clear of any topics that are referred to by the acronym 'PARSNIPS' (politics, alcohol, religion, sex, narcotics, isms and pork). Other sensitive topics could be added to this list, but everything depends on the context in which the material will be used.

First decide if these adjectives describe character or appearance or both. Then mark them P or N, depending on whether you think they are positive or negative.

muscular	flirty	pushy	sexy
plain	macho	forward	unpredictable
warm	dishy	quiet	mature
skinny	cuddly	down-to-earth	hairy

Now describe someone else in your class to your partner using some of the adjectives above. See if they can guess who you're talking about.

From Dellar/Walkley/Hocking. *Innovations Upper-Intermediate*, 2E. © 2004 Heinle/ELT, a part of Cengage Learning, Inc. Reproduced by permission. www.cengage.com/permissions

How To Write Vocabulary Presentations And Practice

Task 6

Look at the list of phrases below. How could you write a communicative practice activity for this set? In order to do this, it may help to think, too, about how you could present these items. It is often the case that you plan presentation and practice materials hand-in-hand. (The level is B1 – Pre-intermediate.)

*afraid of   bored with   fond of   good at   keen on   interested in
terrible at   worried about*

Read the commentary for this task on page 164.

Less communicative activities

Why would you want to write vocabulary materials that are non-communicative, non-interactive and provide only limited practice of the target language? The answer is simple: you may be writing material primarily intended for self-study, such as a Workbook, the 'Review Pages' of a coursebook, or exercises for digital media. In these cases, the student's task will involve writing, not speaking, and the usual preference is for exercises that have a clear right or wrong answer. It is not uncommon for less experienced writers to submit material that would work well in a classroom, but is inappropriate for Workbooks and digital media. I can remember painful occasions when I needed reminding that I was writing for a Workbook, not a coursebook.

I have already considered the standard Workbook-style exercises in *Presentation materials* on page 144. There remains, however, one small, infrequently used category.

In this section, I will list a small number of activities where students talk about the target language, rather than actually use it. Activities like these are typically found in the 'Review Pages' of coursebooks.

1 Students are told to test each other.
2 Students are asked to write definitions of the target items. They then work with a partner, whose task is to say (guess?) the word that has been defined.
3 Students are given pairs (or groups) of words and asked to discuss (with a partner) the difference between them. The pairs of words need to have some sort of connection so that the difference in meaning is not too great! These could be pairs of false friends, or semantically related pairs like *salary* and *bonus*, or *experience* and *qualifications*.
4 Students work in pairs or groups and are asked to find connections between words. Like many of the suggestions in this chapter, this can be turned into a 'game' (as in the example opposite) if you feel that is appropriate.

Work in small groups. Take it in turns to choose a word from each group below and explain a connection between them. For example:

tropical / valley   The explorers made their camp in a valley in the tropical rainforest.

brochure / stunning   There are some stunning views of the resort in the holiday brochure.

If the other students think your explanation is good (believable, interesting or amusing), you win a point. You can use each word more than once.

Group 1

annoying	bargain	brochure	climate	crash	depth
invasion	lightning	naked	rescue	souvenir	staff	stage
symbol	tropical	vanish	weapon

Group 2

adventure	ankle	facilities	fountain	guarantee	headline
identical	injury	lens	obvious	origin	storm	studio
stunning	suburb	truck	valley

Good Vocabulary Material: A Checklist

1. It presents or practises useful (e.g. high frequency) vocabulary items.
2. It encourages the student to think about the meaning of the item.
3. It has a clear rubric and students can understand what is required of them.
4. If it is an activity where only one answer should be possible, it's important that only one answer is possible. It needs to be watertight.
5. It does not contain non-target vocabulary items that are likely to be unknown, and will distract from the focus on the target items.
6. It involves the student in **cognitive** effort.
7. It encourages students to use the item in a meaningful way, and in a way that will foster the forming of mental connections with the item.
8. It requires the student to use the item in a communicative and **discoursal** context.
9. It permits the student to make multiple use of the item.
10. It is not the same as every other vocabulary task type that students are asked to do!

Task Commentaries

Task 1 (page 130)

It seems that most online vocabulary materials are of three basic types: gap fills, labelling and matching. These are often dressed up as games, using Flash animations, for example, but there is very little variety. They are basically tests. Although they could be used in a classroom, there is little to recommend them.

coursebooks tend to devote substantially more column inches to grammar work than they do to vocabulary. The vocabulary work is predominantly 'presentation', although it is often unclear what a student is supposed to do if they do not know the words that are being presented.

Given what we know about the relative importance of vocabulary and grammar in language acquisition, it would seem that there is a need for a much greater amount of vocabulary practice.

Task 2 (page 133)

1

The seven words that are in the top 3,000 are: *best friend, colleague, cousin, daughter, grandfather, neighbour, son*

The three words that some databases list in the top 3,000 and some don't: *aunt, pet, uncle*

The six words that are not included in the top 3,000: *classmate, mother-in-law, nephew, niece, roommate, son-in-law*

It's interesting to note the differences between the different dictionaries/corpora. We need to remember that frequency counts are not 'hard facts': they are only guidelines.

I included the low frequency words when I wrote this material for three reasons. Firstly, it seemed to me to be appropriate to challenge the students a little. At this level, one can expect students to know the highest frequency words like *daughter, son, mother, father*. The *in-law* and *-mate* suffixes are useful, because they are generative. Secondly, I included *nephew* and *niece* because I wanted the list to be more 'complete'. Finally, and most importantly for me, I wanted to include extra items to make the practice activity which follows more interesting.

2

The least common verbs in this list are *see off* and *drop off*. I included these for two reasons. Firstly, the vocabulary work follows on from some work on a text in which the **target** items occur. Of course, I could have rewritten the text to include different items, but these two fitted the topic of the text most naturally. Secondly, I needed to illustrate three different types of phrasal verb (intransitive, separable and inseparable). *See off* and *drop off* worked well in the context and were also further examples that I needed of separable verbs. As is often the case, I wrote the text and the vocabulary exercise at the same time. I wrote a rough draft of both, and then modified both so that they worked together.

3

You need to know your students' own language pretty well in order to predict the level at which they will understand particular words. A tool like English Profile may give us some sort of broad international guidelines, but says little or nothing about particular classes, especially if they are monolingual.

Many of the words in this list are **cognates** with words in Romance languages (although *deceive* is a false friend), so even though *content*, for example, is very low frequency as a verb, it's not hard to guess what it means if you have a similar word in your own language. Similarly, one could expect all students, of whatever language background, at this level to know the word *danger*, so it's not too hard to make an intelligent guess at the meaning of *endanger*.

The highest frequency words in the list are *destroy*, *express* and *remind*. Next, in order of frequency, come *adapt* and *distinguish*. The others do not feature in the top 3,000 lists.

My interest in writing this exercise was less on these particular items than on the generative feature of reflexivity in English.

Task 3 (page 137)

The easiest way these days to find high frequency collocations is to type 'collocations + TARGET WORD' into a search engine. This will take you to a variety of sites which have already sorted the corpus data. For the word *thing*, you will be able to generate a list of examples similar to those below. It will be up to you to select those that you consider most useful to the students who will be using the material you write.

What's that thing over there?

Don't say a thing.

I have a bath first thing in the morning.

You poor thing!

It was the best thing that has ever happened.

I didn't read the whole thing.

The main thing is that we arrive early.

I didn't understand a damn thing.

I want to do the right thing.

Do you think he's the real thing?

The parks are one of the great things about London.

I bought a few things at the shops.

How are things going?

Task 4 (page 143)

Jim Scrivener, who wrote the Teacher's Book to accompany these materials, suggested a lead-in activity. The exercise needed one, and I had originally written one (that was subsequently cut because of a lack of space). Jim's suggestion was a group discussion activity where students talk about their home towns and the sorts of significant features that are not shown on maps.

He also suggested an activity which would allow a teacher to evaluate the students' knowledge of the target activity before doing the printed tasks. This kind of approach (test-teach-test) makes good pedagogical sense, but is usually included in teacher's notes (if at all), because published material tends to follow a **lock-step approach** which is not dependent on the students' response to an activity.

Jim also suggested a management option for stronger classes/students (who can be asked to find at least eight additional items for each category). Finally, he suggested the procedure where students work individually before a whole-class discussion. Such a procedure may be self-evident to many teachers, but not to all.

Task 6 (page 158)

This is one way that I have tackled this set of words. I think the practice works well, but I'm less happy with the presentation, which leaves the teacher with quite a lot of work.

1 Which sentences have a positive (+) meaning and which have a negative (-) meaning?
   1 I was good at mathematics. +
   2 I was bored with my school. −
   3 I was afraid of the older children.
   4 I was fond of my science teacher.
   5 I was interested in science and technology.
   6 I was terrible at arriving on time.
   7 I was keen on sports and swimming.
   8 I was worried about my grades.

2 Think about your experience of school. Change the sentences in exercise 1 so that they are true for you.

3 Work in pairs. Compare your sentences. Were your experiences similar or different?

Extract from: *Straightforward Pre-intermediate* © P. Kerr; 2012, Published by Macmillan Publishers Limited. Used by Permission. All rights reserved

How To Write Critical Thinking Activities

Aims

The aims of this chapter about critical thinking activities are to:

1. understand what a critical thinking approach is and why it is relevant and helpful in English language teaching.
2. give examples of activities that promote a critical thinking approach and examples of activities that may claim to fall into this category, but actually do not.
3. suggest what critical thinking activities may be appropriate to different levels of language ability.
4. provide you with guidelines for writing your own critical thinking activities.

How To Write Critical Thinking Activities

Getting The Right Mindset

Task 1

Before you start this chapter, read this short article and answer these three questions.
1. What kind of book is being reviewed?
2. What is the book about?
3. What does the reviewer like/dislike about the book?

Check your answers on page 181.

In 1714 a rope suspension bridge in Peru snaps and the five people on the bridge fall to their deaths. By chance Brother Juniper, a Franciscan monk, witnesses this tragedy. He is not only troubled by what he has seen but also troubled by why this should have happened. Why at this precise moment? Why these five people? Accordingly, he sets out to find out something about the lives of each person and so to make sense of the tragedy.

This short novel (only 124 pages long) is a beautiful reflection on the subject of destiny. It is not a true story, but some of the characters are based on real people. Written in elegant prose, each chapter describes the life of one of the five people on the bridge: from the aristocratic Marquesa de Montemayor, who longs to be back in her native Spain to the wise Uncle Pio, whose lifelong ambition to make a star of a young actress is in the end frustrated. Our interest is not kept alive by the mystery of their deaths, but the compelling characters that Wilder has drawn so vividly: each eccentric in their own way, and each very human in their virtues and in their faults.

I cannot recommend this book highly enough.

From Heinle ELT. *Life Advanced with DVD*, 1E. © 2014 Heinle/ELT, a part of Cengage Learning, Inc. Reproduced by permission. www.cengage.com/permissions

Now answer these questions.
4. What is the author of the review trying to do?
5. What techniques does he employ to achieve this?
6. How does he succeed or fail?

Check your answers on page 181.

Without knowing it, perhaps, you have just applied critical thinking techniques to understanding a piece of discourse. In other words, you have not only examined the information in the article (questions 1–3), you have also enquired more deeply about the author's motives, knowledge and skills in putting this information across (questions 4–6).

Before we embark on this topic of how to develop a critical mindset, we ought to address an important objection, which is, 'My students aren't really interested in reflecting too deeply. In fact, some of them don't seem to want to express their opinions at all.' This is an objection often raised by people who teach teenagers.

John Hughes makes an excellent point about this in his blog (elteachertrainer. com) on critical thinking. His argument is that learners might a) feel cultural constraints about offering their opinions in open class and b) that they may not have the necessary language to do so. So he stresses the importance of sensitizing students first to the idea of critical thinking and suggests this task. You could include this kind of task as the first task in a series of CT activities.

1   'Young people spend so much time recording their experiences (using digital and social media like smartphones and Facebook) that they forget to enjoy the experiences themselves.'

   Think about your response to this statement.

2   Now choose the response that most honestly matches your initial response to the statement.
   a) *I'm not interested in this topic.*
   b) *I agree. It's true.*
   c) *I disagree. It's false.*
   d) *I'm not sure. I need to think more about it.*
   e) *I agree up to a point but I also disagree.*
   f) *I agree/disagree because ...*
   g) *I agree/disagree for a number of reasons but I'd also like more evidence.*

3   Now read what your response means in critical thinking terms.
   a) *You don't need to be interested but you need to have an opinion.*
   b) *and* c) *OK, you have a strong opinion. But can you give reasons for your opinion?*
   d) *and* e) *This is a safe response. Critical thinkers also need to be active in the discussion and give reasons for their answers.*
   f) *Good. You have a reason for your opinion.*
   g) *Great! You have reasons for your opinion and you want more information.*

These exercises not only sensitize students to what thinking at a more critical level involves, but also introduces some of the language of discussion that might arise in CT activities.

What Is Critical Thinking?

Definitions abound, but two main themes are nearly always present, exemplified in these two definitions. John Dewey, who first coined the phrase in its modern sense in his book of 1910 *How We Think*, defined it as 'reflective thought', that requires a healthy scepticism, an open mind, and the abilities to question assumptions and suspend judgement. The Open University defines CT as 'the process of applying reasoned and disciplined thinking to a subject'. When we put these two ideas together we get: an intellectual approach which helps us to think rigorously, enquiringly and independently about the information put before us. Now, more than ever before, CT is relevant because so much information is available to us through the internet and much of this is either second-hand, unattributed or unverified. It has, accordingly, been called an important '21st century skill'.

So, CT is a **cognitive approach** to learning. As such, it is often associated by educators with 'Bloom's taxonomy', a pyramid of cognitive learning formulated in 1956 which ranks thinking skills in order, beginning with the most straightforward elements of thinking and working up to the highest levels of cognitive thought. It is these higher levels that are often seen as elements of critical thinking. With a couple of recent modifications and interpretations, Bloom's taxonomy basically comes down to this:

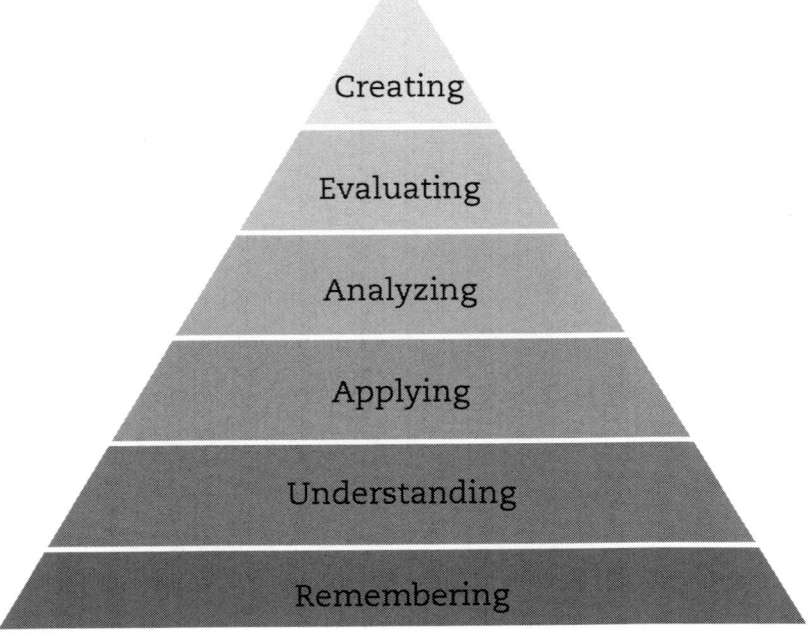

The first step, remembering, is the ability to recall information that has been presented (e.g. *What did the author say about X?*); the next, understanding, is the ability to interpret it (e.g. *What did the author mean by X?*); applying means taking this new knowledge and applying it in another situation (*How could this idea be used in situation Y?*); analysing means understanding how constituent parts relate to each other and the whole (e.g. *Why did the author give example Z?*); evaluating involves making considered judgements about the information (e.g. *Was this a good example in support of the author's argument?*); and the final step, creating, entails the creation of original discourse or ideas from what has been learned and considered (e.g. *Can you think of arguments against the author's position?*).

Now, it would be very handy if we could follow where some others have gone before and simply translate these steps into a series of activities that our language learners practise in linear fashion according to their language level: reserving activities which involve the lower levels of cognitive thought (remembering, understanding and applying) for lower levels of language ability, and asking higher level language learners to apply the higher level skills (the critical and creative thinking skills of analysing, evaluating and creating). But I don't think Bloom ever intended these steps to be used in a strictly linear fashion. Rather, what we need to do, if we are to help students become more critical thinkers, is to foster in them from an early stage a *critical disposition* in both receptive and productive skills. What is a critical disposition? Here are a few examples of what a person disposed to think critically does:

- Questions assumptions (their own included) – this is particularly important when learning a new language because of the cultural assumptions we all make.
- Thinks through the consequences of a line of reasoning.
- Looks for evidence and examines it carefully.
- Considers alternative ideas.
- Is aware of how language choice can influence ideas.
- Tries out and tests new ideas.
- Is sensitive to what is balanced, fair and reasonable.

This could all be summed up by asking the following questions when reading or listening to a given piece of discourse (or, for that matter composing arguments oneself for oral or written delivery):

What's really going on here? What is the speaker or writer trying to do? Are they successful in this and if so, how did they achieve success?

Note!

'Critical' does not mean subversive; the idea is not to promote a cynical or irreverent way of thinking, but a more curious, enquiring and aware state of mind.

Why Is Critical Thinking Relevant To Language Learners?

Learners will need to use their English in one of three contexts: academic life, working life or social life (travel, culture, socializing). In all of these contexts (but especially the first two) it will help if they approach information and ideas in a thoughtful way. Whereas in the UK we tend towards a **guided discovery** approach and to nurturing independent thinking in education, this is not true of all cultures: some still favour a more **rote learning** approach. I am not saying that one approach is right and the other wrong. Indeed, I think there is a place for both, in language learning as well as other areas of learning. CT skills are demanded particularly in university education in the UK and the US and so should form a part of any English language access to university course. Also, by encouraging a more cognitive approach, CT training should help to stimulate discussion and ideas in the classroom. At the same time, it will encourage learners to think more critically and curiously about the language itself, casting aside assumptions and thinking more enquiringly about how it works and how it is used to serve different purposes. This applies to the learning of English grammar especially, where use of a given structure can often be a question of subjective choice rather than objectively right or wrong.

Critical thinking in fact goes to the root of all learning, which is to question. When we question and evaluate information, we trigger deeper processing in the brain, which in turn helps us to commit ideas and language to our longer-term memory. By applying critical filters to the information we gather, we also cultivate reasonableness in our judgement and protect ourselves against developing unfair biases. (I hardly need mention all the information out there on the internet that is being sucked up uncritically and can, in the worst cases, give rise to extreme views.)

Having read all this, you are probably thinking that CT applies to higher levels (B1+ and above) and you would be right insofar as anyone needs to be able to understand the information in front of them before they can begin to think critically about it. But that is not to say that training in CT habits should not begin at an early stage (A2 or B1). In business English classes at these levels, learners are taught basic business communication skills, even if they do not yet have the language at their disposal to exploit them fully. They just need more support.

You may also imagine that CT applies mainly to the receptive skills – reading and listening – and again you would be largely right. But it can also be applied to evaluate the effectiveness of the learner's own writing or speaking against a certain set of criteria.

Types Of Critical Thinking Activity

Task 2

Look at this list of typical CT activities (1–10). Then say which activity each of the CT rubrics (a–h) is practising.

CT aims

1. Identifying the writer's/speaker's aims and whether they were achieved
2. Identifying the main argument and sub-arguments
3. Evaluating whether the evidence provided supports these arguments
4. Understanding the assumptions behind an argument
5. Separating fact from opinion*
6. Inferring meaning
7. Analysing how the organisation of a text affects its impact
8. Recognizing different language techniques **
9. Comparing ideas in a piece of discourse
10. Identifying what is missing or is superfluous

CT activities

a) Reading between the lines. Listen again and say which of these statements (A–C) the author would probably agree with.
b) Emotive adjectives. Look at paragraph 2 and find three adjectives that have an emotive rather than an objective quality.
c) Summarizing. Find a sentence in paragraph 3 that best sums up what the writer is saying.
d) Relevance. Listen again to the introduction. What piece of information does the speaker give which is not relevant to the discussion?
e) Purpose. Who are you writing the letter for? What do you hope to achieve with this letter? Do you think it will be successful?
f) Examples. The writer describes good habits and bad habits. Are these examples from the text (A–D) examples of good or bad habits?
g) Sequencing. At what point in the narrative does the speaker begin the story – the beginning, middle or end? Why is this do you think?
h) Close reading. Read the article again and say if these statements (1–6) are True (supported by fact), False (not supported by fact) or Ambiguous (only partly supported)

Check your answers on page 181.

Now say which level (A2 to C1) you think each of these activities could be usefully used at (the wording in the rubric could be adapted slightly of course). Read the commentary on page 181.

* A strong note of caution needs to be sounded with exercises that ask students to separate fact from opinion. We teachers like such exercises because they draw attention to language that introduces opinion – *personally, it may be that, it seems inevitable, a sensible idea*, etc. but often we are presenting learners with a false choice. For example, in a text about holidays, the assertion *Undoubtedly, activity holidays are healthier* would be difficult to categorise in this way, since, while it appears to be a strongly voiced opinion (*undoubtedly*), it is really a reasoned judgement – a certain degree of activity is generally better for the body than lying around on a beach doing nothing – that borders on fact. So it is often better to ask learners to find supporting evidence for views or arguments expressed rather than asking them if statements represent facts or the author's opinion per se.

** There are many activities that focus on use of language, e.g.
- How a writer uses language (modal verbs, adverbs of probability etc.) to hedge their opinions
- Words with a positive or negative connotation (e.g. *thin* or *slim*)
- Formal vs informal language
- Use of emphatic structures
- Organisation of a text (the order in which ideas are presented)

Writing Your Own Critical Thinking Activities (Receptive Skills)

The list of CT activities in Task 2 (page 171) is not exhaustive, but you should by now be getting a much clearer idea of what CT activities are. If you'd like to look at further examples of CT activities, take a look at some of the following:

OUP's *Oxford EAP* series

National Geographic Learning's *Pathways* series

National Geographic Learning's *Life* series

In all these sources you will see two things: the application of CT to longer pieces of discourse, where ideas are developed and **synthesized**; and a clear distinction between basic comprehension activities and CT activities. We're going to look at some criteria for writing CT activities for both receptive and productive skills, but it's important to keep these two overarching principles in mind.

Remember also that when writing CT activities for lower levels (A2 and B1) the learner will need more support. So rather than asking, *What examples does the author give to support this view?* it would be better to list three examples (A, B, C) and ask *Which of these examples supports the writer's view?* Similarly, try to frame the task in language they will understand: rather than calling a task 'Analysing assumptions', at lower levels say 'Identifying the author's beliefs' and give some paraphrases of what the author probably believes for the students to choose from.

You may occasionally choose a text or listening passage with a clear CT focus already in mind. For example, you come across an article that presents the case for climate change denial in a way that is not very convincing – it's subjective, **polemical** and not backed up by many facts. But more often than not you will have chosen your text for another reason (to stimulate discussion or to practise a particular structure or function). In these cases, you will need to choose the CT activity that is most appropriate to the text. (If none seems to be, because it is a very straightforward text, or a type of text such as a narrative that is not presenting facts or a particular argument, then follow your instinct and do not apply CT to it.) Here are some guidelines for how to do this:

Read or listen to the text and remember to ask yourself these key questions:

1 What's really going on here? What is the speaker or writer trying to do?
2 How effective / successful are they at doing this? Is all the content accurate, relevant and adapted to the purpose?
3 What part does organization and language choice play, if any, in conveying the message?

How To Write Critical Thinking Activities

If we just go back and examine the text in Task 1 on page 166, the answers will be something like this:

The writer is writing a review of a book that he has really liked and wants you to read. As well as saying that explicitly at the end, he does two other things:

1. praises the book throughout ('beautiful reflection', 'elegant prose', 'compelling characters')
2. immediately draws you into the novel by setting the scene and leaving you in suspense.

So either of these following two CT activities would be appropriate:

1. Language choice – adjectives and adverbs. Find and underline adjectives that the writer uses to describe this book. What is the author's aim in using these adjectives?
2. Identifying different elements. The elements that can be included in a book review are:
   - the reviewer's opinion
   - the author's background
   - a general background to the story or subject
   - a brief outline of the plot
   - a description of the writing style.

Which elements does the writer include and in what order? Do you think this is effective? Why/Why not?

Now apply these guidelines in Task 3 and Task 4 in the following section.

Writing A Critical Thinking Activity At B2 Level (Listening)

Task 3

1. Watch an extract (from 08.35–12.45) from the TED talk, *Bring on the learning revolution!* by Sir Ken Robinson about his vision for a learning revolution and say what the main idea is.

2. Imagine that you are going to use this video as part of a lesson on education with a class at B2 level. Ask yourself the key questions you looked at in the previous section (the third one about organization has been removed because this is only an extract):
    - What's really going on here? What is the speaker trying to do?
    - How effective is he at doing this? Is all the content relevant, accurate and adapted to his message?

3. Write a CT activity that lends itself to analysing this extract.

4. Look at the list of CT aims you saw in Task 2. Did the activity you wrote fall into one of these categories or something different?
    - Identifying the writer's/speaker's aims and whether they were achieved
    - Identifying the main argument and sub-arguments
    - Evaluating whether the evidence provided supports these arguments
    - Understanding the assumptions behind an argument
    - Separating fact from opinion
    - Inferring meaning
    - Analysing how the organisation of a text affects its impact
    - Recognizing different language techniques
    - Comparing ideas in a piece of discourse
    - Identifying what is missing or is superfluous

5. Now you've looked at the list again, which of the other CT activities are suited to this extract, do you think?

Read the commentary on page 182.

How To Write Critical Thinking Activities

Writing A Critical Thinking Activity At Lower Levels (Reading)

Task 4

1. Read this article about women Bolivian wrestlers from *Life Pre-intermediate* (B1). Then devise a suitable CT activity for it.

Bolivian Wrestlers

In El Alto in Bolivia, an audience is sitting around a huge wrestling ring. The spectators are getting impatient and so they start to scream: 'Bring them on! Bring them on!' Suddenly, an announcer speaks into the microphone: 'Ladies and Gentlemen. It's time for Yolanda and Claudina!' The crowd shouts and applauds with excitement.

Two women enter. Yolanda and Claudina walk through the crowd like pop stars. They smile and greet their fans until suddenly the music stops. Both women jump into the wrestling ring and within seconds, Claudina hits Yolanda. Yolanda grabs Claudina. Claudina tries to escape, but Yolanda doesn't let her go. She spins Claudina round and throws her down on the floor. The audience goes crazy!

As Claudina lies on the floor, Yolanda is smiling and waving to the crowd. She doesn't see Claudina get up behind her. Then Claudina pushes Yolanda onto the ropes. The crowd shouts at her. Claudina is the baddie in this competition so when Yolanda – the goodie – gets up and throws Claudina out of the ring, the crowd cheers with happiness. One minute Yolanda is winning. The next minute, Claudina is winning.

Wrestling in Bolivia is incredibly popular and after a hard day's work many people love watching this mixture of sport, drama and entertainment. Usually, the wrestling matches are between men wearing masks and special costumes. But in El Alto, where it's especially popular, you can also see women wrestling.

Yolanda is one of the top women wrestlers. Her father was also a wrestler so it's a family tradition. During the day she makes clothes. She also has two daughters who both look like her. Would they like to become wrestlers one day? Yolanda doesn't think so. 'My daughters ask me why I do this. It's dangerous and they complain that wrestling doesn't bring any money into the house.' But Yolanda loves wrestling because of her fans, and she has lots of them!

One fan called Esperanza Cancina pays $1.50 (a large part of her salary) to sit near the ring. She explains why she likes watching the wrestling: 'It's a distraction. The women wrestlers fight here and we laugh and forget our problems for three or four hours. At home, we're sad.'

From Heinle ELT. *Life Pre-intermediate with DVD*, 1E. © 2013 Heinle/ELT, a part of Cengage Learning, Inc. Reproduced by permission. www.cengage.com/permissions

2. Now compare your activity with the one that is in the book. See page 182.

3. What support has been given to the learner in this activity? What support did you give in your activity? If you didn't give much, think of ways you could rectify this.

What Is NOT A Critical Thinking Activity

It's already been pointed out that critical thinking is not just a qu...
answering a series of comprehension questions. In fact, a better wa...
it is that a critical thinker *asks* questions rather than answers questio...
are put to them – questions such as those we have seen already: *Why is...
author arguing this? Am I approaching this with an open mind? Where's the evide...*
etc. If you look back at Task 1 on page 166, you will see that the first three questions about the review were straightforward comprehension questions. As mentioned when discussing Bloom's taxonomy, CT falls into the two categories of higher order thinking skills called 'Analysing' and 'Evaluating', rather than the 'lower' order skills of Remembering, Understanding and Applying.

To help your students understand the information in a piece of discourse, you might:

- ask comprehension questions to identify the ideas presented.
- ask questions about the meaning of certain items of vocabulary.
- ask them to discuss if they agree with the ideas presented.
- get them to do a role-play based on this topic.

To get them to think critically about it you will:

- ask why the author presents these ideas.
- ask if the author supports their ideas with accurate, relevant and fair evidence.
- ask why the author chose certain items of vocabulary.
- ask them what an alternative, reasonable position could be.

This is not to say that you should not include both comprehension and CT activities when treating a particular piece of spoken or written discourse. Indeed, it would be perfectly legitimate, and even desirable (with the goal of deeper processing), to deploy all the steps in the taxonomy. E.g.

1 Before reading the text about drones tell your partner what drones are used for, and what they could be used for. Then read the text. (creating)
2 Which uses of drones that you discussed in question 1 are mentioned in the text? (remembering)
3 Now say if these statements are true or false according to the author. (understanding)
4 Which of the uses of drones would you find useful in your daily life? (applying)
5 What do you think was the author's purpose in writing this article? Choose the reason (A–D). (analysing)
6 Did the author convince you that drones were a positive technology? How did he do this? (evaluating)

Comprehension And Critical ...ing Activities

... say which you think came from a general ... from a CT activity.

... paragraph 2 which summarizes the writer's main ...

2 Often a final paragraph gives a conclusion. Is that the function of the final paragraph in this text? Or does it have another function?

3 The author argues that money is a poor motivator. Do you agree with her? Tell your partner.

4 Look at these statements and say if they are true (T) or false (F) according to the text.

5 The author gives a detailed description of how a Camera Obscura works. Does he do this a) to explain how the results are achieved? b) so you can make one yourself? or c) to compare it with a modern camera?

6 Read the article and write down the events before, during and after the fire in the correct order.

7 Look at these phrases. Find them in the article and discuss what each one means with your partner.

8 The article lists both advantages and disadvantages of foreign travel. Find and underline adjectives that give a positive view of it and adjectives that are more negative.

Check your answers on page 183.

Identifying General Comprehension And Critical Thinking Activities

Writing Your Own Critical Thinking Activities (Productive Skills)

As mentioned earlier, for learners to apply critical thinking to their own output, they have to set their speaking or writing against certain criteria and see if it passes the test of reasoned and disciplined thinking. I think we have all probably done this with our students, though we haven't called it critical thinking.

Let's take the example of a discursive (or opinion) essay at B1+ level.

> 'Good social skills are more important for success in working life than formal qualifications and experience.' Discuss.

Criteria or questions to be tested.

1. What do I really think about this?
2. What is going to be my main argument?
3. What evidence can I supply to support this argument?
4. Are my examples really true and relevant?
5. What arguments could there be against my main argument? How can I successfully refute these?
6. Is the finished essay convincing and objective enough?

Or, using the example of a three-minute speech at B1 level describing the education system in your country and if it works well, the criteria or questions to be tested might be:

1. What do my audience know about this thing already?
2. How can I make this description as clear as possible? With only words or with visuals (diagrams, pictures, etc.)?
3. How can I check that they have understood my explanation?

The criteria will of course vary according to the task involved and there is no need to concentrate on all the criteria at once (e.g. in one lesson, you could concentrate only on giving relevant examples) but the main criteria will always be the same:

- What message or idea am I trying to convey?
- What is the clearest, most logical, truthful, thorough, fair and effective way to do this?

Break these terms down for the learner and discuss their meanings:

Clarity = clear sentence structure, clear pronunciation

Logical = organizing ideas in a clear sequence

Truthful = checking facts and signalling to your audience what are subjective comments

Thorough = covering all aspects of the issue

Fair = taking into account other views and addressing possible counter arguments

Effective = adding 'colour' – examples, illustrations, rhetorical questions, powerful vocabulary, etc.

Writing A Critical Thinking Activity For A Student Talk

Task 6

1 You would like each of your students in a B1+ class to give a 2–3-minute talk describing what they think is their nationality's greatest characteristic and why they admire this. Write a set of critical thinking criteria for them to follow.

2 Could these criteria also be used to evaluate the success of each talk? What other criteria might be appropriate in such an evaluation?

Read the commentary on page 183.

Task Commentaries

Task 1 (page 166)

Standard comprehension question answers

1. A historical novel
2. Following the death of five people on a rope bridge in Peru, a monk sets out to research the lives of the victims to discover if there was a reason for their deaths.
3. The reviewer likes the vividly drawn characters and the elegant prose.

CT question answers

1. The author is trying to persuade you to read the book.
2. He praises the book throughout (*beautiful reflection, elegant prose, compelling characters*) and draws you into the novel by setting the scene and leaving you in suspense.
3. He succeeds in arousing your interest but he spoils some of the suspense by saying '*Our interest is kept alive not by the mystery of their deaths, …*' implying that their deaths remain a mystery.

Task 2 (page 171)

a 6, b 8, c 2, d 10, e 1*, f 3, g 7, h 5

* this is the only productive CT activity listed here, although other CT aims could be applied to students' production, written or spoken, e.g. Analysing how organisation affects the impact of an opinion essay or Understanding the assumptions behind an argument in a student's presentation.

The question of what can be used at lower levels is often a question of how much support you give the student. If you are asking them to identify the author's opinion, for example, you could give them a choice of three opinions, one of which is correct. For reading between the lines you could ask *Which of these statements would the author agree with and why?* and list several ideas. Here is a rough guide, however, to the level for each CT aim:

1. Identifying the writer's/speaker's aims and whether they were achieved A2
2. Identifying the main argument and sub-arguments A2
3. Evaluating whether the evidence provided supports these arguments B1
4. Understanding the assumptions behind an argument B2
5. Separating fact from opinion B1
6. Inferring meaning B1
7. Analysing how the organisation of a text affects its impact B2
8. Recognizing different language techniques B2
9. Comparing ideas in a piece of discourse A2
10. Identifying what is missing or is superfluous B1

How To Write Critical Thinking Activities

Task 3 (page 175)

1 The main idea is that our society is too fixed on the idea of a linear progression in education where the ultimate aim is to go to college.
2 Information and entertainment! He is trying to get his point across using humour; to what extent he cares more about the former or more about making his audience his laugh is an interesting point.

Clearly he is good at making people laugh; the question is: does this get in the way of the serious point he is making?

3 This last question is perhaps the most relevant CT angle here: What methods does the speaker use to get his point across? You could give a list, e.g. stress, repetition, humour, real life examples, visuals.
5 The following Items are all possible:
   - Identifying the writer's/speaker's aims and whether they were achieved
   - Evaluating whether the evidence provided supports these arguments
   - Recognizing different language techniques
   - Identifying what is missing or is superfluous

Identifying what is missing or is superfluous is related to Recognizing different language techniques in that learners are looking at the question of whether the examples he gives are relevant or just to get a laugh.

Task 4 (page 176)

2
Critical thinking: reading between the lines
An article doesn't always tell us everything about how the people feel, but we can often guess. Match these people from the article (1–3) with the sentences (a–c).

1 Yolanda
2 One of Yolanda's daughters
3 Esperanza
   a I don't like the days when the wrestling is happening.
   b I get a wonderful feeling every time I go out there.
   c Life is very hard for people like me.

3 The learner is supported by the introductory sentence in the rubric, which is helpful and sensitizes the learner to the type of CT they are going to do. The structure of the activity allows students at this lower level to do the easiest two matches and by default work out the answer to the third. The activity heading (reading between the lines) also guides the learner to the right approach to the task.

Task 5 (page 178)

1. CT
2. CT
3. General comprehension
4. General comprehension*
5. CT
6. General comprehension
7. General comprehension
8. CT

* True/false activities can also be CT tasks if they involve a more detailed look at the evidence supporting the statement, e.g. Say if the sentences are True, False or not enough information is provided to be certain.

Task 6 (page 180)

Suggested answer

1. CT criteria:
   - Is it clear *who* thinks this is our greatest characteristic?
   - Have I given examples of this greatest characteristic?
   - Are these good examples?
   - Will the audience remember my talk? For example, did I start and end powerfully?
   - Is my speech clear and effective? (Use of stress, pausing, checking understanding etc.)?

2. The criteria in 1 could be used to evaluate the success of the talk. Other criteria could be based on language use – fluency, grammatical accuracy, appropriate vocabulary, etc.

How To Write Audio And Video Scripts

Aims And Introductory Task

The basic aims of this chapter about writing audio and video scripts are to:

1. provide an overview of the theoretical and practical issues involved in writing audio and video scripts for ELT materials.
2. provide you with a framework which can guide you in the writing of scripts for audio and video components in ELT materials.
3. provide practical suggestions on writing scripts for audio and video and to provide a wide range of models.
4. encourage you to think critically about script writing for audio and video.

Note
This chapter focuses primarily on materials for adult and secondary school learners.

Task 1

Before you start reading this chapter, make notes about your answers to this introductory task. Keep the notes somewhere safe so you can refer back to them later.

1. To write audio and video scripts, materials writers need a number of skills and abilities. Look at the following list and rank these abilities in order of importance from 1 to 6 (1 = most important, 6 = least important):
   - ability to grade the language to the correct level
   - ability to target language to include in an audio script
   - ability to write scripts that sound authentic
   - ability to listen to real speech and identify features of discourse
   - ability to create credible dramatic narratives and characters
   - ability to format audio and video scripts using scriptwriting conventions

2. Can you think of any other skills or abilities a writer of audio and video might need to develop for ELT materials writing?

3. Which of the above abilities do you feel you already possess to some extent? Which will you need to work on and develop while you read?

A Short History Of Writing Scripts For ELT Materials

Writing scripts for language learning materials is one part of what the modern ELT writer is required to do. Scripts often take the form of monologues or dialogues which are then recorded and which make up part of a coursebook package or appear in the form of online self-study materials. Increasingly, ELT writers are also writing scripts for video materials. Whether it's for audio or video, for a CD or an MP3 file, for a DVD or a video on *YouTube*, scripts are often something we tend to associate with the modern world of ELT. However, writing scripts (and especially dialogues) is not just a feature of modern ELT materials. In fact, they appear in some of the very earliest materials written for language learners. This section provides a brief overview of how scripts have evolved in materials writing over the last five centuries and illustrates the reasons why it's such an important – and influential – aspect of materials writing.

Early scripts in language learning materials

In *A History of English Language Teaching*, Howatt and Widdowson provide examples of language learning materials taken from early handbooks written for learners of English. Many of the earliest extracts take the form of scripted dialogues on the page; for example, the following dialogue is set at a dining table and appeared in a handbook published in 1554 called *A Very Profitable Book*. Written specifically for Spanish learners of English, the English version and the Spanish translation would have originally been placed side-by-side on the page:

Hermes *John, I pray God send ye a good day.*
John *And I, Hermes, wish unto you a prosperous day.*
Hermes *How do you?*
John *Ask you how I do? I fare well, thanks be to God, and will be glad to do you pleasure. I say, Hermes, how go matters forward?*
Hermes *Verily I fare well.*

Quoted in Howatt, A.P.R & Widdowson, H.G. (2004)
A History of English Language Teaching Oxford, p15

Although the English is old, the actual context and rationale behind this text feels quite contemporary; after all, it provides students with the language for meeting people for the first time and making small talk so if updated it wouldn't feel out of place in any modern business English coursebook. Another book from the same century contains nothing but scripted dialogues. Published in 1586 for French-speaking refugees entering England, *Familiar Dialogues* is a collection of dialogues which 'have a domestic setting with a strong emphasis on shopping…The book ends with some useful travel phrases.' (pp22–3)

What's interesting about many of these early examples of scripted ELT materials is how they focus on the learners' needs and provide functional and useful phrases in a context, much in the same way that the modern ELT writers try to do today. The only difference is that they were not recorded but probably read aloud by the teacher and the students had to memorise the dialogues by heart.

Later textbooks also include scripted dialogues which weren't necessarily functional but were used in a question-and-answer approach in order to explain points of grammar or other areas of language. This example of such a dialogue is from a Russian textbook published in 1795 (p71):

Teacher When is g pronounced?
Pupil G is pronounced soft when it precedes e, i, and y, for example, gender, ginger, gipsy.
Teacher Are there exceptions?
Pupil The letter g is pronounced hard before e and i in the following words: gelderland, gibbons, gilman …

Howatt and Widdowson also report on another book published only two years later in 1797 designed to aid pronunciation by listing sets of words (including nonsense syllables) for the student to practise such as *lip, nip, pip, rip, sip*. This kind of listing of words for students to pronounce is not greatly different from what modern ELT writers do when they script simple 'listen and repeat' type pronunciation exercises for low-level materials.

The 19th century is generally associated with the period of the **Grammar Translation Method** and the growth in languages as a formal school subject. Typically, we think of rows of pupils reading and translating long written texts on the page and therefore little room for students learning to speak with the use of scripted conversations. Whilst there are in fact examples of materials from the 1800s which include phrases and question-and-answer dialogues in a semi-scripted format, the end of the 19th century and the rise of the **Direct Method** and the **Natural Method** is more significant in terms of script writing.

Both methods placed the emphasis on asking the student genuine questions that require a real answer; for example, *What's the time?* The coursebook writer and school owner Maximilian Berlitz is probably the most famous name associated with these movements. While he didn't invent the Direct Method, he introduced it to many language learners via his many schools and textbooks. His famous *First Book* (first published in 1906 with many new editions printed in later years) contains a variety of scripts which a teacher and student would have read aloud in class. Many of these scripts are formulaic and artificial language drill exercises which introduce a grammar item, like this one in the ninth lesson of the book:

Me, him, her, us, them
I give you a book. What do I do?
Give me a pencil. What do you do?
I give a box to Mr White. What do I give (to) Mr White? You give him a box.

M.D. Berlitz *First Book* (333rd Edition 1924), p27

In the second half of the book, there is a section of reading passages which often take the form of mini-conversations. Unlike the language drills earlier in the book, these scripted conversations have a context. Here is the opening extract aimed at introducing students to the language of travel:

The arrival
A. – *We shall soon be at the station. We had better roll up our rugs and get our valises down.*
B. – *At what hotel shall we stop?*
A. – *We can stop at Charing Cross, because it is so centrally located, not expensive, and it will be very convenient when we leave for Paris, as it is connected with the station.*
B. – *The train is stopping. What an immense station! Shall I call the porter?*
A. – *If you please.*
B. – *Here, porter! Take these two bags to a cab. You can carry the rugs also.*
Porter – *Here is the cab, Sir. Have you anything besides your hand-luggage?*

M.D. Berlitz *First Book* (333rd Edition 1924), p67

By writing materials like this, Berlitz didn't need to employ highly trained teachers with an understanding of the student's first language (as had been the case with Grammar Translation) but, instead, Berlitz teachers simply needed to follow a script. This conversational approach or Direct Method proved especially popular with the growing number of students who needed English (or other languages) for business and travel purposes in the early part of the 20th century.

The introduction of recording technology in the classroom

About 20 years before Berlitz's first publication, Thomas Edison had invented the phonograph which could record human speech. Years later, as recording technology evolved, it eventually became a central feature of the language classroom but by the 50s and 60s the Direct Method had 'metamorphosed into **audiolingualism**.' (Thornbury, S. (2006) *An A–Z of ELT* Macmillan Education, p66). Essentially, the Audiolingual Method stressed the value of having students listen to and repeat sentences in a continuous drill pattern.

The natural manifestation of audiolingualism was the language laboratory. By the 1970s classes of students might be found in rooms of cubicles, each with a set of headphones. The teacher's role was to play a variety of recordings and – in theory – monitor each student's individual progress. Many language laboratory sessions began with the student listening to a scripted passage and completing comprehension tasks. As the class progressed however, a student would be expected to listen and respond.

In the passage below, the student has listened to model versions of questions and sentences based on a series of small pictures of grocery items bought while shopping. Now it his/her chance to play an active role in the scripted dialogue. Note that the student would have heard the exercise number and rubric given at the beginning – a mechanical but nonetheless important aspect of this type of ELT script writing:

Exercise 3. Now play the part of a customer. Look at picture 1. Listen.
Voice   Good morning. Can I help you?
Student   I'd like five oranges. How much is that?
Look at picture 2.
Voice   Good morning. Can I help you?
Student   I'd like half a dozen eggs. How much is that?
Look at picture 3.
Voice   Good morning. Can I help you?
Student   I'd like two loaves of bread. How much is that?

Dakin, J. (1973) *The language laboratory and language learning* Longman, p124

Despite criticism for its lack of authenticity and drilling, we can still see the influence of this kind of audiolingual scripting on modern language learning materials, especially those sold for self-study such as 'listen-and-learn-a-language-in-the-car' type audio recordings or teach-yourself computer-based programmes. In other words, it is a type of script writing that many modern ELT writers still write from time to time.

Writing scripts for communicative language teaching (CLT) materials

Towards the late 70s, there was a growing demand for materials to include audio recordings which, if they weren't entirely authentic, at least reflected the need for learners to achieve communicative competence. As we have already seen, writing scripts with model dialogues was nothing new but there was a renewed emphasis in communicative language teaching on authenticity and **functional/situational** type language. However, what made materials around this time distinct from the past was that coursebooks started to focus on skills development; in other words, the contents page of a book might include a column on developing the skills of reading, writing, speaking and – most relevantly – listening. So the tape cassettes which were sold with these books not only included dialogues and mini-conversations but also longer spoken texts which were scripted to develop listening sub-skills in some way. Many of these listening scripts were written in the style of news broadcasts or journalistic interviews but graded to the target level. Such types of listening script still appear in coursebooks to this day, like this extract from a book preparing students for the Cambridge ESOL First (FCE):

Listening 13.1
Newsreader *Have you heard about a new report on education which says these are the worst results in over 20 years and one ex-headmaster said the situation is appalling? That's the verdict on the spelling ability of school children in Great Britain after the results of last year's national tests were released. The report reveals that pupils who were tested, aged 11 and 14, made more spelling errors than they did four years ago ...*

Extract from Hughes, J & Naunton, J. Spotlight on FCE (2009)
National Geographic Learning

The emergence of video

In the 1980s, a newer technology was starting to have an impact on ELT publishing and materials writing. The growing accessibility of VHS video meant that language schools might have at least one video player and TV in their school. The 'video lesson' proved a popular draw for students and some language schools even used it as a unique selling feature of their courses. In response, publishers brought out whole courses based around learning from a video, or produced video as an add-on to a coursebook. The author Ben Goldstein in his article *A History of ELT Video* comments on one such early attempt to teach English via video:

'*Follow Me*, the BBC video crash course from the late 70s, is a revealing way to see how video was used in the beginning. The series commonly showed functional language contexts with heavily scripted and rather unnatural dialogue. The purpose of the video was language focus. Learners would watch the sketches and use them as a model for their own output. In fact, the video was exploited no differently to audio.'

That the exploitation of ELT video is often no different to audio is a criticism often levelled at ELT materials and it's an issue to which we'll return again later in this chapter. In fairness to a series like *Follow Me*, while many of its episodes (some of which you can still watch on *YouTube* today) did cover predictable functional language, its scripts did attempt to add drama and intrigue, and many of the locations and settings were ambitious.

By the 90s, other ELT video courses such as the *Grapevine* (OUP) videos had become very popular but video had a long way to go before it became commonplace in every classroom and most ELT script writing remained confined to writing for audio, not video. In an interview with the co-author of the successful *Grapevine* videos and 12 other video courses, Vicki Hollett asks Peter Viney to look back at his period of video and script writing and he remarks that, 'For years I'd tell [teachers] that in the future teachers would use video in every single lesson and I was completely wrong. It didn't happen.' You can watch an extract from Vicki Hollett's video interview for Simple English Videos on *YouTube* by searching for 'Interview with Peter Viney'.

In the period that Viney is describing, video tapes were relatively expensive and the cost of the equipment to play it on was a significant amount for the average language school, which may explain why video remained the 'fun' lesson and not a common feature of any lesson. However, the arrival of YouTube in 2005 and the increase of digital projectors or IWBs in classroom suddenly made it more possible that teachers might use video in every lesson.

Reflecting the growth in video usage in the classroom, more and more ELT writers are now writing video scripts; some of these still have a functional language focus as in the past but increasingly ELT video script writing is more varied. For example, this script is an extract from a video about a real school which trains butlers. It contains documentary footage of the trainee butlers talking and narration that has been scripted for the level of the learners who will watch the video. The job of the script writer here is to script the narration and to mix it in with the authentic language of the people in the video. The script also contains reference to what we can see on screen.

Narrator Long ago, England was a land of country houses, palaces, gardens and afternoon tea. Every real gentleman had servants, especially a butler. Just 70 years ago, there were tens of thousands of butlers in England. Now there are only a few. So where does one find a good butler nowadays? The Ivor Spencer International School for Butler Administration, of course.
Butler 1 Good evening, sir. My name's Michael. I'm your butler.
Butler 2 My name is José.
Butler 3 I'm your butler.
Butler 4 Can I bring you some refreshments, sir?
Butler 3 I'm your butler.
Butler 5 Good evening, sir.
Narrator It's the first day of class and the students are learning how to introduce themselves to their 'gentlemen' or 'lady'. A proper butler must also learn how to carry himself correctly.

Extract from Butler School, National Geographic Learning

The present day

So in this short history, we've seen the origins of script writing for ELT materials and how it has evolved (or not at times). Nowadays, Student's Books, Workbooks and online materials still require audio scripts. In addition, the dramatic rise in video over the last decade and the fact that it is relatively cheap to produce means that ELT courses will want more and more video scripts. From drills to dialogues, dramas to documentaries, the aim of this chapter is to help you write them.

Task 2

Choose a mainstream coursebook or online course that you are currently using or are familiar with. Consider the following questions about the audio and/or video scripts of the course in relation to the brief history you have just read:

1 Can you see any similarities between the approach to some of the scripts in the early course materials and the scripts in the course you are looking at? For example, how much does it use dialogues? Listen-and-repeat drills? Videos with drama or documentary?

2 How much difference is there between the ELT scripts in the modern course and those from the past?

3 What do you think the earlier attempts of materials writers and their scripts can tell us about how we should approach scripts for language teaching nowadays?

How To Write Audio Scripts

Types of audio scripts

> **Task 3**
>
> 1 Make a list of all the different types of things you have listened to in the last few days; e.g. the news, a quiz show.
>
> 2 Compare your list with the types of listening scripts in published materials; e.g. in a coursebook. How similar or different are the types of listening in real life and in the book?

The types of audio script you might be required to write either for your own lessons or for publishers can be quite varied. Here's a list of listening text types that can appear on the Cambridge English Language Assessment First (FCE) exam Listening paper 3. It's a good reflection of the types of listening texts that often appear in many ELT materials.

Monologues: answerphone messages, radio documentaries and features, news, public announcements, stories and anecdotes, talks

Interacting speakers: conversations, interviews, discussions, radio plays

Cambridge English First Handbook For Teachers 2015

The purpose of the audio

Before you start writing your own audio script, you obviously need to understand how it will be used in the teaching material; in other words, what is the language aim?

Most commonly, ELT audio scripts are written for the following reasons:

1 To develop listening skills (e.g. listening for gist, listening for detail)

2 To practise an aspect of pronunciation (e.g. listening for the stressed syllable of a word)

3 To introduce an item of grammar and/or of vocabulary (e.g. the target language is contextualised in the listening and given higher frequency than you might hear in an authentic script)

4 To introduce useful expressions for a real situation (e.g. asking for directions in the street)

Task 4

Read four audio scripts taken from a pre-intermediate level general English coursebook. For each script, decide what the primary purpose of the script is. For example, do you think it is used to develop listening skills in general or is it to introduce a language item or practise an aspect of pronunciation? Also try to imagine what type of rubric and exercise would accompany the script in the main part of the book; for example, would the student be asked to listen and fill gaps, answer comprehension questions, or listen and repeat the words or sentences?

Audio script 1

Nick Veasey takes photographs of ordinary people, places and objects but no one could describe the final photographs as ordinary. In fact, they are very creative. Nick uses X-ray photography and, as a result, you see inside the object. The final images are often beautiful, strange or surprising. Working with X-rays can be dangerous because of the radiation. So safety always comes first for Nick. His well-equipped studio is a large black building. It has thick concrete walls to stop the radiation. Inside he has different X-ray machines for different sizes and types of images. But not everything he photographs will fit in the studio so sometimes he has to travel to them. For example, he has photographed an aeroplane, a bus and an office building with people working inside. These kinds of projects take many days and many different X-rays. Then, he takes the best image back to his studio and spends a lot of his working day improving the image on his computer until it is ready for an exhibition. You can see his photos in galleries all over the world and many companies also use his images in their advertisements.

Audio script 2

J = Javier, T = Ticket office clerk

J   A return ticket to the airport, please.
T   OK. The next train goes in five minutes.
J   Right. That one, please.
T   First or second class?
J   Second.
T   OK. That's £14.50.
J   Wow! Can I pay by cheque?
T   Sorry. Cash or credit card.
J   Oh no ... Oh, one moment. Maybe I have enough left.
T   OK. Here you are.
J   Which platform is it?
T   Err, platform six.

Audio script 3
1. Single or return?
2. Window or aisle?
3. Credit card or cash?
4. Bus or train?
5. North or south?
6. First or second?

Audio script 4

I = Interviewer, E = Engineer

I   How long have you worked for your company?
E   For 25 years. Since I left college.
I   So, when did you study engineering?
E   I started college when I was 19 and I qualified as an engineer about four years later.
I   And have you always lived in Pennsylvania?
E   No. I've lived in lots of different places. In the energy business, you live where the work is.
I   So when did you move here?
E   In 2007. Just after they found the gas here.
I   So, how many different places have you lived in, do you think?
E   I'd say about 15, maybe 16 places.
I   Have you ever lived abroad?
E   Yes, but only for about three months.
I   And how does Pennsylvania compare with other places? Has it been easy living here?
E   Yes, it has, overall.
I   Have the local people been friendly?
E   Yes, they have. Well, most people anyway.

You can read a commentary on this task on page 227.

Extracts from Dummett, Hughes, Stephenson
Life Pre-Intermediate (2013) National Geographic Learning

Task 5

Look at six language items taken from the contents page of a general English coursebook. In each case, think of an audio text type which naturally incorporates the target language. For example, item 1 would lend itself to a presentation about how something technical works or a dialogue between two people in an office in which one person asks the other for help with a piece of equipment.

1. Verbs for giving instructions (e.g. *press, turn*, etc.) with sequencing language (e.g. *First of all, after that*, etc.)
2. The first and second conditional
3. A lexical set of film genres (e.g. *sci-fi, romantic comedy*, etc.)
4. Collocations with the verbs *make* and *do*.
5. The pronunciation feature of contrastive stress.
6. Useful phrases for asking for directions.

You can read a commentary on this task on page 228.

Balancing real speech with graded speech

As we have seen, scripted audio is often written so that it presents target language in context as well as providing listening practice. However, this kind of scripted audio recorded for use in coursebooks and student materials is sometimes criticised.

Task 6

Think about whether you have ever heard teachers and/or students complain about the recorded audio in course materials? What kinds of comments have they made?

One major complaint is that the listenings in the course materials are not authentic enough and don't prepare students for listening to real speech. Such a criticism is to miss the point about graded, scripted audio. It is written to the current level of the students or slightly above their level in order to improve their English. If the purpose of the audio were simply to reproduce authentic speech or listenings, then a teacher could simply play authentic recordings; however, the reality is that many students at B2 level and below would not be able to understand them.

However, there is an important issue here that part of our job as audio script writers is to try and include some elements of real speech in order to help students prepare for the real world. In this way, we need to try and find a balance. For example, imagine a writer has produced this listening script for a unit in an A2 coursebook which aims to teach students the language for finding somewhere to eat:

Tourist Is there a good place to eat near here?
Local Yes, there is. There's an Italian restaurant on the corner. It serves delicious pasta. Go straight down the street and it's in front of you.
Tourist I prefer Indian food. Are there any Indian restaurants near here?
Local Yes, there are two. My favourite is on Gower Street. Go straight ahead, take the first right and it's on your left.

Extract from Life Elementary Video, Unit 3, National Geographic Learning

The script is at the right level and it introduces some useful vocabulary and expressions for giving directions. You can probably picture the type of exercise that might go with it; perhaps a simple gapfill exercise where you listen and write in some key missing words or phrases, or a map which you have to label with the names of the restaurants. In fact, overall, it's very typical of what you might find in many low-level course materials.

Now compare it to two more conversations which were recorded with real people in a street in Oxford. The interviewer walked up to them and asked them to talk about places to eat that they'd recommend in the local area. So these two scripts are 100% authentic and illustrate some key features of real speech:

Speaker 1 Yeah, there are some places, I mean there are some choices which is Italian, Turkish, Greek and, err, burger, pizza places.
Speaker 2 There are several good places to eat round here. It's a good road for it. There's the Greek place err just there, err there's the Italian over the road, there is the American style Atomic Burgers down there who also have a pizzeria at the other end.

Extract from Life Elementary Video, National Geographic Learning

These two short authentic scripts illustrate some key features of real speech which are often omitted from scripted audio. They are as follows:

False starts and repetition

Speaker 1 makes a false start in his response when he says *there are some places, I mean there are some choices …*

He begins speaking and then decides to start again. He also repeats the words, *There are … there are*. This kind of feature is common in everyday speech but rarely reproduced in graded scripts.

Error

Both non-native and native speakers alike make 'errors' in natural speech. In the examples above, the verb (*to be*) doesn't agree with the subject in Speaker 1's opening sentence so he uses is instead of *are*:

... there are some choices which is Italian, Turkish, Greek and, err, Burger, Pizza places.

Fillers and filled pauses

Both speakers use the most common filler *err* while they think for the next word. Speaker 1 also uses the filler *I mean*.

Contracted and full forms

Most audio scripts include contracted forms such as *I've* or *He's* instead of the full forms *I have* and *he has*. It's such a standard feature of real speech and many written texts that it has to be incorporated. However, Speaker 2 illustrates a contrast of contracted forms and full forms that a scripted audio text is unlikely to include. Notice this part of the text where the speaker contrasts different restaurants:

There's the Greek place err just there, err there's the Italian over the road, there is the American style Atomic Burgers down there.

He uses the contracted *there's* as he lists different restaurants but then uses the full form *there is* to refer to the American burger bar. This use of the full form indicates that the speaker thinks this place is especially good. It's a very subtle use of word stress in a sentence and one that many students would not notice so it would not appear in many scripted audio texts.

Idiom, slang, jargon

Real speech tends to include more frequent instances of local idiom, slang or jargon related to the speaker's background. Quite often this kind of language is cut in published materials because it dates and it's often very local or regional. Neither speaker uses the word *restaurant* but instead refer to *pizza places* or *the Greek place*. For a lower level student in another part of the world, this usage might well be confusing as it isn't a global term.

Pronunciation and accent

When recording real speech you cannot control the pronunciation features or accents of the speakers. In fact Speaker 1 has a strong Italian accent in the recording and Speaker 2 speaks in a southern English accent. Most coursebook recordings will tend towards neutral accents with standard British English (or equivalent in US publications) or other accents which are not too pronounced.

Conclusions about balancing real speech and graded speech

Having identified the key features of real speech, a writer needs to decide how much these need to be added into a script which is being written for a certain level. Here are some tips for incorporating features of real speech:

- Contracted forms are a common part of everyday speech, so a lot of your scripts, especially dialogues and conversations will include them.
- If you decide to include features such as fillers, filled pauses and false starts to add authenticity, then write them into the script so that an actor knows where you want them to be added.
- As a general rule, don't include an error even though it is a feature of real speech; it's expected by teachers and students that a scripted text will demonstrate 'correct' English and including an error – unless it is clearly part of an error recognition exercise – will cause unnecessary confusion.
- As with errors, slang, jargon and idioms should only be included if they are part of the teaching aim, and usually only in scripts for higher level learners.
- If you need a particular feature of pronunciation to be added in (e.g. a certain stress), then make sure it's clearly indicated in the script. For example, underline a stressed word or indicate intonation by adding an arrow above a word or write [rising] or [falling] after the word or sentence.
- For accents, include notes on using particular accents in square brackets.

Task 7

Read this audio script for students of English for Academic Purposes at a B1/B2 level. The aim is to present the language needed for giving a presentation. Rewrite the script so it includes more features of real speech and sounds more authentic but without increasing the level of difficulty for students at this level.

Good morning everyone and thank you for coming. I am currently studying for my degree in Media Studies and so today I would like to present part of my dissertation on the subject of web-based media. Before I go into too much detail, I would like to give an overview of what we mean by web-based media for anyone who isn't familiar with this aspect of media studies.

> etc
> Basically, web-based media refers to anything on the internet. So when we look at a website, we need to think about the purpose of a website, analyse its target audience, and think about the conventions that most websites follow. To show you what I mean, take a look at this slide ...
>
> You can read a commentary on this task on page 228.

Other Considerations When Scripting Audio

Obviously, the linguistic purpose of the audio is uppermost in your mind when writing a script – does it need to illustrate a language point in context or is it being used to develop a listening skill or aspect of pronunciation? However, there are other factors to bear in mind when scripting. But before reading about what those factors are, try this task.

Task 8

Compare two drafts of a script prepared for a unit in an Elementary coursebook on the topic of using technology in the workplace. What are the key differences between them, and why do you think the writer made the changes to draft 1? *natural, Introduce vocab slower, more features of speech*

Draft 1

A Sorry, can you help?
B Sure.
A How do I use the new Intranet?
B First of all, you need a password and remember to use lower case letters. Don't use upper case letters. So when you log in, here is Company news. And you can also send messages like this. First of all, click on *My intranet*. Next click on *Messages*. So it's similar to email. You have an inbox and you can send messages to people at work. OK?
A That's great. Thanks.

How To Write Audio And Video Scripts

Draft 2

Magda	Sorry. Can you help me?
Chen	Sure.
Magda	How do I use the new Intranet?
Chen	Do you have a password?
Magda	Yes, it's here. I'm trying to key it in, but it doesn't work.
Chen	That's because the password is in lower case letters. Don't use upper case letters.
Magda	Oh!
Chen	That's it. So here is *Company news*. And you can also send messages.
Magda	How?
Chen	First of all, click on *My intranet*. Next click on *Messages*. So it's similar to email. You have an inbox and you can send messages to people at work. OK?
Magda	That's great. Thanks.

You can read a commentary on this task on page 229.

Reproduced by permission of Oxford University Press.
From *Business Result Elementary Student's Book* by David Grant,
John Hughes and Rebecca Turner © Oxford University Press 2009

Adding context

It will help the listener's comprehension if he/she knows where a monologue or conversation is taking place. For example, if the conversation is happening at a conference, then you could put that information in the rubric in the material, e.g. *Listen to the conversation at a conference and answer questions 1–6*. Alternatively, you could include a photograph showing people talking at a conference. However, it can also be helpful to make the context for the listening 'overt' by having a character say something like *The conference is busier than last year*. Or *Have you been to this conference before?* There's a danger that such sentences make the script less authentic but nevertheless it can help.

Sound effects

Another way to help with context and add some authenticity is to provide notes with the script on using sound effects. For example, if the conversation takes place in a railway station, the listening could begin with the background noise of a station announcement. Although ELT audios can't be too ambitious with background sound effects, most recording studios can add in effects such as background street noises, types of transport, doors closing, etc. For telephone calls, they can make the speaker sound as if he's talking down a phone. Indicate any sound effects using square brackets in your script.

Turn-taking and responding

When writing conversations between two or three people, as a general rule, keep each turn short. The danger of one person talking for a long time is that a listening student can lose track of what is being said. If the other characters often respond, ask clarifying questions or even echo something, it helps the listener to follow.

Numbers of speakers

Because it is for audio, having too many speakers will confuse the listener. Two people in a dialogue is ideal. Three people is manageable for a listener as long as the conversation uses names overtly to help distinguish between who is speaking. Four speakers becomes a real challenge and should be avoided in most cases. Any more speakers than that in one **track** and you'll confuse teachers and students alike.

Gender

Other than the obvious reasons for having a fairly equal balance of male and female speakers in your scripts, one particular reason is so that the listener can easily distinguish who is speaking. For example, if you write a dialogue, using one man and one woman avoids any potential confusion. As soon as you increase the number of speakers then it becomes even more important to mix the genders; for example, with three speakers, one of them should be the opposite gender to help the listener follow who is speaking.

Naming the speakers

It's common in many scripts to see the speakers referred to as A, B and C, etc. Typically, this notation is used when the conversations are short or the purpose of the recording is a listen-and-repeat drill or a short pronunciation exercise. However, naming the speakers can be useful when a conversation is longer and especially when there are more than two speakers. With three speakers you often need to insert a name here and there to help students identify who is speaking. It's also useful for the design of a comprehension exercise because students can listen to what a particular person says and write it down.

Accent

Using different accents is another way to make it clearer who is speaking but – more importantly – it reflects the use of English as a form of international communication and exposes students to a range of voices. In the past, the speakers in ELT scripts were often given the names of native speakers because the settings were often in the UK or USA. Nowadays however, scripts tend to reflect the fact that English is the lingua franca used between non-native speakers across national borders. So scripts might include someone with a French accent talking to someone else with a Japanese accent. As a result, you will also need to find names from different countries to use in your scripts. One way of doing this is to do an online search for lists of first names and surnames from different countries. Also make sure you check the gender of the names you're using; it isn't unheard of for coursebooks to include a male speaker with a female name for example. Something a student from that country will gleefully point out to their teacher once the material is published! (See also the *Resources And Further Reading* section (page 225) for more sources of names for speakers.)

Note: In the section on writing video scripts (page 205), you will also find information on developing narrative and characters, some of which are also relevant when writing audio scripts.

Preparing the finished script for a recording studio

If you are recording your audio scripts for use in your own lessons, then modern technology allows you to produce reasonable quality recordings at little cost. At a very basic level you can record voices with a smartphone. For something more professional – but still free – download the software *Audacity* which allows you to make and then edit a recording. With regard to the actors, you can probably ask colleagues, friends and family to read out the various parts.

However, if you are writing the script for a publisher, then the publisher will hire the services of a recording studio which specialises in producing audio for language learning materials. Although you will have very little direct contact with the studio until (possibly) the day of the recording it's useful to understand the process of preparing a script for the recording and how the recording sessions will work.

The producer of the recording will request a copy of the entire script in order to give a quote to the client/publisher. That quote will include the cost of hiring actors, the studio, a technician, editing time and facilities, and even the cost of delivering the copies of the recording. Once the price is agreed, the producer will go ahead and hire the actors and prepare for the recording. So at this stage the editor will need to make sure the script includes all of the following information:

- accents required (UK, US, French, Japanese, etc.)
- gender and approximate age of characters
- any particular personality or character types
- the location of a script which might require certain sound effects (e.g. background noise in the street)
- the level of the material and therefore how this affects the actors' speed of delivery and use of pauses
- notes on the main purpose of a track or how it will be used; for example, if it is being used to highlight an aspect of pronunciation then certain words might need to be in bold to help the actors get the desired result.
- notes on difficult or unusual pronunciation, e.g. for proper nouns or names.

The finalised script is the responsibility of the editor who will add in features such as narrator lines. These include rubrics if they are to be recorded before the main listening, track numbers and **idents** (e.g. A, B, C, Speaker 1, Speaker 2, etc.) and any copyright information that has to go at the start or end of the complete recording.

Here is part of a listening script to accompany a business English coursebook which has been prepared for the recording studio. Notice the information that is included in addition to what the speakers will say:

Sample script for recording studio
[Track 32]
Narrator Unit 3, Track 12

[One male and one female voice – Alex is early-50s and has a Spanish accent. Josey is from Canada and in her early-30s. They are meeting for the first time at a conference in Toronto. Sound of people talking in the background.]

Josey Hi! Are you Alex by any chance?
Alex That's right. Pleased to meet you.
Josey I'm Josey from Roxbo. We've spoken on the phone a few times.
Alex Of course! Hi Josey. Nice to meet you at last!

The day of the recording

Once the actors are hired and the studio is booked, everyone receives a **call sheet** which gives details of time and place. On the actual day of the recording you will need to arrive at the studio in good time before the scheduled recording start time – this will give you an opportunity to meet the producer and the audio technician and discuss any queries they have about the script, etc. You will also meet the actors as they arrive.

During the recording you will sit behind the producer with your editor. The actors will be working on the other side of the glass window in the studio. The producer is the person in charge and will lead the recording. After each track has been recorded he/she will ask for your opinion to check that it achieves what you wanted; this is especially true of pronunciation recordings where a specific result is required. All being well, for large parts of the recording, you won't need to comment. At this stage, everything should be evident from the script and it isn't the time for a writer to suddenly change a script. The cost of hiring a studio and the time involved doesn't allow for this, and any changes that do arise will be discussed with the editor before being implemented as they will possibly create knock-on effects for other elements of the material such as artwork, answer keys or associated exercises. A writer should only interrupt the recording proceedings if something is completely wrong; for example, if an actor is delivering the script in a way that won't work within the context of the exercise in the material.

How actors will read your script

When actors record materials for language learning, they are briefed to read only what is on the page. This means that you cannot assume they will add any features of real speech that are not written into the script. If you require a speaker to use a false start (e.g. *I mean, I mean, what I want to say is ...*) then you need to write it in. This issue is especially important with regard to writing in any pronunciation features. If you expect a particular word to be stressed in a dialogue then you need to indicate that stress (perhaps by underlining it or even inserting a note to the actor in square brackets. (Square brackets [ ] are used in scripts for notes that aren't meant to be read aloud.) In a very few cases, some ad-libbing is allowed by actors but this is typically only done for advanced level material and you will need to make this clear in your scripting.

Once the recording session is over, it is left to the producer to edit the tracks and send them to the editor for checking; you might also receive a copy to listen to and check; note that re-recording of a track will only take place if there is something totally wrong such as an error in pronunciation recording. Otherwise, this is the final version and you won't hear it again until it's published.

That's the end of this section on writing scripts for audio recordings. As we have seen, it is a fine balancing act between writing a script which includes the target language at the right level and the authenticity of real speech. In addition, you have to bear in mind that audio doesn't allow for any visual context and the fact that there are limitations imposed by the realities of recording the script in a studio.

Now we will take the principles of script writing for audio and develop them for writing scripts for video materials.

How To Write Video Scripts
Why video?

> **Task 9**
>
> Before you start reading this section, make a list of reasons why teachers use video in the classroom.

In the past, video used to be used to teach language but also to add fun to a lesson; it was notoriously used in lessons at the end of the week when it was thought students would enjoy a 'video lesson'. It's important to note that lots of students didn't necessarily have access to video at home, nor did they have videos in English so watching video in your English lesson did indeed have a novelty value. However, fast forward to the present day and any student with access to the internet has access to videos in English any time of the day. In addition, teachers with projectors or IWBs in their classroom can add in video to any lesson; in other words, the novelty factor has diminished.

You can watch me outlining typical uses of video in the classroom on *YouTube* by searching for 'John Hughes talks about using video in the classroom', but in general there are the four main reasons that teachers use ELT video:

Language input
As with audio, students can listen to the spoken words in a video and use this as springboard into an area of grammar or vocabulary; for example, they could watch two people in a shop and learn expressions for shopping via the dialogue. However, since this is video, we could also show some of the different items in the shop on screen and use this as a way to introduce a variety of countable and uncountable nouns.

Skills
In many materials, video is used to develop (or test) students' listening skills. Many of the comprehension exercise types that accompany video resemble those used with audio. Of course its advantage over audio is that what's happening on screen makes the listening more accessible and students have a better chance at guessing meaning because they have a context or can see the people speaking.

Activating language
Video is also used in the classroom as a way to get students speaking or writing. For example, a teacher can start the lesson by playing a video with the sound off and students have to predict/imagine what the people in the video are saying. Alternatively, students are only played the soundtrack and don't see the screen; then they have to speculate about what is happening on screen.

Topics and content

For teachers who want to help students to understand a topic or new subject matter, then video can be very effective. For example, in business English teachers could show a class a documentary about a company or an interview with a CEO. In other words, we use videos in English to teach *about* something as well as teaching English.

Having seen how teachers are using video in the classroom, it's clearly important to know in what ways the teachers and students will use your videos. Diarmuid Carter is the script editor for Oxford University Press. His advice for any ELT script writer starting out on a project is to 'know the function of the video. Some courses use the videos to kick-start debate. They want exciting videos, and they're often willing to sacrifice some vocabulary or grammar points to get them. For others the learning points are paramount, and while they will also want engaging videos, the language and grammar must take priority. The earlier you know how the video will be used, the better for the script.'

How is writing for video different from writing for audio?

> **Task 10**
>
> Think about using video instead of audio in the classroom. What does video offer that audio can't? How can it improve language learning?
>
> You can read a commentary on this task on page 229.

The key difference between writing for video and audio is that you have to consider the visual elements and write those into the script. To some extent, we can transfer some of what we know from writing scripts for audio and apply that to writing for video. However, the danger with merely transferring an audio script onto video is that it's potentially quite dull; for example, if you take an audio script of two people ordering coffee in a café and turn it into video, then all you add is a view of a café and two actors at a table. In a way, you have gained little from the conversation taking place on video.

One of the early rules taught to students at film school is to 'Show, don't tell'. In other words, if it can be shown on the screen visually, then don't script words to express it. Let's consider how this might be applied to an ELT video script. Imagine you want to teach the language for asking for and offering help. Your script might begin with something like this:

A *Can you help me move this box?*
B *Sure. Where are we taking it?*

But in a video, the script might read (and be laid out) like this:

We see an enormous cardboard box blocking the corridor in an office. Man A is struggling to lift it. Man B rushes up, looking at his watch. He tries to get round the box.
Man A Can you help?
Man B Sure.
They lift the box and move up the corridor to a doorway. Man A tries to turn into the doorway but the box is much too wide.

Task 11

Compare the two previous scripts. What does the video script offer the viewer that the audio script doesn't offer the listener?

You can read a commentary on this task on page 229.

You'll have noticed that the layout of the two scripts are different. This will be addressed in more detail later in this section.

Although the video in the previous example might be memorable because of the problems caused by a ridiculously large box, we also need to consider whether the students recall any of the language used if the main focus is visual. In other words, does the 'Show, don't tell' rule apply to ELT videos in the same way it does to movie making?

This issue faced me some years ago while working on a script for elementary students on checking in at a hotel. I wrote a dialogue between a visitor and a receptionist with useful phrases for checking in and dealing with some minor difficulties. I added notes on what the camera might show (e.g. hotel entrance, reception area, type of person behind the desk and so on).

The script was passed on to the director who went off to film it. The next time I was involved was for the final edit. The video started very much how I'd imagined it with some very nice outdoor **establishing shots** of a taxi arriving at a hotel and the visitor stepping out and entering the hotel. What came as a surprise was the additional (and previously unscripted) voiceover narration which explained something to the effect of: *A visitor is arriving at the hotel to check in*. Why include this when the video already shows us this information?

When I questioned why this voiceover had been added to the script, the director argued that the 'Show, don't tell' rule doesn't always apply in ELT videos because the primary job of the video is to provide language input so sometimes it's necessary to add it in where you wouldn't normally include it; in other words, scripted ELT videos have a responsibility to 'Show AND tell'.

Whatever you think about the two views of video, I do think there's a balance to be struck between 'Show, don't tell' and 'Show and tell'. Certainly, for video which is being written in order to introduce key expressions, then there is a responsibility to include more overt language than you might normally. On the other hand, if the aim of the video is to stimulate interest or class discussion, something that's more visual with fewer words might be preferable. James Tomalin is a producer of ELT video with Oxford Digital Media and considers this balancing act: 'If your script includes a car broken down on the side of the road, then you have to ask yourself why a character needs to say *That car's broken down*. If the aim is to teach the verb *break down*, then you can justify it. Otherwise, why say it when we can see it?'

Task 12

As we have seen so far, in ELT videos we usually need to keep in mind the target language we want to teach. Nevertheless, the following exercise is a useful way to raise your awareness of how to script visually. It's a task that is often given to new students at film school. Read each phrase and consider how you might show it in a video without using any of the actual words. In particular, think about how you would use the context, character, gestures, location, etc. to achieve this.

1. I'm so angry, I could scream!
2. Sorry, can you repeat that? I didn't understand you.
3. I'll give you $10 for it.
4. Would you mind moving your car? It's in my space.
5. The bus is leaving. Run or we'll miss it!
6. I've never been to Paris before. It's wonderful!

You can read a commentary on this task on page 230.

Practical Points To Consider About Writing For Video

Writing visually is the obvious way in which writing for video is different to writing for audio, but if you are used to writing for audio, then there are some other key points to note when writing video scripts. They tend to be practical issues and all indirectly related to the budget. It's hard to overstress just what an impact the budget of filming has on what is possible. Unlike recording an audio, filming involves many more costs including one or more camera operators, a sound technician, the director/producer, actors, a place to film (studio or on location), props, costumes, and even transportation; as one video producer said to me: 'If you write that you want a helicopter in your video, then you need two helicopters because you need the other to film it from.'

So before you go off and write a script, you need to be aware of what limitations there may be on the video as a result of the budget. The following points should help you with this. Ideally, they are all points you will be made aware of in a brief from your publisher and – if they aren't – then ask about them. It will save a lot of time and heartache later on, if you do.

Location

When writing a script for audio, you can place it in any location you like. On the side of a Himalayan mountain with the wind rushing past or inside a helicopter flying across London. When writing a video script, your choice of location will affect the amount of time it takes to organise the filming and, in turn, the cost. So a lot of the time you have to ask yourself why the dialogue has to be filmed in a particular place; for example, if your script says that a conversation takes place between two people in a moving car, you have to ask yourself if it's crucial that the car is moving. Could they have the same conversation in a parked car because it will be much easier and therefore cheaper to film?

Mari Tudor Jones, who directs educational video, also points out that 'shooting on location is often less efficient because – for example – you're waiting for the noise of an overhead plane to pass or an interruption by a siren. Filming in a studio is easier and cheaper.' She also argues that 'filming against a white backdrop with creative use of props and objects can often achieve your purpose just as effectively as being in a real location'. In recent years many ELT videos, including the *New English File* videos (OUP), have used the white backdrop. Alternatively, you can shoot against a green screen in the studio which allows you to film actors and then insert images (still or moving) behind them afterwards.

Number of actors

Recording an audio script for a coursebook within the region of 100 different tracks requires lots of different voices. However, it can all be achieved with around six actors all playing different parts with different accents. In video this is not the case and new ELT video script writers often make the mistake of having too many characters. For example, if you are filming a hotel scene, you could include a business person arriving in a taxi, the taxi driver, the doorman, other guests in the lobby and a receptionist. To justify all these people you could give them all something to say. However, for such a short sequence it would be too expensive. In reality, the main target language needed for checking in at a hotel is that of the guest arriving and the receptionist. So while including all these extras might suit a Hollywood blockbuster, you can't include them in an ELT video script.

Writing scripts for different levels

Another point to consider is that the publisher might be filming video materials to go with different levels of a course. So you are probably going to write a series of scripts used at elementary, pre-intermediate, intermediate and so on. If this is the case then keep in mind that the same actors and locations can appear at different levels so try to write the different scripts in a way that they might reuse actors (or their characters) and the same locations.

Describe, don't tell

Writers who have moved from writing audio to video also have a tendency to overwrite their scripts according to script editors and directors. James Magrane of OUP's media department gives this advice: 'One thing worth remembering about writing for video is that you should 'describe, don't direct'. This means that in the narration sections of a drama script, for example, don't write that you want tracking shots or pans across vistas, just describe the vista. This is partly practical – you may not know the specifics of the location and what's possible – and partly politics – directors are by and large touchy folk who don't like to be told what to shoot.' His view is supported by the comment of another video director that inexperienced ELT writers have a tendency to 'overwrite when less is often more'.

Types Of Video Script

'Language teachers are using *YouTube* in class and so your scripts are competing with that.' Mari Tudor Jones (MTJ Media)

To spend an hour or so idly clicking through *YouTube* is to discover a vast range of different types of video. It's currently such an evolving form that it would be hard to define every type. In ELT, many teachers are now producing their own videos with their students writing scripts and performing them. Another trend in education video is to produce video content which teaches students something. Perhaps the best-known examples of this can be viewed at the *Kahn Academy* website which offers video lessons in 'maths, science, computer programming, history, art history, economics, and more'. Out of the idea that a student can watch the input for a subject at home has developed the **'flipped classroom'** approach where the input is delivered by video before the lesson so that lesson time is spent doing practice activities. The flipped classroom has an obvious attraction for English language teachers. It's easy to present a grammar point on the board and video it. Then students watch the presentation at home before the lesson so that during the lesson they can focus on using the new grammar in communicative activities. In fact, you don't even need to record it yourself because there are countless teachers on *YouTube* who have already scripted and recorded their own language presentations.

When it comes to writing video scripts for ELT publishers and a professional media company, writers are often required to script certain types of video and Diarmuid Carter (OUP script editor) suggests that there are times when one is more appropriate than another: 'Short mini-dramas often suit beginners because you can contrive a situation to best suit what's in the book. Voiceover documentaries often suit profiles of things and places and presenter-led documentaries often suit abstract concepts that are difficult to illustrate visually but that a presenter can help to explain.'

As well as drama or documentaries, an increasing number of ELT videos are also making use of graphics and animation and so you will need to adjust your approach to the script according to the needs of the project. However, we can broadly categorise the type of ELT video scripts we write into two main categories: Dramas and Documentaries. So the section that follows presents some examples of scripts written for these genres and how writers might develop their skills accordingly.

Drama scripts

The term 'drama' in ELT script writing has quite a broad meaning. At a basic level it is a fictional situation between fictional characters; for example, you might write a script in which two friends meet at a café and order coffee and a sandwich. It's a useful way to present the language in a visual and contextualised situation even if it's somewhat lacking in originality or what we might call 'real drama'. At a more sophisticated level, ELT video drama should also aim to present target language in a dramatic context with interesting characters and a strong narrative thread.

Not surprisingly then, writing drama scripts is probably the most challenging (and expensive) type of ELT script writing because to be successful it requires the balancing of three different skills:

- grading the language level and target key language.
- understanding the basic principles of how video scripts are written and constructed and how they are essentially different from an audio script.
- writing dramatic scripts with interesting characters and narratives.

The first skill of grading the language is the least challenging for us because we have presumably honed that skill after years of teaching and writing course materials and audio scripts. The second skill is something that can be acquired by working with experienced script editors and video producers (and of course by reading this book!). However, the third skill of writing real drama needs the skill of a TV script writer.

The layout of a drama script

Let's begin by considering how you might construct a basic script for a drama. Many ELT writers submit their scripts in the same way as an audio script with the speakers' lines and a few notes added about what's on the screen. Your publisher will be happy to accept your script in this way and then they will pass it on to a script editor who turns it into a finished document. This final script might follow certain conventions so that everyone involved in the process understands what will be filmed. Here is an extract from an ELT drama script that has been prepared for filming.

Task 13

Read the script and note the layout. How is it different from, for example, a script written for audio? Why do you think these conventions are used?

You can read a commentary on this task on page 230.

Episode 5
PART ONE
1 EXT. THE HOUSE – NIGHT
Establishing shot. The house is mysterious and dark. We see a flicker of torchlight inside.

2 INT. THE HOUSE: HENRY'S STUDY – NIGHT
Jenny and Luke are frantically searching through books on the bookshelf using torches. We see Jenny pulling out several books from the shelf.

JENNY   *The Iliad, The Poems of Lord Byron, The Complete Works of Shakespeare … nothing about an old man!*

We see Luke doing the same.

LUKE   *Not even a picture on the front cover.*
JENNY   *(pointing torch to paintings) What about those paintings? Anything there?*
LUKE   *I've already checked them. Nothing. Luke turns around to the bookshelf.*
LUKE   *Should we look through each book?*
JENNY   *That could take forever and we don't have time. (frustrated) Oh, this is hopeless.*

Jenny's mobile rings. Jenny and Luke suddenly freeze. She checks the caller ID.

Reproduced by permission of Oxford University Press.
From English File Intermediate Plus Student's Book by Christina Latham-Koenig,
Clive Oxenden and Mike Boyle © Oxford University Press 2014

Developing dialogue, characters and narrative

As mentioned previously, developing the third skill of writing intrinsically interesting drama is probably the toughest challenge for most of us. As Mari Tudor Jones remarks on some of the scripts she works with: 'ELT writers are naturally good at writing drama at the right language level, but what's lacking is character and narrative.'

It is not within the size and scope of this book to provide a whole course in developing the skills of narrative and character. There are in fact many more books available which can help you to do this and some are recommended in *Resources And Further Reading* on page 225. However, it is worth looking at a few quick techniques that can be applied to your scripts in order to develop characters and narrative.

In the previous section on writing scripts for audio recordings, we looked at the balance between writing dialogue for the students' level and writing dialogue which feels authentic and includes features of real speech. However, it's worth noting that good drama doesn't necessarily rely on authentic dialogues but instead the writer needs to concentrate on what makes good dialogue.

In an article on how to write good dialogue for ELT materials, the ELT author Nicola Prentis comments: 'Aiming for authentic dialogue is impossible. What a writer should be focusing on is good dialogue. By that I mean dialogue that's entertaining enough to want to listen to for its own sake and not purely for the purpose of learning how to say something. Students have heard Hans the Wooden Businessman check into Hotel Anonymous and enquire when breakfast is a million times. Just because they're in a classroom shouldn't mean we sacrifice some kind of entertainment value. For that, taking tips from screen and fiction writers is the key to success.'

Prentis, N. Writing good dialogue for audio and video
(Jan 2015) Modern English Teacher Volume 42, Issue 1

The key starting point for 'good dialogue', according to Prentis is 'strong characters'. In her article she suggests a variety of ways to develop your characters such as cutting out a collection of photographs of interesting-looking people from magazines. Then choose two and imagine them having the kind of dialogue you need to write for your video (or audio). How will their gender, age, race, clothing style, etc., affect the way the lines are spoken?

Video producer Mari Tudor Jones endorses this view that ELT scripts need developed characters. Partly because it naturally aids the dialogue but also because it helps the actors who have to deliver the lines to the camera: 'It's much harder for an actor to act if there's no character. In that situation, it's just words and language but an actor naturally wants to do something with it.' She suggests that ELT writers try adding more detail about characters in their scripts; so instead of a line like *Man in shop – middle aged*, try expanding the detail so the actor can bring it to life.

Imagine you have to write a dialogue between two people meeting in a café. How can you develop the characters? One way is to create a **backstory** for both people by asking questions about them, for example:

- Who are they?
- Why are they meeting each other?
- Have they met before?
- Do they often meet at this particular café? Why? Why not?
- What were they doing five minutes before this scene?
- What does one of the characters want to get out of the meeting?

How To Write Audio And Video Scripts

The novelist Kurt Vonnegut also believed that character was central to all good stories and that the main character always wanted to get something by the end of the narrative. So a useful technique when writing your script is to consider want the main character wants by the end. Of course if the setting is a café or a hotel, then the main character may only want to buy a coffee or to check in to a comfortable room. If that's the case, then one way to add narrative to a mundane situation is to introduce problems and obstacles for the main character which prevent him/her from getting what he/she wants.

To understand how introducing problems can add narrative to an ELT script, compare two versions of the same script. In version 1, a hotel guest checks in with no problems. In version 2, things go wrong.

Version 1

Receptionist Hello, can I help you?
Guest I have a reservation. My name is Long. Jane Long.
Receptionist Ah, yes. For two nights.
Guest That's right.
Receptionist Can I have your passport and a credit card?
Guest Sure. Here you are.
Receptionist Can you fill in this form?
Guest Of course.
Receptionist Here is your key. Your room is 301 on the 3rd floor. Breakfast is between 7 and 10 on the first floor.
Guest Thank you very much.

Version 2

Receptionist (unsmiling) Hello?
Guest I have a reservation for two nights. My name's Bond. Jane Bond.
Receptionist types into computer.
Receptionist Sorry, you're not here. I have a reservation for James Bond.
Guest I think that's a mistake. It happens a lot.
Receptionist (suspicious) Really? Can I have a credit card and your passport, please?
Guest Sure. Here you are …
Receptionist swipes card.
Receptionist Sorry but the machine won't accept it.
Guest I don't understand. Can you try again?
Receptionist And also this isn't your passport …

Types Of Video Script

As you can see, there's nothing wrong with the dialogue in version 1 and it gives students the target language they need. But in dramatic terms, version 2 is more interesting. By creating conflict and therefore tension, the two characters also become more interesting. Arguably, your students need to be prepared with the ordinary formulaic language in version 1 but sometimes they might need to deal with problematic situations so version 2 also offers a useful (as well as a more engaging) context. Note that the technique of introducing difficulties for main characters is tried and tested, especially in comedy. Watch some classic visual comedy such as *Mr Bean* and *Fawlty Towers* which are based around the main character trying (with or without eventual success) to get/do something.

As I said at the beginning of this short section on character and narrative, you can discover more ideas for developing your characters and narrative by looking at *Resources And Further Reading* on page 225, which lists some useful titles. Perhaps the combination of what I've suggested above and the ideas of others can help to inject some drama that is sometimes lacking in ELT videos.

Documentaries

As mentioned earlier in this chapter, the use of documentaries in ELT materials has become very popular in recent years. It reflects the popularity of similar videos on *YouTube* as well as a modern fascination with watching reality. Another attraction for ELT publishers must also be the relative cheapness in producing documentaries in comparison to producing drama.

As far as the materials writer is concerned, your role in the process of creating a documentary script will feel very different to writing drama and will depend upon the nature of the project. In many ways, writing documentary scripts won't feel as much of a challenge as writing drama because you are writing about something real. You will also apply similar skills to those you use when selecting interesting texts and topics for coursebook writing. You want a subject that is intrinsically interesting and that offers students the opportunity to learn certain target language; the key mantra is that 'students should learn ABOUT something as well as learning English'.

The style and format of a documentary can vary. On screen there is a range of ways subjects can be illustrated, including:

- filming original footage of the subject
- using existing footage which can be edited
- using an existing documentary but replacing the narration so the language is graded
- interviewing an expert on the subject
- interviewing people in the street
- using photographs and images with narration
- creating graphics and animation which are added to live action documentary or used instead of live action (sometimes referred to as *kinetic typography* videos).

In the rest of this section I'm going to outline the way in which three documentaries were written and developed for ELT courses. This will illustrate some of the different approaches that can be taken when scripting video documentaries.

Documentary 1: The city of Santiago
Approach: filming and editing footage with narration

The aim of this OUP video for *International Express* was to introduce the city of Santiago and the language students need for describing a city. Footage of the city was filmed specially for the video though sometimes publishers will use so-called 'stock footage', film that already exists and is purchased and edited in. (Another way of achieving a similar documentary effect for less money would be to use still photographs combined with narration.)

As a basic layout, the script is written in two columns with the narration on one side and notes about what we can see on the other. (Note that the abbreviation *GV* means 'general views'.) You can watch the finished video on *YouTube* by searching for 'International Express Elementary, Unit 6 – Santiago, Chile'.

How To Write Audio And Video Scripts

Voiceover	Images
Santiago is the capital of Chile	GVs Santiago
It's a large, busy city in a beautiful location.	View of mountains from Santiago
To the east of the city are the Andes, the longest mountain range in the world.	The Andes from Santiago
To the west, there's the Chilean Coastal Range. It's shorter than the Andes, and the Andes are more famous, but the Chilean Coastal Range is just as beautiful.	The Chilean coastal range from Santiago
An hour away is the Pacific Ocean, the largest Ocean in the world.	The Pacific
Almost five and a half million people live in Santiago.	People in Santiago
It's by far the largest city in Chile, but it's not the biggest in South America. It's smaller than São Paolo, Bogotá, Lima, Rio de Janeiro and Caracas.	GVs
Santiago combines the modern with the traditional.	Modern buildings in Santiago Old building in Santiago
This is the city centre. It's the busiest area of the city and the buildings here are taller and more modern than the buildings in Santiago's older areas.	Santiago city centre
But there are lots of beautiful, historical buildings here too.	Classical architecture
This is La Moneda palace. The Chilean President lives here, and it's almost as old as the city itself.	San Francisco church
It has a bell tower and a old clock.	Bell tower and clock
As well as the interesting old buildings, Santiago also has beautiful scenery.	
The mountains in the distance are pretty to look at, and they're home to some of the best adventure centres in Latin America.	Sports in Santiago
Inside or outside, there's always something to do in Santiago.	GVs
It is one of the most exciting cities in South America and lies in one of the most beautiful areas of the world.	Panoramic view of Santiago

Reproduced by permission of Oxford University Press.
From *International Express Elementary Student's Book* by Angela Buckingham, Alastair Lane and Bryan Stephens © Oxford University Press 2014

Documentary 2: Women in space

Approach: using an existing documentary and rewriting the narration

Unlike the previous documentary about Santiago, this documentary about the first ever female US astronauts reuses existing video footage and so there was no need to film new material or do any editing. Instead, the writer watched the original documentary and wrote a narration which was recorded and added to the film. This replaced the existing narration which was inappropriate for the target students in terms of level.

Task 14

The script below shows the timings for the film in the first column. The second column contains the original narration from the documentary and the writer's new version is in the final column. You can watch the video with the original narration on the National Geographic video website (video.nationalgeographic.com) by searching for 'women in space'.

Compare the two scripts and think about how and why the writer adapted the narration for elementary level students.

You can read a commentary for this task on page 230.

Timing	Original narration	Narration for Elementary level*
0.00 – 00.18	Since the US space program began in 1958, NASA has achieved much in the realm of space exploration. From lunar landings to voyages into the depths of our solar system, NASA has built a storied history.	NASA began in 1958. It put a man on the Moon in 1969. Spacecraft like Voyager 1 and 2 discovered new places in our solar system and the space shuttle flew into space and back again.
00.19 – 00.50	In the early days, space was a man's world. All that changed on June 18, 1983 when Sally Ride became the first American woman to rocket toward the heavens aboard the space shuttle Challenger. A doctor of Physics, she was recruited by NASA as one of six female astronaut candidates for the shuttle program. While her first job was as a mission control communicator to orbiting shuttles, Sally Ride soon found herself in orbit during 1983's STS7 mission.	In the early days of NASA, space was a man's world. But on the 18 June 1983, Sally Ride was the first American woman in space. Sally was a doctor of Physics and she was part of a group of six candidates to be the first female astronaut. Sally soon got the job and went into space on the Challenger space shuttle.

00.51 – 01.28	And although the Russian space program had sent women into space as early as 1963, Ride's journey into space was a first ever for the US. Aboard the shuttle Challenger she served as a mission specialist, helping deploy two satellites and perform scientific experiments over six days. Shortly after her return. Ride reflected on what her journey into space meant. (Ride speaking:) 'I was asked at a press conference just before our flight what I thought about being the first US woman astronaut. I was quoted as saying that it was no big deal.'	The Russians sent the first woman into space in 1963, but Sally Ride was the first for the USA. She helped to launch two satellites and did scientific experiments over six days. After she returned from the journey, Sally gave talks across the USA.
01.29 – 01.58	What the astronaut meant to say was that technically as far as NASA's concerned it was no big deal. 'On another level, the United States sending a woman into space was a very important event for at least 53% of the population and I'm very proud of that.' Sally Ride would venture into space once more, in 1984. And since that time others have become trailblazers as well.	In particular, her journey was important for women and many travelled to listen to her. Sally went into space one more time – in 1984. And after her, there were other women astronauts and other 'firsts'.
01.59 – 02.32	Physician-turned-astronaut Mae Jemison became the first African-American woman in space during shuttle Endeavour's 1992 mission. During orbit she performed experiments involving life sciences, materials sciences and bone cell research. In 1990, astronaut Eileen Collins became the fist female shuttle pilot aboard Discovery. Collins commanded two space shuttle missions including the important return to flight mission in July 2005, the first after the 2003 Colombia disaster.	Mae Jemison was a physician and became the first African-American woman is space with the space shuttle Endeavour in 1992. Then, in 1995, Eileen Collins became the first female pilot, with the space shuttle Discovery. And she flew two times in 1999 and 2005.

02.33 – end	Since Sally Ride's momentous flight into space the ranks of female astronauts have grown. And in a male dominated field they hold a special position as role models for young women everywhere who dream of reaching the stars.	So as a results of Sally Ride, and many more female astronauts after her, young women – as well as young men – now dream of becoming astronauts and a journey into space.

From *Life Elementary*, National Geographic Learning

Documentary 3: Memory and language learning
Approach: vox pops and animation graphics

Many ELT videos, and especially the documentaries, include interviews with real people. These are either short interviews interspersed with related footage, or the entire video is made up of short interviews. These interviews are sometimes with an expert or they are sometimes ordinary people in the street expressing an opinion; these types of interviews are often called 'vox pops' from the Latin *vox populi* which means 'voice of the people'.

The advantage of the vox pop format over the longer interview is that they are short, require less specialist content knowledge on the part of the student, and the kinds of responses given will often reflect those of the students themselves so the vox pops have intrinsic interest and model the type of language a student might use. The role of the writer is to script questions that will elicit useful answers; this writing combines your ability to grade the language level of a question with the skills of a journalist to formulate effective questions. You may also be called upon to brief the people being interviewed.

In the following example I wrote three questions for a short video about learning languages. We interviewed four people who had experience of learning another language 'off the street' in a studio. They were briefed on the questions in advance but the responses were their own. In every case we filmed them at least twice and in between takes we made suggestions on how they might make their responses clearer given that the materials were for students at around a low A2 level. Here is part of a transcript of the final version:

Question: *When you hear or see a new word in the language, how do you memorise it?*
01.36–01.47 [Spanish speaker talking about learning English] I've got a book and every time I learn a new word I write it down and I also write the definition so I can go back to it and memorise it.
01.48–02.03 [English speaker talking about learning French] I use different techniques. I might think: 'Does it sound like something I know? Does it look like something I know?' For example, un plat is 'a plate' and I think: 'It's like a plate but without the e.'

Extracts from *Life Elementary* Unit 10 Video, National Geographic Learning

Whilst the vox pops speakers gave useful, clear answers, as it stands the above script would work nearly as well if played on audio. However, we filmed the speakers against a green screen in a studio which allows any kind of graphic image to be placed behind the speaker after the filming has been done. This is a relatively quick, cheap and straightforward way to add visual impact and interest to a video. For example, for a drama you could film two actors against a green screen and then put a picture of the Eiffel Tower behind them in order to suggest the dialogue is taking place in Paris. In the case of these vox pops we wanted to add visual interest by adding small animation sequences next to the speaker. So after the initial scripting of the questions, the next stage was to script instructions for animation to be added.

Here is the same part of the video above but this time the script includes notes on the animation and graphics which were then added at the editing stage afterwards.

Vox pops script	Animation and graphics to be added
When your hear or see a new word in the language, how do you memorise it?	Put spoken question on the screen with background music.
01.36 – 01.47 I've got a book and every time I learn a new word I write it down and I also write the definitions so I can go back to it and memorise it.	We see a pen and notebook to the left of the speaker. The pen starts writing.
01.48 – 02.03 I use different techniques. I might think: 'Does it sound like something I know? Does it look like something I know?' For example, *un plat* is 'a plate' and I think: 'It's like *a plate* but without the e.'	Draw a plate, a fork and a knife to the right of the speaker. The word *plate* appears above it. The letter *e* drops off the end of the word *plate*.

Extracts from *Life Elementary* Video 'Memory and Language Learning, National Geographic Learning

Final Checklist

That nearly brings you to the end of this chapter. To sum up the main content, here is a checklist of 20 questions to consider when writing an ELT script. Clearly, not every question will be relevant to every type of script since, as we have seen, this will depend upon whether you are writing for audio or video, listening skills or speaking skills, documentary or drama, and whatever other types of scripts are set to emerge in the future. However, it will be useful to refer to this list from time to time and remind yourself of the key points.

1. Do you know the purpose of your script?
2. What level is the script for?
3. Will the script need to include certain target language?
4. How much will you grade the language to the level?
5. Can you include features of real speech and make it sound authentic?
6. Is the context clear from the script?
7. Are you going to include any sound effects or music?
8. Is there the right number of speakers without it becoming confusing for the listener?
9. Is there a good range of genders, names, nationalities and accents?
10. Does it need pronunciation for any words, expressions or sentences?
11. For a video script, how much emphasis will be on the visual elements? (e.g. 'show, don't tell' or 'show and tell')
12. Are the choices of locations realistic in terms of practicalities and budget?
13. Have you described your locations clearly but not to the extent of telling the director how to film them?
14. Is the number of characters in your video script realistic and/or necessary in terms of budget?
15. How interesting are the characters in your video script and will an actor know how to play them?
16. Can you improve the storyline or narrative in any way?
17. For a documentary, will you make use of photographs, footage or any other types of graphics or animations?
18. Will the documentary make use of existing footage or will new footage need to be filmed?
19. If the video includes interviews with real people, have you prepared the questions which will encourage useable responses?
20. Have you laid out and formatted your final draft of the script (audio or video) clearly so that an editor and producer can easily work with it?

Task 15

In Task 1 on page 184 you were asked to consider the types of skills that someone writing ELT scripts might require. Look back at your notes and reflect on what you have read and learnt since. Have any of your views changed with regard to the importance of certain skills? Are there any skills that you would add to your original list? Which areas of ELT scriptwriting do you think you will need to develop further in the future?

Resources And Further Reading

Writing scripts

Kenyon, S. (2010) *The Writer's Digest Character Naming Sourcebook* **Writer's Digest Books**

This book contains over 25,000 first names and surnames for more than 45 countries. It was written for novelists and authors but is useful when you need a name for a speaker from a specific country or region of the world. One word of warning is that it includes historical and legendary names which will sound dated nowadays, so you'll need to cross-check.

Field, S. (2005) *Screenplay* **Delta**

Syd Field's book is considered the bible of screenplay writing by the Hollywood film industry and is used in film schools. Chapter 13 is about the form of a screenplay with details on conventions for formatting your video scripts. The book is aimed at writing a full-length film but you will also find ideas on developing areas such as character and narrative.

Online software for formatting screenplays

www.celtx.com and www.finaldraft.com offer online and downloadable tools for formatting screenplays.

This download is a style guide to writing video scripts. It is published by the BBC but the guidelines can also be followed for writing scripts for ELT video. For more examples of different formats for scriptwriting also see the BBC's *Writer's Room*.

ELT authors mentioned in this book

Peter Viney

When publishers eventually stopped selling his video titles from the 80s and 90s, Peter Viney started distributing them himself via his website and they continue to be used in classrooms around the world. In addition to this, Peter has a blog (peterviney.wordpress.com) with a section of articles on ELT and ELT videos. Although some of the references in the articles feel dated in places, many of the ideas and comments are still very relevant and of interest and use to writers of video material.

Vicki Hollett

The well-known ELT author Vicki Hollett began writing video scripts for publishers but now produces her own independently made videos at *Simple English Videos* and she also writes about video in ELT on her blog (www.vickihollett.com).

Ben Goldstein

Ben has written various articles and books about using images in ELT. His website (www.bengoldstein.es) also includes articles about video.

ELT audio and video production companies who contributed to the research in this chapter

MTJ Media (www.mtjmedia.com)

Oxford Digital Media (www.oxforddigitalmedia.co.uk)

MGvdo (www.mgvdo.co.uk)

Tom Dick & Debbie Video Production (www.tomdickanddebbie-video.co.uk)

Task Commentaries

Task 4 (page 193)

Audio script 1

This text type falls into the category of 'talk' or 'documentary'. In the book, students could look at the photographs taken by Nick Veasey and then listen to how they were taken. It's an example of an information-rich text type which is often used to develop listening skills in some way. Students will probably listen once for gist and then listen again for more detail. This kind of script also lends itself to teaching items of vocabulary or grammar. For example, in this case, the text is full of references to ways of working and includes some useful vocabulary that could be focused on in accompanying exercises.

Audio script 2

This is typical of dialogues which have been written to model useful expressions in a real transactional situation. This kind of script normally has exercises in the student's book which focus on students listening for and identifying the key phrases and the functional purpose. Then they do a roleplay activity in which they recreate a similar dialogue.

Audio script 3

This script is written for pronunciation practice. Students listen to each phrase and try to reproduce it. In the actual recording, the emphasis is on the intonation rising on the first noun and falling on the second noun. (The script writer would have supplied notes on the rise-fall patterns in the original draft so it could be recorded correctly.)

Audio script 4

This script uses the format of a journalist interviewing someone. This kind of interview format is a favoured vehicle in many ELT materials because it's a useful way to introduce a particular language point. In this example, the script is clearly aimed at demonstrating how the present perfect is used in question forms and the tense is also contrasted with the past simple. While this overuse of a language point makes the script sound inauthentic, it does nevertheless provide a contextualized way to present the grammar.

How To Write Audio And Video Scripts

Task 5 (page 195)

Here are some possible text types for items 2–6:

2 **The first and second conditional**

   These two grammar structures are often presented in the context of a negotiation between two people because this type of conversation often requires the use of conditionals (e.g. *If I offer you $50, will you sell it?*)

3 **A lexical set of film genres (e.g. *sci-fi*, *romantic comedy*, etc.)**

   A radio programme about the latest film releases would include this lexical set.

4 **Collocations with the verbs *make* and *do*.**

   These collocates could occur in a range of text types. However, someone describing or being interviewed about everyday routines or what they do in the workplace would guarantee the use of *make* and *do*.

5 **The pronunciation feature of contrastive stress.**

   To present the use of contrastive stress in an authentic situation requires a context in which someone needs to check information; e.g. *Did you say thir*ty *or thir*teen? For this reason, it is often presented in the context of a telephone call with the caller asking for and writing down information.

6 **Useful phrases for asking for directions.**

   The obvious context here is to have a tourist lost in a city and asking a passer-by for directions. Alternatively, it could be a message left on a person's voicemail giving directions to a house.

Task 7 (page 198)

Here is an example of how you might include more elements of real speech in the rewritten script. Note that the key language and structure remains the same but with minimum changes it feels a little more authentic. Also, making the speaker from a distinct region or country and adding notes on the accent to be used all add to the script's sense of authenticity.

[*Middle East accent*]

Mujahid: Err, OK. Good morning everyone. Thanks for coming. I'm currently studying for my degree in Media Studies and so today I'd like to present part of my dissertation on the subject of web-based media. OK? Now, before I go into too much detail, I'd like to give an overview of what we mean by web-based media. You know, for anyone who isn't familiar with this aspect of media studies.

Task Commentaries

Err, basically, web-based media refers to anything on the internet. So, erm, when we look at a website, we need to think about the purpose of a website, analyse its target audience, and we need to think, err … to think about the conventions that most websites follow. Right. To show you what I mean, take a look at this, err, [clicks on slide] slide …

Task 8 (page 199)

First of all, notice that in both scripts the first three lines of the dialogue remain unchanged because we are establishing the context for the conversation and the relationship between the speakers. However, in draft 1, Chen goes on to give a monologue about how to use the new company intranet. If the script was for video, the visual elements would make this easier to follow. However, for an audio recording, his monologue would be hard to follow in isolation. Instead, draft 2 is much more conversational with Magda and Chen turn-taking. Although dialogues of this kind can have a feeling of inauthenticity, within the limitations of audio and the level of the target student, this is often necessary. In draft 2 the speakers are given names, which helps to add a sense of context.

Task 10 (page 206)

ELT author Peter Viney talks about what video brings to a classroom that audio can't:

'When I can see people, when I can see visual signals, when I can see contexts, I can see facial expression, everything becomes clear … . You know if people are joking, if they are serious, angry, gestures, stance, movement, all this information comes with video. With video you are taking the blindfold off.'

Watch Vicki Hollett's interview with Peter Viney on *YouTube* by searching for 'Interview with Peter Viney'.

Task 11 (page 207)

- As you can see from the video script, the speakers' words can be briefer because we infer so much more meaning from the visual elements. It's also noticeable how much more we can add with video in a short space of time in terms of content, characters, plot and humour; within 30 seconds of video we discover the box is comically enormous, we are in a workplace, one person is really struggling, the other person is in a hurry but has to help because the box is blocking his way.

How To Write Audio And Video Scripts

Task 12 (page 208)

Here are some suggested ways to replace the spoken words with something visual:

1. I'm so angry, I could scream! – A close up on an actor's face looking angry at a situation.
2. Sorry, can you repeat that? I didn't understand you. – A quizzical look from one person to another.
3. I'll give you $10. – Holding out $10 and gesturing towards the object for sale.
4. Would you mind moving your car? It's in my space. – Pointing a finger at the car and then pointing in the opposite direction.
5. The bus is leaving. Run or we'll miss it! – A bus pulling off from the bus stop and two people running to catch it.
6. I've never been to Paris before. It's wonderful! – A person looking up in awe at the Eiffel Tower.

Task 13 (page 212)

Unlike an audio script, the layout for a drama script makes it very clear for everyone involved to see what is happening on screen and what is being said. Note that locations are given in capitals with some abbreviations like INT. and EXT. (interior shot and exterior shot). The action sequences are described in sentences going across the whole page. Character names (in capitals) are in the centre of the page with spoken words centred beneath, so as not to be confused with on-screen description. For a more detailed description of the conventions for the format of a written screenplay including details such as visual effects, etc., refer to *Resources And Further Reading* on page 225. Remember that when you work with a publisher and video producer, they will also advise you on layout or edit the script themselves to fit the exact format required.

Task 14 (page 219)

In order to write a narration that can be used with Elementary level students, the writer has:

- kept the key facts (names, places, dates, etc.) from the original where possible
- simplified the sentence structure
- removed low frequency vocabulary and expressions (e.g. *the realm of space exploration*)
- increased the number of higher frequency words
- made the target language more overt; in this case the video was used to recycle the past simple tense from an earlier grammar presentation in the book.

Glossary

The following glossary items are all emboldened the first time they appear in the text.

21st century skill   21st century skills are learning, literacy and life skills which students need to succeed in the information age. For example, critical thinking, media literacy and social skills.

anagram   An anagram is a word with the letters jumbled up. The students' task is to rearrange the anagrammed letters to make a word.

artwork brief   An artwork brief is a set of instructions that explain the kind of illustration (drawing, photo, etc.) that you want to accompany the material that you have written. Artwork briefs need to be unambiguous and realistically do-able (e.g. within budget).

audiolingual approach   A style of language teaching which relies heavily on drilling sentence patterns. It is based on behaviourist theory – the idea that learners could be trained through positive and negative reinforcement.

audiolingualism   (also Audiolingual Method) Audiolingualism was based on the belief that language learning was about habit formation. Learners listened to and repeated dialogues in the form of a drill. As recording technology developed, the idea of classrooms as language laboratories emerged with rows of learners wearing headphones and the teacher controlling what each student was listening to.

authenticity   In recent years, ELT materials have put an emphasis on the use of authentic texts in the classroom. For example, using articles from real newspapers or recordings from TV documentaries. In contrast, coursebooks have been criticised for their inauthenticity with their gapfill exercises and drills. Nowadays, most teachers and writers assume that a mixture of authenticity and inauthenticity is desirable. As a result, many published texts and scripts tend to be 'realistic' rather than '100% authentic'.

backstory   A term referring to the story behind a character in a story; writers will develop backstories for characters in order to develop their personalities and to make them seem more real.

backwash effect   The direct and indirect effects of tests and examinations on teaching methods and curriculum.

call sheet   This is the document sent out by the producer of the audio or video to the actors, listing when and where the recording or filming will take place, at what time and who is required to be there.

Glossary

chunk Chunks are sequences of two or more words that are processed by the brain as a single unit. Examples of chunks (lexical chunks) include idioms (e.g. *more than meets the eye*), formulaic phrases (e.g. *know what I mean?*), discourse markers (e.g. *as a matter of fact*) and collocations (*lexical chunk* is a collocation!).

closed A closed question or a question in a closed task is a question which has only a very limited number of possible answers. We can usually identify a right or a wrong answer. For example, the question, What is a closed question?, is a closed question because there is a correct answer. Compare with open questions or open tasks.

cloze test A cloze test is a test in which every (for example) 5th, 6th word is removed and learners have to complete the gaps. This is slightly different from a gap-fill where gaps are chosen to test specific things.

cognate A cognate is a word which has a very similar form in two or more languages. The English word, Englisch, for example, is cognate to the German word, Englisch. It is a true friend. Some pairs of words look like cognates (e.g. the English word language and the French word langage) but have rather different meanings, or different parameters of meaning. They are false friends.

cognitive Cognition is what the brain does: it processes information. A cognitive challenge, therefore, is the way that a task challenges the brain (e.g. a lot of memorisation or reasoning is required). It is generally agreed that learning a language requires cognitive effort, but it is important in materials design that the cognitive effort required by a particular task is neither too great nor too little.

cognitive approach A cognitive approach to learning is a logical, reasoned approach to the understanding of information and ideas. It involves understanding the connections between ideas to improve our retention, understanding and ultimately manipulation of them.

coherence A text has coherence if it makes sense, and if the sections follow logically one from another.

cohesive If a text is cohesive the elements within the text are connected using linking words, reference words, and so on.

collocation A collocation is a group of words (two or more) that commonly occur together. Examples of collocations include prepositions that typically follow a particular noun (e.g. *example* is often followed by *of*), or two content words that are often found together (e.g. *coursebook writer*).

communicative A communicative activity or task is one which requires students to communicate with each other, either by speaking or by writing. It is only really communicative if there is a non-linguistic reason for them to communicate with each other (i.e. they are not simply required to speak to show off their language knowledge).

Glossary

communicative approach A style of language teaching where the emphasis is less on teaching language systems (grammar and vocabulary) and more on encouraging real communication.

corpus A corpus (plural = corpora) is a database of language that can be searched to find patterns in language use. Modern corpora contain many, many millions of words of both spoken and written language, and corpora exist for native speakers, for learners, and for specific kinds of English.

co-text Co-text is the language which surrounds other language. The co-text of a word is, at least, the sentence in which it occurs. The co-text of a sentence is, at least, the paragraph in which it occurs.

diagnostic A diagnostic test is used to identify a student's needs, strengths and weaknesses.

Direct Method / Natural Method The Direct and Natural Methods were two approaches that emerged in the late 19th century in reaction to Grammar Translation. They emphasised use of the first language only in order to reflect the way a first language is learned 'naturally'. Learners were exposed to the spoken form before the written form so teachers often followed scripted dialogues with students.

discourse Discourse is spoken or written communication, which is more extensive than a single sentence. A discoursal context is the wider context of a particular act of communication.

discourse marker Discourse markers are words or phrases (e.g. *by the way, anyway, right, however*) used by speakers/writers to show the connection between what they've said/written and what they're about to say/write.

double-page spread Most (but not all) coursebooks present sequences of activities (texts and tasks) so that they are divided up into sections that fit neatly onto a double page. This double-page spread is usually intended to represent about 90 minutes of classroom teaching time.

EAP EAP is an acronym which stands for English for Academic Purposes. This means studying English in order to use the language as the medium of study, at university for example.

English as a Lingua Franca (ELF) English as a Lingua Franca is sometimes referred to as English as an International Language (EIL). It is the variety of English that is used when people whose own language is not English use English to communicate. Some academics insist that these terms describe different things, but the precise differences need not concern us here.

exponent An exponent is an example of a language function. For example, *If I were you …* is an exponent of the function of 'giving advice'.

false friend See *cognate*.

Glossary

flipped classroom The 'flipped classroom' refers to the idea of students studying formal input before the lesson and then using the lesson time to take part in more interactive tasks. In other words, instead of the teacher formally presenting some new language, students work on this at home, and then try out using it in the classroom with the teacher monitoring. This has become more realistic as an approach with the increasing use of technology; for example, a teacher can film him/herself presenting some grammar and students watch this at home. Then during the lesson, the teacher gives students freer practice exercises to do.

formulae Formulae, or formulaic language, refers to groups of words that operate as a single unit, for example, *In conclusion* or *In my opinion*.

frequency The frequency of an item or structure is how often it occurs in spoken and/or written language. Writers (and teachers) can use data taken from a corpus to determine the frequency of a word or phrase.

function A function is a communicative purpose such as apologising, inviting or giving advice.

Functional/situational This refers to the approach in a syllabus or materials to present language as functions and/or in a situation. For example, you might have the function of 'asking for information about a product' and the situation is 'at the shop'. This way of organising language is typically used in tourist phrasebooks and materials that help learners prepare for using English in specific contexts (e.g. travelling abroad).

genre A genre is a type of spoken or written discourse that has recognisable features. For example, a formal letter is organised in a very specific way, and has typical phrases used for opening and closing. These kinds of features mean that people in the community which uses the genre will recognise it easily.

genre approach The genre approach is superficially similar to the product approach, in that it involves analysing features of a model, but it is rather more sophisticated. Whereas the product approach is mainly about copying the model, and focuses mainly on using language correctly, the genre approach is also focused on the purpose and the audience of the piece of writing.

Grammar Translation A method of teaching based on the way in which Latin was once taught. Grammar is regarded as being at the centre of language teaching and is formally presented to the students and then tested by having students translate sentences either into their own language or from their own language into English. This method of teaching was highly influential on the language classroom into the early and middle part of the 20th century.

guided discovery A process whereby the teacher gives clues or directions to help the learner make their own discoveries of how the language works. In this way the learner develops better and more independent cognitive skills

Glossary

hyponym A hyponym is a word that is a kind or type of another word. Oranges and apples, for example, are hyponyms of fruit. The category word, fruit, is the superordinate of oranges and apples.

idents In scripts, idents refer to the identities of the speakers. They might only be a letter such as *A* or *B* or *Speaker 1* and *Speaker 2*, or they could be real names.

learnability The learnability of a piece of language is how easy it is to learn. Cognates, for example, are easy to learn. Some tenses, on the other hand, may be hard to learn because the concepts that they express are not expressed by tenses in the learner's own language.

lexical chunk A (lexical) chunk is a group of words commonly found together.

literacy Literacy is the ability to read and write.

lock-step approach A lock-step approach is one where the teacher requires all the students to do exactly the same thing at the same time at the same speed – irrespective of the students' abilities. It is often used to describe repetitive and mechanical drills.

low-frequency low-frequency words are words that aren't often used

mind-map A mind-map, or spidergram or spidergraph, is a way of organising information visually by putting words into a series of bubbles that are joined up by lines that show connections between the information in the bubbles.

open An open question or a question in an open task is a question which has many possible answers. There is no single correct answer. For example, the question, *Why do you use open questions with your students?* is an open question because there is a huge number of possible responses. Compare with closed questions or closed tasks.

parallel text In the ELT context, a parallel text is a text with very similar content and features. For example, if students are shown a model text of an invitation to a party, they might then be asked to write a parallel text which is an invitation to a different event.

polemical Using or supported by strong arguments.

process approach The process approach emerged in the 1990s and took as its starting point the cyclical way that people write in real life. In a process writing lesson, students will begin by brainstorming ideas, then write out a brief plan before drafting, and redrafting, until they reach a final version.

product approach The product approach is a traditional approach to writing, very much in line with the idea of Presentation – Practice – Production. Typically, there will be a model text which the students will analyse to see how it is organised or what language is used. The students will then carry out a quite controlled activity either focusing on the organisation (such as putting paragraphs in order) or on the language (perhaps completing gaps in the model). Finally, they will write their own version of the model.

pronominal questions Questions in which the question word functions as a pronoun; often referred to as *Wh-* questions. When we ask a pronominal question, we usually want a piece of information.

ranking Ranking exercises ask students to put things into a particular order. If this order is personal in some way (i.e. there is more than one single way of ordering the information or the words), this task-type can be a very communicative activity if students do it in pairs or groups.

rote learning The learning of information by heart.

rubric The rubric is the set of instructions at the top of an exercise which tells students what to do.

scaffold If we scaffold an activity, we provide temporary support to enable learners to perform a task that they might not be able to do completely unaided.

scanning Scanning is a kind of reading. When you scan a text, you read it quickly to look for particular information. Some people call this a sub-skill of reading; others call it a reading strategy.

script A script is a particular alphabet or system of writing.

semantic The word semantic refers to the meaning of something. If two words are semantically related, they have some similarity in meaning. A semantic set of words is a set of words for teaching purposes that are related in terms of their meanings.

shot / establishing shot The shot is what the camera needs to film and what we see on screen. An establishing shot refers to the first shot in a film sequence which tells us where the action is taking place. For example, an establishing shot might show the outside of a hotel before we see another shot inside where the main action takes place.

skimming Skimming is a kind of reading. When you skim a text, you read it quickly to get the general gist. Some people call this a sub-skill of reading; others call it a reading strategy.

substitution drill A substitution drill is a drilling technique where the teacher models a structure and then prompts small changes. E.g. T: *I went to the cinema.* S: *I went to the cinema.* T: *theatre.* S: *I went to the theatre.*

summative A summative test measures a student's achievement. Compare this with a diagnostic test.

superordinate A superordinate is a word which is related to other words by being the category description of the other words. Fruit, for example, is the superordinate of oranges and apples. Oranges and apples (examples of the superordinate) are hyponyms of fruit.

syntax Syntax is the sequencing of words so as to show the relationships between them. It is part of grammar (the other part is morphology, or the way that words can change to show different tenses, agreement, etc.).

synthesize Combining a number of different things or ideas into a single coherent whole.

tagging Tagging is a way of adding a digital label to something you write so that it is easy to index and find. For example, you might tag an activity as 'speaking', 'pairwork' or 'picture description'.

target language Target language is the language that a piece of teaching material or a teaching activity sets out to teach to the students. This could be, for example, a tense, a rule of grammar or a set of words.

thesis statement The thesis statement summarises the focus of the essay and tells the reader what the essay is going to be about.

topic sentence The topic sentence expresses the main idea of the paragraph.

track / track numbers A track is one recording on a CD or within an online file library. For example, a coursebook might come with around 60 tracks. Each of these will have a track number which appears in the book for ease of reference.

true friend See *cognate*.

vocabulary breadth Vocabulary breadth refers to the number of words a student knows. Vocabulary depth refers to how well the student knows these words.

word family Word families are groups of words that share the same base, but have different suffixes and prefixes, and are often different parts of speech. An example is *differ, different, difference, differentiate, differentiation*, etc.

writing brief Instructions from the publisher about what to write and how to write it. In ELT contexts, it often contains some or all of the following: target market, syllabus, information about methodology, number of units, etc.

writing frame A writing frame is a kind of scaffold, with key phrases given. For example, a writing frame for a letter of complaint might begin *I am writing to complain about* … . Usually the beginning of each paragraph is given.

Other titles in this series are ...

How ELT Publishing Works

How To Plan A Book

How To Write And Deliver Talks

How To Write Audio and Video Scripts

How To Write Corporate Training Materials

How To Write Critical Thinking Activities

How To Write EAP Materials

How To Write ESOL Materials

How To Write ESP Materials

How To Write Exam Preparation Materials

How To Write Film And Video Activities

How To Write For Digital Media

How To Write Graded Readers

How To Write Primary Materials

How To Write Reading And Listening Activities

How To Write Speaking Activities

How To Write Teacher's Books

How To Write Vocabulary Presentations And Practice

How To Write Worksheets

How To Write Writing Activities

For further information, contact us via our website at
www.eltteacher2writer.co.uk

Printed in Poland
by Amazon Fulfillment
Poland Sp. z o.o., Wrocław